A NOVEL BY

BALACHANDRA RAJAN

The Dark Dancer

GREENWOOD PRESS, PUBLISHERS
WESTPORT, CONNECTICUT

Contents

The Dark Dancer

CHAPTER ONE

Homecoming

IT WAS where he was born, but where he was born didn't matter. There was nothing in the cracked, arid earth to suggest that he belonged to it, or in the river, shrunk away from the banks, that seemed almost to wrench its way through the landscape, startling the brown anger into green. The rail tracks ran forward like an act of will, straining across the flat, baked plain to the first muddle of houses, and then the road forked from it, driving relentlessly through the mantle of dust to an end that might have been reached from any beginning.

In the distance, hazing, and under the white blaze of an almost venomous midday, the sheer rock of the temple rose, with the houses clustered around it, carved out of the cliff, seeming to thrust it upward, proclaiming the pride and defiance of the earth. He looked at it and felt no tide of emotion at returning. He had been born in its shadow, but he could have been born anywhere else, anywhere in that parched infinity where the roads narrowed and the gutters wormed among the congested houses, or wherever the scream filtered through the laboring rice fields, and the thatch was pierced by the anger of the first cry.

He was coming back, but not to an identity, a sense of being rooted, not even to an enmity like that of sun and earth, a struggle against circumstance, a creative confronting, which would open his mind to its depths of repossession. He was coming back to an indifferent sky, an anonymous teeming of houses, the road striking forever into a distance which not even the clenched thrust of the temple could make real.

Krishnan's stride tightened a little, an unconscious bracing against the heat's pressure and the tensing of his thoughts. He had chosen to walk from the station, which, being the pride of the railway authorities, found its natural place on the fringes of the cantonment, suburbia, exurbia, the necessary aloofness of the white men and their mimics, and four miles outside the old city with its ambiguous savors that the rock temple immemorially dominated. With a faith in human nature that stupefied him now that he recollected it, he had consigned his belongings to one of the only two taxi drivers at the station, given him his destination, buried deep in the town's heart, and trudged off down the grimy road while the man watched him in scandalized amazement. This was the day of his homecoming, a day earlier than it should have been, but he had told nobody of the difference, for he was anxious to avoid the clusterings and the inanities, the aggressive aunts who would survey him like a prize cow and the garland he might embarrassingly have to wear. He would come home unannounced and unexpected, slipping quietly into his appointed place, like any man's feet into accustomed slippers.

He walked now to acclimatize himself, to ease long absence into familiarity. But the heat of the sun on his uncovered head struck at his theories with inconsiderate violence as he watched the children frolic unconcernedly in the heat, which malevolently attached his sports shirt to his body. A *topee* would have protected him, but he had disdained it as a confession of foreignness. It was a mistaken and petulant refusal. One could not avoid estrangement simply by rejecting its symbols. The perspiration was streaming off his face now, dimming his glasses. Ten years before he would have walked barefooted and undistressed on the macadam. Now the heat came sizzling off it, burning through his shoes and riveting them to his feet. He began to appreciate the merits of not coming home in the hardest possible way.

He looked up the dusty road with its wilting trees. As was to be expected, no taxi was in sight. A rickshawallah stared at him hopefully and almost hungrily. He was a small man, emaciated to essentials, and Krishnan, himself slightly built, seemed almost indecently robust in comparison. He knew what was going on in the man's mind and breaking into his face. This wasn't the time for misdirected sentiment. The ride into the city meant the night's food for the rickshawallah and his family. It was all that mattered or ought to matter yet Krishnan, realizing it, was neither tired enough nor acclimatized enough to go home pulled in by someone else's shoulders. His choice fell eventually and thankfully on a passing *jutka*. That at least facilitated the anxieties of adjustment, as the harness clanked against the horse's bony body and the cart wheels shivered in the rutted road. Supreme, he sat in the caparisoned tunnel that was the vehicle's body, with its matted base and the cushions sprawled around him, while the crouched figure of the man outside shouted invective and endearment at the apathetic beast. The cantonment was dropping behind now, and the pock-marked houses huddled closer together, red, blue, yellow and father-in-law's fancy, with a door in violent ocher where rummaging had brought forth a forgotten tin of paint.

The *jutka* jolted its way through the bazaar and, missing the open gutter by inches, took the sharp turn into Periya Kovil Street. This was the center of the city, too narrow for two-way traffic, and in the middle two cars that had entered hooting and obstinate, from opposite directions, were acquainting themselves with this incontrovertible fact. The car nearest to Krishnan was a ten horse-power and that on the other side was an eight. Conscious of the superior facilities for purchasing influence implied by the five-inch-longer wheelbase, the minor contestant gracefully withdrew. Thus could Krishnan proceed uninterrupted while his triumphant vanguard passed to the other end, flourishing itself around the narrow corner.

Now a sudden rush of music in the heat haze. Drums beating, children running. Two horses, better fed than usual, garlanded and festooned, pulled into sight a king-sized *jutka* from which the rotund prescriber, embodiment of Ganesha, god of bounty, dispensed the formula for the day's contentment. Positively your last chance to see *Valli's Wedding!* Mighty mythological made at unmentionable cost! Fifty-six minutes longer than *Gone with the Wind*. Forty-eight songs, gods, demons and palavers and stupendous battles on the reacting stage. Verily will the nightingale of the Carnatic strike at your heartstrings as you contemplate the spectacle of India's ancient glory in the blithe anterior before evil triumphed and the age of Kali descended. Drumming and dancing, the procession passed, the wide-eyed children eagerly coursing behind for extra copies of those gaily colored notices which would grace with the proud performances of *Valli* the drab interiors of so many homes.

Krishnan watched the festivities disappear around the corner. His memory heard the dimming of the music as it had done repeatedly in the past. He remembered how often he had rushed into the street, leaping dangerously down the worn steps with their tilting surfaces, timing his exit to coincide with the crescendo, joining the procession, fighting his way to the donor of consolations in the *jutka,* weeping with chagrin as the child ahead of him, in a supreme effort, seized the last blue poster. Ten years had passed and the movie was still *Valli's Wedding,* longer, more lavish, this time in color, perhaps, but unchanged enough for his own response to remind him of the extent to which he himself had altered.

He shook himself out of his thoughts, becoming aware that the *jutka* was approaching its destination. The entrance to Fourteen Periya Kovil Street was where it always had been—immediately adjacent to the rear end of a cow.

The cow was probably not the same cow that had been there ten years before, but the architectural relationship was necessary and constant. Four steps rose from the street to the level of the ground floor, flanked on either side by plinths of black Cudappah stone. From each plinth a pillar of the same stone rose to support the first floor, giving the house front its traditional solid formality. Krishnan had often clambered up those pillars, the giant trees of the Vindhya forests, where in the brilliance of his imagination Tarzan the ape man and Hanuman the monkey, servant of God and savior of Sita, would grapple together in the coexistence of cultures. Now the pillars were bare and the plinths empty, a fit podium for Socratic discourse. The emptiness suited his mood. It was not simply the moving away from his past that had left the severe, peremptory spaces vacant, unpeopled by the imagination even in remembrance. It was a different journey, a more alien detachment, so that thinking of childhood would not bring the dream back or allow it to be held in affectionate nostalgia. He could summon the images, but he could not make them move him. Home was for him a more disturbing vacancy without even the expected leap of longing tensing in him to bridge the separation. Home was his beginning, no more than a point of departure. It could have been anywhere and any shape. He was too far from it to come in joyously as if the house were his, a place that had bloomed into significance around him, an experience he lived in and an affection he wore. He could only come in abstractly, knowing bloodlessly that he had already been there. The familiarity would not desert him; it would stay with him, like the mocking remembrance of a past life, a receding shore in which he must strive to be rooted.

He looked at the *kolum,* the decorative emblem patiently drawn each morning on the water-sprinkled floor, the symbol of the universal design, giving each house its particular geometry of perception. Behind it the door stood, burglar- and bullock-proof. Age had blackened its weather-scarred teak to the hue of the massive iron ring that functioned as its handle. Krishnan hesitated in front of it, then told himself brusquely that he had no right to hesitate. He pushed it open and stepped inside the cave.

The darkness was also coolness. The house was a refuge from the outer inundation, furnished in the fashion of refuges with arbitrary salvage from the wreck. It was rescued from anonymity not by a sense of purpose but by a collection of accidents, this inherited pot and that atrocious doll, everybody's good taste jumbled into anarchy, the worst things most prominent because they were the free ones.

Krishnan made himself recognize the confusion. It was an act that, he realized, should have been automatic. He had lived in it and it had grown up around him. There should have been a feeling of identity however remote, a sense of familiarity however patronizing. He looked at it more closely. Some of the details had changed; but essentially it was like the cattle in the streets, the propaganda for the perennial movie, the aged elephant that probably still stood at the temple gates, unaltered, or the difference not in it but in the foreign eyes by which it was valued. There was a time when he would have found the lack of order capricious or, at the worst, chaotic. But bringing to it the sense of removal engendered by long absence, he seemed now to find it almost disturbing. It was an exaggeration, of course, the projection of an artificial sense of purpose, but looking at the jumble, he found himself tempted to see it as a deception instinctively stage-managed. It seemed almost as if the organization of the house were deliberately pushed below the level of discipline because there were more dangerous and more effective ways for the family unity to express itself.

The center of the tableau was, as usual, the great swing, long enough for a man to lie upon and creaking dismally from its four rusty chains. Behind were the inevitable pictures: Lakshmi on the lotus, Saraswathi wrapped in study, and a slightly effeminate Krishna playing his flute to an enraptured milkmaid. Bhawnani, the *ghee* merchant, had provided the first two. The third had come from the calendar of the Gem Emporium. Loving hands had bedecked Lakshmi in a turquoise-colored sari, the cloth sewn and sequinned with devoted delicacy on to the outlines of the picture. Beneath Saraswathi's feet were deferentially placed two novels by Rider Haggard, the S. I. R. timetable, the *Mahabharata* done into galloping English verse and *Paradise Lost* opened at the ninth book.

Krishnan's mother came forward hesitantly out of the darkness, with the uncertain, shuffling gait that was his last remembrance of her, when she had stood on the platform bidding the train farewell. Her memory seemed to grope around the familiar silhouette which the flood of light in the doorway had unexpectedly let in. The welcome broke into her care-lined face eventually, but it did so qualified by a vague distress.

"Oh, Krishnan, Krishnan! You were supposed to come tomorrow."

"I wanted to surprise you. I thought I'd come a day earlier."

She spread her hands characteristically. It was the same gesture as ten years ago, and remembering it made him realize how the hands themselves had altered. The skin was loose now and the flesh discolored. Time pushed its way slowly through the constricted streets, and a year on the calendar was a far longer trial lived through.

"But we were going to meet you," she protested, her voice trembling and by no means with fondness. "Your uncle was coming here specially this afternoon. Now he isn't here and Father has left on business and won't be back till this evening. What sort of welcome is this to give a son returning after ten years?"

"I don't want that kind of welcome, Mother. All I need is your affection and your blessing."

It was the right thought and reflected a sturdy sense of proportion, but to his discomfiture the words had no effect. All the upset plans were struggling in her face now, and in her eyes he could see the bruised garland which would be brought home only to be given away, or left reproachfully at Lakshmi's feet.

"We wanted to be there," she said. "All of us wanted to stand there and take you among us and then go to the temple, all together, and thank Lord Ganesha for your safe return. Now it cannot be done. You have been away a long time and don't know what it means to us."

He did know, or thought he did, but he had believed that the pleasure of seeing him a day earlier would more than offset the loss of ceremony. He had thought of his homecoming as an emptiness filled, a resurrection of memories, the arranging of new shapes in a familiar, affectionate circle. He had taken it innocently for granted that the whole process centered around himself. The ceremony was merely a carpet over which he could walk to his welcome and which he could dispense with if he preferred a different approach. He had been mistaken, and this was one way to find out. He did not matter, or, to be more precise, he only mattered as the foreground of the festivities he was supposed to occasion. He would begin to count and to deserve his welcome only when he agreed to come in through that frame.

Her eyes in the lined face were still those of a young girl, clear enough for him to see the damage which the wrong sense of proportion had wreaked.

"I'm sorry," he said. "I'm terribly sorry."

The words came out of him limp and unconvincing. The cruelty of ill-will was better than that of ignorance.

All of a sudden she seemed to see who he was. It was as if her mind had gone around the corner, beyond the obstruction, to the right side of his homecoming.

"Oh, Krishnan," she wailed. "You have not looked after yourself. You have become so miserably thin."

She disappeared precipitately into the storeroom, returning with a silver plate, a plank, a tumbler and three biscuit tins from which high-calorie sweets were disgorged. She knelt by him as he sat on the plank diffidently nibbling at the Mysore Pak, stroking his head in a monotonous, consoling rhythm of reminiscence. Feeling her fingers, he realized that she had not forgiven his ignorance; she had disposed of it by making him ten years younger and too innocent of responsibility to know.

2

Dinner was delayed by the need to have something slightly more elaborate than usual for the occasion; also by his mother's discovery, having divested her mind of its luggage, that her only son had no luggage whatsoever. She wrung her hands piteously, reducing his mental age further in the process. His trousers were all lost and so were his testimonials; but even more important, by his reckless confidence in the honesty of taxi drivers, he had lost the photograph of his prospective bride and the only available copy of her horoscope. Her lamentations reminded Krishnan that the inevitable subject was around the corner. It was the second time something in the air had told him that he himself, as a person, might not matter. He had not come home simply to be at home. He had come home in order to get married.

After various wanderings, the luggage eventually arrived, and his mother plunged chaotically into its orderly depths to retrieve with jubilation the blueprint of his future. Watching her, he had for the first time a curious sense of detachment, of seeing himself take part in a procession, of belonging himself to that insistent collectivity by which his own actions were to be decided.

Dinner was undoubtedly the proper occasion, sitting with the family in vegetarian splendor, contemplating the right way to dispose of the body. But it was still odd that Mother should choose the time when Krishnan was engaged in munching ladyfingers to begin reciting the specifications of the lady.

"She is satisfactory as far as features go. Her nose is a little too broad, but fortunately it is no longer than the distance from the tip of it to her chin. Her complexion is comparatively fair. I should say it's the color of oatmeal, wouldn't you?" She paused to look inquiringly at Father.

"If you ask me, it's more like the color of Peek Frean's biscuits."

It was Father's kind of retort, bluff and hardheaded, but all the while accepting the order it sought to deflate. Like everyone else, he had done what he had to. Realism and responsibility, the pragmatism with which he liked to be credited, were merely his particular form of resignation, the clothes he had chosen in order to live with his defeats.

Mother was accustomed to these sallies, and the shrug of her shoulders was almost instinctive as she continued with her catalogue.

"Anyway, pedigree is more important than complexion. There's an O.B.E. on the maternal side and two uncles in Government service."

"That's important," said Father. "That almost makes up for the grossly inadequate dowry."

"What does my only son think?" inquired Mother with intimidating fondness.

"I haven't had the time to think," said Krishnan. "I arrived only this afternoon and I wasn't supposed to arrive until tomorrow. My luggage has been unpacked, thanks to Mother, but I haven't yet been able to unpack my mind."

"My only son," wailed Mother. "He's all I have and he doesn't care for marriage."

Father intervened with pompous matter-of-factness. "Marriage is only a means to an end. It is part of a career and the bringing up of a family. The proposed alliance serves these purposes also."

Krishnan's uncle decided that it was time for his contribution. "It is better to marry than to burn," he announced unexpectedly.

Everyone looked suitably astonished, so he went on proudly to explain his cryptic remark. "The quotation is from the Epistle to the Corinthians. In view of your Western education, Krishnan, you are no doubt familiar with the teachings of St. Paul. The saint was mostly saintly and undoubtedly well informed. Unfortunately he spoke only part of the truth. It has remained for your father to say the rest."

He looked back at Krishnan, satisfaction at his sally glowing in his eyes, tentatively fingering his half-handlebar mustaches. They suited his name, but nothing else about him did. He had been christened Kruger after the First World War, following the defeat of an extremist faction that had sought to name him Bismarck. After this distinctive gesture of defiance the briefly awakened patriotism of the family had subsided, satisfied, into its normal torpor. Kruger was left with the memory of schoolboy taunts and a mounting dislike for the nationalism that had contrived to give him his remarkable name.

"There is a practical consideration," Kruger added. "Her second uncle will see to it that you're not rejected because of your poor eyesight."

"Rejected from what?" asked Krishnan.

"From Government service, naturally." Father's tone showed the beginnings of impatience.

"But I don't want to be in Government service," said Krishnan. Consternation grew in the surrounding faces. Gone were all thoughts of marriage and four-day feasts as the family pondered this ominous announcement.

"Don't want to be in Government service! What else, may I ask you, can an educated Brahmin do?"

"I want to be a teacher, Father."

Father's face relaxed into a grin. He had obviously been thinking of more dangerous alternatives, such as politics or even gentlemanly idleness.

"Only imbeciles teach," he observed with hearty decisiveness. "If you're not good enough for Government service, if you can't remove a man's tonsils without also cutting his throat, if you haven't the memory for law, or the acumen for business, then, of course, you degenerate into teaching. But though the English weather has obviously softened your brains, it cannot yet have brought you to that degree of incompetence."

"Government service isn't the measure of everything," protested Krishnan. "I want to teach in order to express myself. I want to have the creative satisfaction of planting the right things in someone else's mind and training them to grow according to his character."

They were the right thoughts, yet, looking for some hint of a change in attitudes, he was conscious only of his father's effort to be indulgent. He paused a little as if to allow Krishnan the courtesy of having weighed his argument. Then he plunged heavily into his crushing retort.

"You won't have much creative satisfaction after six months of living on a teacher's salary. Idealism is all very well for students, but you're a responsible person now, and you also have to be practical. You can't have self-respect unless you have the respect of your community. And if you persist in being a teacher, your community will judge you a failure whether you are or aren't. I am sure you will understand," he concluded, with the finality of a judge dismissing a case that was too trivial to be worthy of the Court's time. "I am arranging to start your riding lessons on Monday."

"Riding lessons?" asked Krishnan, astonished. "Whatever for?"

Father replied with what he obviously thought was infinite patience. "Everyone has to pass a test in riding before being admitted into Government service. If the British don't like your background they'll flunk you in the *viva*. And if that isn't enough to offset your written papers they'll probably do their best to reject you because of inferior horsemanship. There have been reports about your becoming involved in politics, and we must be prepared to meet the strictest standards."

"The greatest sage in modern India, Father, was unable to ride a horse and, falling from it, was exalted into philosophy."

"He fell off his horse then," interjected Kruger scornfully. "Now all he does is fall off his ideas."

"You only said that to be witty, Kruger."

"Not at all," replied Krishnan's uncle. "I wasn't trying to be any more than objective. Sooner or later you have to realize that falling off ideas is part of the Indian character."

"There are some ideas," Krishnan pointed out scathingly, "that this family could very well fall off."

Kruger was unperturbed. "I was referring to the *modern* Indian character. The ancients and this ancient family know better. In this respect even the British have more sense than our moderns. They get hold of an idea, a myth—something, for instance, like the white man's burden. It may be false but it doesn't matter. They ride it to its conclusion and that matters. Push anything to its end and you have achievement. The Congress will compromise and temporize and go on uselessly mixing oil with water. That's what we'll get—misgovernment by reason when all we need is a solid foundation of prejudice."

He was more right than he knew, thought Krishnan. The foundation of prejudice was here and now and unshakable. They didn't argue with him. They didn't even threaten him by implying that resistance to the family will was futile. They went further, and by some tacit collective assumption that he could not challenge since it was never stated, they made even the basis of his opposition frivolous. In the circle of faces there was neither sternness nor pity. There was only the detached understanding of him as a misguided soul fuddled by individualism and unable to discern the clear light of truth.

"On Friday," Mother was saying with the unperturbed perseverance that was so much stronger than rivers. "On Friday, we'll go to Madras. Then if Krishnan doesn't approve of Kamala there is still Menaka and Parvati and perhaps even Shakuntala. But I think we should consider Shakuntala only in the last resort. After all, the family lives in Dindigul and the father isn't even in income tax."

"He's in railways," said Father. "That virtually makes him into an Anglo-Indian."

"On the other hand," said Kruger judiciously, "her nose is undoubtedly superior to Kamala's. In fact, her whole face conforms precisely to those specifications laid down in our most ancient and authoritative texts. I must also point out that notwithstanding the Dindigul sun she has preserved a complexion that is wheaten rather than biscuit."

"And her figure?" asked Krishnan indifferently.

"Her figure?"

"If I am to marry the girl, I trust I may presume to some interest in her body. Do not the ancient and irrevocable scriptures ordain certain optimum dimensions?"

"The face reveals character," said Kruger, "the body only lack of it. We will consequently confine our scrutiny to the face."

"But you will see them, won't you?" Mother asked appealingly.

What was he to say? That any person had the right to be himself? Yet what was himself but the truest of many reflections, the way those who had borne and raised him saw him? That every man was entitled to create in his own way, to express himself as his own nature dictated? But the roots of expression

stretched into being recognized, into belonging, and was not belonging acceptance of a pattern, the privacy real only by living
within it? He ought to rebel, but rebellion seemed inadequate
when the forces opposing him were counterbalanced by the force
within him that conformity claimed. A career arranged, a marriage predetermined. His private and public life inexorably charted.
It should have shocked him, and to some extent it did, but was
the shock anything more than superficial, a tingle on the skin of
his upbringing? And under the skin did his muscles not move
to surrender, did his blood not sing in that deep, fascinated curiosity of acceptance that his reason resisted while his emotions
curved to the pull? He had the strange sense of detachment once
again, of being both the dancer and the dance, of being the ritual
and the ritual's object. He had to wade through, to let the singing flow through, to know what fragment of the truth there was
on the calm far shore where the tide of surrender ended.

He heard his mother's voice anxiously repeating the question.
"Krishnan, you aren't listening, dear. You *do* agree to see them,
don't you?"

"I suppose so," he replied, and wondered who was replying. "I
suppose that if I have to, I must."

3

The house at Madras was larger than that on Periya Kovil
Street. It was Krishnan's acquired home as distinct from his ancestral one, acquired when Krishnan's father made his modest pile
in Government service, before the cost of living doubled and the
salaries halved. Property was able to survive inflation, and property
in the Nungambakam area had a certain prestige. Father's position had advanced enough to save his investment from the charge
of ostentation, and he was also tired of the narrow alley with its
open gutters, swept through by smallpox every sweltering summer
and leaving the scars after the screaming subsided. The new
house had a sanitation system that was still imperfect but superior

to the ancestral method of naked manpower and a makeshift spade. It was a large building, unintelligently designed, with a compound that must have been close to an acre, and a driveway to the portico, bordered by whitewashed bricks with their corners facing upward. In front of the portico was a bed of multicolored zinnias, and on the west side of the house a tamarind tree, which could not quite prevent the evening sun from streaming through the dark-green, lowered chicks. The house had been built by a man who was undecided whether to construct a home or a fortress. The floors were concrete, as was the terraced roof, and one looked at a dilapidated tennis court through massive windows with assault-proof iron bars. The rooms themselves were larger than normal, the cane furniture in the front tasteless and only moderately expensive and the brass in the rear rooms plentiful and ornate. Under Lakshmi's picture was a short-wave receiver with Batavia and Buenos Aires hopefully marked on the dial. White ants had long since found the condensers good eating, but as an expression of prosperity the massive-inlaid cabinet was so intimidating that no visitor had ever asked if it worked. Substance and security were supposed to be the dominant impression, but for all their actual solidity the rooms were tremulous, tremulous not only with the heat but with the animation of the approaching event. *Who* it was to be was still an open question; but that it *was* to be was evident from the processions of aunts and the gambolings of urchins, the consultations of amateur astrologers, the mounting pile of *appalams* in the storeroom and the smoke that billowed from under the great urns on the kitchen fire.

Krishnan sat on the swing while the seventh aunt surveyed him. It was a process to which he was uncomfortably accustomed. It had begun in his infancy, when he was entitled to stick out his tongue at seventh aunts and was brought down proudly, hair brilliantined, skin burnished with coconut oil, to be set before the admiring audience like the crown jewels or a family heirloom. The annual display had taken place every *Deepavali,* the compliments growing fewer, the stare more hostile and the retort receding into an impossible impertinence which he could only recollect with nostalgia. "How thin he is," the reproving faces would say. It was true enough; but it would have been said even if he had been completely spherical. "He's very, very shy," Mother invariably replied. "We mustn't do anything to make him feel self-conscious." The circle of faces would cluck its assent, and he would shuffle off, ears burning, bored with playing marbles, back to the black morocco books where people spoke sense and spoke it in pentameters. Now she was staring again, and what was she staring at? Did she see V. S. Krishnan, five seven, one hundred and thirty-six, brown-eyed, slim-waisted, scarlet-eared and, in a sensitive way, without the glasses, good looking—did she see that or simply the welcome return of the traditional focus for her condescension? She looked at him and then at the divine flutist, Lord Krishna, his immortal namesake, whose portrait hung in silent reproach behind him. Krishnan shuffled his feet and sucked in his abdomen. He could imagine how unfavorable the comparison must be. He was thankful to have her scrutiny arrested by the entrance of his mother and Kruger.

"My only son," said Mother breathlessly. "I've been looking everywhere for you."

The swing was, of course, the obvious place to look, but Mother always began in this way when what had to follow was particularly important.

"Are you sure, Krishnan, that this is what you want? You *have* gone over *all* the considerations?"

"Naturally," said Krishnan, "And what's so terribly wrong about it anyway? Six months ago you were all in favor of Kamala."

"But her horoscope," protested Mother. "We mustn't ignore her horoscope."

"If her horoscope weren't adequate you would never have sent me her photograph."

"Of course it's adequate, my precious boy. But adequacy isn't enough. When an only son is involved can a fond mother be satisfied with mere compatibility?" She paused a little proudly on the word *compatibility,* making it apparent that Kruger was her mentor. "I've nothing against Kamala personally," she continued. "It just happens that there is a better alternative. Besides, I never knew about Menaka's father's cousin. What a powerful figure he is! Soon, very soon, he may be taken into the Government. Just imagine," she said, her hands sweeping out, "my only son the relative of a Cabinet Minister!"

Krishnan intervened hastily. "I'm sorry to disappoint you. I've given way on the principle of marriage. But that was on condition that the right of choice was mine, and Kamala remains the person I choose."

"You tell him," Mother said imploringly to Kruger. "When he was five years old he listened to nobody else."

Kruger cleared his throat, wagged his mustaches and searched in his memory for a sonorous sentence.

"I have nothing to add," he finally said judicially, and Mother's face showed her obvious disappointment. "Nothing, that is, to what Desikan has stated." He surveyed his audience commandingly looking the picture of an orator as he thrust his thumbs behind the lapels of an imaginary coat. "I need not introduce Desikan to this gathering. No astrologer commands greater respect in the Carnatic, and Desikan has recorded it as his conclusive opinion that Kamala should marry no one born west of the Cauvery."

"You see," said Mother with triumphant satisfaction.

Kruger continued floridly with his argument. "Menaka, on the other hand, is an entirely different story. Let the flawless reciprocation and conjunction of your horoscopes be the augury and portent of your union. Moreover, the very same Desikan, after a typically masterful survey of the evidence, has put before us his emphatic conclusion that Menaka can marry any man south of the Indus."

"In that case," said Krishnan, "she can afford to live without me."

Mother threw up her hands despairingly. "Woe is me, alas! My son no longer listens to my voice. Youth has no longer any respect for Age."

When her feelings were intense she always went back to literary-sounding phrases as if thereby she could add to her own emotions the emotions of others who had also used the words. Krishnan wished he could console her. He tried to go over the basis of his resistance.

It had been Menaka who had attracted him the most. She had height enough to carry the formal, heavily bordered sari that she wore. Her slim figure was handsomely proportioned; she disposed of it with a dancer's natural grace and a confidence which her breeding saved from vulgarity. In the fumbling ten-minute interview, broken by interruptions from apprehensive relatives, through which compatibility is normally decided, Menaka had fortunately displayed no particular brilliance and neither forced wit nor well-rehearsed profundity. She was unaffected and relaxing. Krishnan could see her as an enviable hostess. He could imagine the grace of her flowing beneficently and tolerantly through his life. Perhaps that was what the conjunction of horoscopes meant: the mutual creation of tranquillity so that the dark energies latent and challenging in one remained rooted and flowering in the circle of decorum.

Was tranquillity belonging? He remembered the brown wastes which the train had passed through, after the green slash of the Cauvery ended. Brown, baked earth and the endless, venomous sky. Dust and desire and the chain of the soil's crippling poverty when the green blades burst gallantly through and the rain never came that the villagers forever prayed for. Scum in the temple tank and burning the steps going down to it, to the reflection of the sky and its eternal enmity. The *gopuram* dark as the hungry earth, up up into the wolfish stare of the sun. Prayer or thrust or declaration of war? Was there a place for contentment in the temple's heart, in the kindling core of the mind where Shiva dances, in the circle of flames on the dead earth's shuddering body? A place for contentment or a haven for anger? For discontent flowering into the will to transform?

With Kamala there would be no tranquillity. He knew that from the moment he entered the room and she rose to greet him, her hands together in the *namaskar,* but with a quiet pride entirely foreign to the gesture. It was not rebellion, not even resentment against the constrictions of an arranged marriage, but, on the contrary, a strange strength of acceptance. His mother accepted also, accepted the old because it was so ordained and the new in the helpless hope of understanding. Kamala accepted with an undeceivable innocence, as if she knew better than the giver the character of his gift, better than the demander the roots of his demand, as if by the force of her receiving she might bring what she accepted to its essential nature. In a petite way she was good looking, not in the sharp-nosed, almond-eyed manner of the classics, but with a gaze gentle and yet intense and a mouth just too fastidious to be sensual. Her figure was lithe, exactly formed, slimness fined down to nearly the point of thinness, definite and firm beneath the clinging georgette. Patently, hers would be the unyielding yielding. Her body would serve its purpose, Krishnan thought, and realized with a start that he was not being cynical. In other circumstances her womanhood might attract him. At present it could not distract him from the deep psychological recognition that established the terms of their meeting. Complementing her power of acceptance, he felt in himself a capacity for commitment, a compulsion to the irrevocable act, a will to burn bridges and create his island. In infinity what is belonging? Indus or Kistna? Creek of Cochin or the ice-blue waters of the Ganges tumbling through the northern gorges? Belonging is a body, a place, a problem, a responsibility; acquire them as you can, endure them as you must, and with the passion of your attachment change them. A man creates when he is unable to escape. When what one is is taken and thrust and hunted into a meaning. When a barrier is thrown across the flood of one's loneliness, controlling it to patience while the green acres grow. She would not change him. She would accept him. She would leave him nothing but himself, no mask, no pretense, no illusion. Without harshness, perhaps without love also, she would lead him to the precipice of belonging, the point of no return and no escape.

He knew what the choice had to be, that it wasn't a choice, that what he wanted was not happiness but that stubborn and strengthened freedom that derived its force from the restrictions of conformity. Her acceptance was the temple pool, the pitiless mirror, the unclouded truth that would yield him that reflection.

"It has to be Kamala," Krishnan suddenly said. "It has to be because there is no alternative."

4

"It's a waste of time and, even more, of money," said Krishnan. "All you'll do is to give succor to scoundrels and urchins."

"Four days," Mother had said. "When the conjunction is not perfectly auspicious it is tempting fortune to make do with less."

"Professional wedding guests, that's all they'll be. You won't find a single indigent Brahmin among them. How can you possibly think of such a thing with the harvests failing, the rice ration down to ten ounces and the cows too famished to give milk?"

"Four days," said Father. "It's the least they can do after such a ridiculous dowry."

"There's a Government edict restricting wedding guests to twenty-five people."

"Seventy-five Government officers will come nevertheless. Then they can explain how they violated their own edict."

"Four days," said Kruger. "Manu, the lawgiver, says so, and so it has always been. You have crossed the dark waters and eaten flesh with the foreigner. You have probably even ceased to perform your ablutions. But the Brahmin never ceases to be such. From the time that the triple thread is laid across your shoulder the call of the priesthood is in your heart and no defection from that voice can still it. Four days it has to be. The thread is the first reminder of your calling. Let the marriage be the second and be done as the ancient books ordain."

Krishnan had other objections. He was going to say that the expenses of so prolonged a ceremony would be enough to set him up in business or to attend to his livelihood while he compiled some monumental work of scholarship which, far more than any four-day ceremony, would bear witness to the nature of a Brahmin. But he had looked at the expectant faces and thought of the splash of color that a wedding made to the poor, wide-eyed relatives from the village, the widows in their white robes of bereavement, the hungry children with the sweets clutched in their fists. Suddenly he thought that perhaps he understood something of the significance of a wedding. It was not simply that circuses were more important than bread. Men otherwise prudent and frugal could hardly be expected to squander their lifetime's savings or put themselves in bondage to moneylenders merely because of a curious passion for spectacle. Was it not that the carnival helped to loosen for a moment the rigid and priestlike compulsions of austerity which seemed to claim even the wealthiest of his community? Loosened them in the name of religion and the ordained procedures. Was not the throbbing of the drums a calling together of the clans, giving them for the moment cohesion and an identity, seventh aunt and sixth cousin each their particular status, able to bless and be received with dignity? Then they would return with the wind, like withering leaves in the moonlight, each to their separate and anonymous lives. Krishnan could appreciate how they too might wish to belong. He became aware that what was behind his objections was not horror at waste, or an awakened social conscience, but simply that capricious dislike of ceremony with which he had ruined the first day of his homecoming. And what was it but capricious? If he wished to offer resistance it should have been to the principle, to the conception of conformity, not to the details. Both logic and regard for the interests of others required him to acquiesce in what the sacred texts demanded.

So the marathon had begun. The gifts were ceremoniously exchanged on the preceding evening between the bride's party and the bridegroom's. Then, on the morning of the first day, Krishnan had set out on his token pilgrimage, twenty steps along the road to Benares. As it turned out, it was not even the right road and continuing on his erroneous course would only have landed him in the Bay of Bengal. He was still several paces from the gate when his father-in-law-to-be rushed up to him, presented him with a copy of the *Gita* (in Shri Aurobindo's translation, he noted with amusement) and acquainted him with the existence of Kamala,

which fact apparently made unnecessary the course of renunciation on which he had embarked. Krishnan, told of his duties the
previous night, had seen this incident reflecting the struggles between the world and the spirit, but his father had chided him
with typical insensitivity: "Why must you see symbolic meaning in
everything?" And Kruger had been critical: "Symbolism, yes;
but, like a Western metaphysician, you simplify the issue. You
think that there are only two sides to any problem. In India there
are at least five hundred." And Kruger had gone on characteristically. "That's another proof of the bankruptcy of reason. What
choice can reason make among five hundred alternatives? Without prejudice all action is impossible."

Krishnan still could not respond seriously to Kruger's familiar
argument; but as the ceremony went on he became aware of the
dangers of simplification and of the complex yet organized balance
of forces which the pattern of the ritual subtly embodied. He had
proceeded first into the small marquee, the *pandhal,* at the foot
of the bride's house, four pillars of plantain stalks festooned with
mango leaves holding the blue silk roof aloft over the fragrant,
water-sprinkled earth. On the ground the *kolum* in red and white
had been drawn with the controlled, anonymous sense of loveliness that comes to the ordinary on exceptional occasions. He
stepped across it to come face to face with Kamala. The previous
encounters did not exist; this was their first meeting in the sight
of God and the family. They placed the garlands on each other,
recognition blossoming into welcome. He still did not look into
her eyes. Up the steps they walked, toward the swing, the red
and white *kolum* on the teak surface also, discipline and devotion
their firm earth, wherever they paused, wherever their feet rested.
The water was sprinkled around them, hallowing the place. Then
the rice balls were thrown, exiling evil to the four imagined corners. Their feet were washed and stained with henna. They went
down to where Kamala's father sat on his pile of hay, incongruous
yet with a touching solemnity as he yielded Kamala, his supreme
endowment and his pearl beyond price, watching her pass beyond
the circle of his possession.

In the larger marquee, the bricks were laid in the prescribed pattern; the twigs piled into the hearth were soaked with *ghee* before they were ignited. The *Muhurtham,* the ceremony of union, was beginning, and the two sat before the fire on rosewood planks while the circle of witnesses gathered expectantly around them. They looked at the priest's face. It was an ordinary face, the face of many ascetics, yet the occasion seemed to make it timeless, giving it that statuesque serenity in which the eyes alone lived, veiled in the rising smoke, the deep-set reflection of the fire they answered. He recited the Sanskrit verses to them. It was not a language that Krishnan understood, but he was still able to respond to the deep diapason which was its characteristic current, the rolling polysyllables and pervasive alliteration molded subtly to the ceremonial cadences. Their sound brought back to him the image of the *gopuram,* pointing upward like a squat finger of loneliness. Was that not one's virgin condition—the marriage of solitude with the unknown? For a little that aspiration could be civilized, curbed to its responsibilities, a family growing and cared for, a career fashioned with decorum and diligence and brought to its unostentatious ending. Was not man's course like a river blessing the land, helping to bring forth its harvests but, in the deep compulsion of its nature, thrusting always toward a different element —its very deviations a strategy of approach?

Kamala looked at him out of the corner of her eye. She had exchanged no glances, the reason being not only modesty but the embarrassment of being a scholar in Sanskrit and so of understanding only too clearly the unprogressive elements in the ritual. When Krishnan put the marriage yoke against her and with blithe ignorance declared, "With this I beckon thee to my dominion," she was aware of some strain upon her self-esteem. "He for God only, she for God in him." "The man is the image and glory of God, but woman the image and glory of the man." She had flung the phrases from *Paradise Lost* and St. Paul priggishly at the Mother Superior in the mission convent whenever the latter spoke to her about the inferior position of Indian womanhood. Such contemptible nonsense! How about she who led the Rajput armies? How about those who were in the vanguard of civil disobedience? As if marriages weren't arranged in the West! The

fact that another civilization shared your errors didn't make
them any less erroneous, the voice of self-esteem insisted clearly
and coldly, and Kamala squirmed a little, trussed up in her
gold tissue sari. Why couldn't she wear it in the ordinary comfortable way? A wedding was not a *Bharata Natyam* performance.
She looked at Krishnan and saw that he too was far from comfortable. At first she had thought of him as the least of four evils.
The first evil had greasy hands, the second was paunchy and the
third moronic. But on closer inspection he did not seem evil at all.
In fact, he appeared to be even less happy than she was. The
thought that he might have made an even bigger mistake nearly
sent Kamala off into a peal of laughter. Her elders looked at her
scandalized, but Krishnan smiled, and it wasn't a bad smile, Kamala
decided. After all, there was logic in an arranged marriage,
none of those illusions of romantic love. Two people came together at random (well, almost) and remained together till the
fire died in its ashes, and they were successful because success
was perfectly normal if one brought good will and the desire to
understand into the relations of any two human beings. Wasn't
that a practical view of human nature? She would tell that to the
Mother Superior. But how fortunate that the laws of chance were
about to give her a husband with an appealing smile and a reasonable figure and one whose ignorance of Sanskrit made him happily unaware of the position of dominance which the marriage
ritual gave him.

They took the seven steps around the fire, she knowing as he
did not that the ceremony was over and that the same fire which
was their witness would burn in their home, witness to every consequence, everlastingly, inescapably, the fire of unity and of Sita's
ordeal.

5

The four days of feasting were in progress. Under the marquee
were gathered the civil service, the intelligentsia, men from the

professions and the *cognoscenti,* who, by some mysterious faculty, could tell exactly when and where a wedding was in progress. Krishnan circulated despondently among them. Some of these people, he decided, he could only have met in a previous incarnation. Kamala introduced him to Vijayaraghavan, the mathematical prodigy. Once he had been an assistant in a *pan* shop. He was too poor to buy any books, so to save money he had invented trigonometry and rediscovered calculus. A group of public-minded Brahmins, impressed by these accomplishments, had got up a subscription to send him to Presidency College, where, much to their dismay, he had revealed an erratic but unproductive brilliance and an altogether frivolous interest in that *femme fatale* of the intelligentsia, politics. Now he glared belligerently at Krishnan through thick horn-rimmed lenses.

"Fine feast you've got here. Don't you know that the people are starving?"

"I haven't noticed you eating any the less for that."

"These are positively my last *jilabis.* The marriage season is over and I have no other means of support. Next week, consequently, it is my intention to become a guest of His Majesty's Government."

"You seem pretty sure they'll look after you," said Krishnan. He liked the man. He could sense that the flippancy was not meant as bravado but as the protection for an underlying earnestness.

"Demonstrations," Vijayaraghavan replied, "are fortunately smaller these days. In forty-two they were on much too large a scale and it was extremely difficult to get the cell that one wanted. In fact, some of us couldn't get to jail at all. The British found it simpler to crack our skulls." He looked at Krishnan skeptically. "You will join us, won't you, in a gesture of non-co-operation with the nefarious *Raj?*"

"Where and when?" asked Krishnan. He hadn't taken part in a demonstration before, and the prospect generated a certain sense of excitement. Carrying sandwiches in Trafalgar Square was one thing; but the reality of civil disobedience, the supreme expression of discipline in defiance, appealed to him as an embodiment of the creative power of conformity. He wanted now to share in that discipline not as a nationalist but more ultimately as an Indian, for reasons that oddly had nothing to do with politics.

"It will be on Tuesday," Vijayaraghavan told him. "Symbolically, before the ocean itself. The sea," he explained for Krishnan's benefit, "is the means by which the British will quit India. There we shall assemble and a Congressman will lecture to us tediously on the demerits of the latest British proposals. After which, with remarkable self-restraint, we shall march remorselessly toward the nearest policeman. If it's the speaker I fear it will be, doing that may even be something of a relief."

Still uncertain of Krishnan's response and pretending to a lack of interest in it, he wandered off in search of a *jilabi*.

Sundaresan came up and tapped Krishnan's arm. "If I were you I wouldn't be seen with that character. It's no way to improve your prospects for Government Service."

Krishnan turned hotly on his university colleague. He had no strong objection to people who stayed out of politics in order to protect their careers. That was part of the pressure of responsibility. But when a university radical who led all others in scorn for the imperial edifice became, without any apparent inner struggle, an enthusiastic upholder of that edifice, he felt there was something indecent about the *volte-face*.

"You've got a nerve to say that, haven't you? When you were in Cambridge I remember your screaming louder than anyone else about Jallianwalla."

"Times change," said Sundaresan suavely. "Let's simply assume that I've grown up."

"In that case, praise be that most of India hasn't."

Sundaresan shrugged his shoulders in what was obviously meant as a gesture of good humor.

"I know what you are thinking—turncoat, renegade. Others have said it, and it makes no difference if you do. I'm doing a job. It has to be done, no matter what the Government, and I do it a little better than the next man. When the British leave—as they must—and Congress comes in, I'll still be doing the job two notches better and teaching it to immature hotheads like you."

Krishnan looked at him with all the scorn he could muster. "Do you seriously think," he said as scathingly as he could, "that Congress will want to co-operate with people who've spent their adult lives putting Congressmen in jail?"

Sundaresan was unruffled. "My dear fellow, it isn't at all a question of what they want. Every government needs a functioning machinery. It's a problem of efficiency, not of likes and dislikes. If we're useful to them they'll be obliged to use us."

"You and your steel frame," retorted Krishnan. He was uncomfortably conscious that there was no basis on which to argue with the other man. His only response could be one of indignation, and that evidently was without effect. "Don't be patriotic," he continued, repeating the words in the hope that they might hit harder. "Don't be patriotic. Just be indispensable. If that's your philosophy you can keep it."

Sundaresan looked at him blandly. It had trickled off him many times before. "When you've been in India a little longer, Krishnan, you won't feel so ill-disposed toward us. The law is there and so is the authority to enforce it. If we don't apply it someone else will. We at least will apply it with humanity."

Krishnan was trying to think of an effective retort when his venerable uncle from Palghat rushed up. "Is it true that the British bathe only once a week?"

Krishnan found himself not averse to explaining the sanitary deficiencies of Western Europe.

The festivities went on. Night fell with the suddenness typical of the tropics, and the gathering drifted out from the marquee, under the stars' natural canopy, the moonlight softening the lavish brilliance of heavy jewelry and brocaded gold. The nightingale of the Carnatic was not present, but her heir-apparent sang, a plump, stocky figure seated in front of a microphone, clapping her hands in unison with the music. She sang of Shiva dancing in the great temple of Chidambaram, the timeless dance in which each gesture is eternity with every movement of that mighty form expressing and exhausting the history of a universe. "You who danced with your limbs held high, the moon in your forehead and the river Ganga in your matted locks, lift me great Shiva as your limbs are lifted." In the beginning was rhythm, not the word. Not darkness, but moonlight and the radiance of creation. There had never been nothing without form and void but always form in its essence, everlastingly changing. He heard, half heard, the drums and the *tamboura* accompanying the voice—throbbing, civilized, sophisticated frenzy. He saw the great figure of the Nataraja, one leg arched in that supreme expression of energy, the dying smile of the demon beneath the other's lightness, all that infinite power of destruction drawn back into the bronze circle of repose.

> *neither flesh nor fleshless*
> *Neither from nor toward, at the still point there the dance is.*

Paradox, contradiction, miracle—they were the barriers to which explanation was driven. But at least in that hypnotic figure the paradox was a radiance in one's senses, the intense union of power with tranquillity, not captured but liberated in that eternal dancing. And the miracle was not that of a single individual's unrepeatable insight, Ozymandias lost beneath the seventh city, there to be disinterred by the sure hands of Blenkinstauffer and placed in the great vestibule for millions to gape on, by courtesy of fruit juice and vanadium and even your best friends wouldn't dare to tell you. Again and again, century after century, thousands of times in city or in village, the molten metal would settle into solidity and the craftsman gazing upon it would feel the strange light of a vision not his own. Feel it perhaps in parched earth and prowling jungle, in the marriage drums of the sea's far-off thunder, tranquillity where the surf breaks, in the cave of loneliness with the glaciers grinding. Creation, Destruction. Two concepts but one dance, the trampling leg, the outthrust arms asserting the law invincibly, ecstatically, the drums beating, the strings plucked in supplicating monotony, raise me, raise me into the mystery's center; for something to be born something must die.

"Something must die," he told Kamala abruptly.

She did not at all understand what her strange husband was saying, so she decided to reply with equal elementality. "Nothing ever dies. It says so in the *Gita*."

That was the end of the conversation. The gulf was too wide for repartee to bridge it. But as his mind went over it, he wondered if it were really a gulf, if the opposing formulations hadn't meant the same thing, like the two concepts united in one dance. The generalizations were nothing in themselves, only the abstract poles of a situation between which the tension lived and fructified. And when a man, discovering, sank down into his own reality, was it not the tension alone that mattered, the pull in the nerves and the beckoning song in the blood?

The song died away, the resonance of the *tamboura* decayed into the silence, the genteel applause flared generously up, restoring the right world and its reassuring correctness. He wondered how strong the disciplined surface was, a man's life foreseen with all the precision of ages, stretched taut as the skin which the drummer's fingers caressed, over the energy of the dark, jubilant waters.

6

Four days the feasting continued. Morning and evening the guests flowed, the gifts were given, hands together in respectful greeting, your relatives even if you've never seen them, no man is an island and every man his uncle. Cloth of gold, cling of georgette, gleam of shot silk upon the burnished ocean, bangle and spangle and the clinking anklet, diamonds leading the inquiring noses, earrings from the plump lobes like double umbrellas of scandal. I have met you before, you of the *choli* of alarming brevity, with your midriff flat as the Rajputana desert. Permit me to introduce myself: V. S. Krishnan, humble student of belonging. Gaze and gauze, cast not upon me the diamonds of your dowager disdain. Kind Sirs, venerable antiphonies, *Shri* and *Sow,* we who were churned together out of the milk by Mount Meru, Krishnan salutes you with the wrath of *Kaliyuga*. Shall I go and return, farewell, farewell, by all means yes, same place and same commotion, forget me not, for I shall know you never. Slippers clattering on the gravel, the cars moving away, moonlight gratefully on the very last anklet. Then suddenly the loneliness, the house still and waiting, everyone asleep but the two on the cement floor with the bright barrier of naked steel between them. That was Kruger's inspiration. He had found it in a book of unchallangeable antiquity: a drawn sword had to lie between the married couple for four nights. Of course, no one had done it for as long as one could remember, but there it was, indisputably in the text, and the omissions of others were no license for one's own.

Madras was a pacific town, and a sword was not easy to acquire. A fruit knife perhaps, said Mother hopefully, but Kruger was adamant, so the sword was procured and the situation explained to the uneasy official in Fort St. George whose job was to prevent the illegal possession of arms. There it lay edge up between them, the embroidered scabbard thrown behind the pillows and four volumes of Freud's works at the base holding the handle in position. Krishnan would lie there wondering which was more desirable, to be stabbed in the back or sliced open at the tummy. Then he would fall asleep turned toward the weapon, on the principle that it was more dignified to die face to face with one's enemy. Once he had put his hand across to stroke Kamala's hair, but after the vitality of her response had nearly deprived him of his elbow they had both decided to endure their situation.

So the golden days went by, brocade and satin sweeping for the last time through the massive iron gates. The lights were switched off. Next day the marquee would be dismantled. All the mendicants had been fed and had blessed the union with hyperboles, each according to the intensity of his hunger. Tomorrow one would shrink from the leper on the street; but today he too was fed and his felicitations also were part of a tissue of benediction, with no discordant thread. For Krishnan an exhausting carnival was over. For Kamala a page could never be turned back. The family house of her mother was a thing of the past, and before her rose the house of Krishnan's father, bleak, massive and forbidding.

A servant had opened the twice-bolted wooden gate, and the car drove slowly into the portico, the tires crunching on the loose gravel. Krishnan's father greeted them almost perfunctorily. His mother embraced them, but a little abstractedly, as if her emotions were elsewhere. For them the climax was over. Now the consequences had to be measured and sifted, a structure of responsibilities modified, a new member integrated into the tight, almost ruthless hierarchy of the family. Had it really been Krishnan and Kamala that mattered? Or was it their marriage, satisfying Father's resolve to maneuver his son into his proper station, satisfying Mother's inarticulate longing for prestige, Kruger's lust for antiquity and the common hunger for significant spectacle? The multicolored cloth of festivity was gone now and there remained only the pretexts on which it hung.

The hall was lonely and the lamp high and dim as they climbed the quiet stairway, their shadows merging in the flickering space beyond them. In the room itself there was relatively little furniture. It was an innocent room, the heavy corners yet to be filled with memories. Sticks of incense burned fragrantly, the points glowing like fireflies, merging with the odor of sandalwood and the fitful coolness of the air borne in spasmodically from the far-off beaches. Kamala walked to the window. She loosened her hair, and in the moonlight it tumbled about her like a waterfall of darkness, down her back to the taut firmness of a waist so slender that one was reluctant to touch it. But it was not Kamala's intention to be provocative. Her thoughts at this moment were not even of Krishnan but of the whole new world into which she had come. The room was hers; she had agreed to its confinements. What life would grow now in its sullen spaces, what wall of loneliness would she stumble against in the endless, pitiless search for understanding? She was the bride now, the housewife, the keys were all there in the silver ring at the waist of her sari. Which was the door that they could never unlock?

She turned back into the room, and as the tears brimming in

her eyes subsided, she looked steadily at Krishnan with an intense tranquillity that seemed the dispassionate mirror of his loneliness. Her arms were held out toward him. Her body shivered as he encircled her waist and she moved against him tense and tremulous, not with eagerness, not even with curiosity, but with a deep force of commitment to the unknown beyond her. The moonlight streamed through the windows, brilliant enough almost to throw the shadow of the bars upon her, white surf of moonlight pounding at the body and the rock pools of her eyes with their impregnable gentleness. Krishnan could hear the ocean's muffled thunder. It was miles away and centuries behind him. But the drums of the dance were there remorselessly beating, the tattoo blurred like an ancestral memory.

For a moment Krishnan was tempted to withdraw. What did they know of each other? Frail, conventional, arbitrary fragments pieced together between the peepings of relatives. Was that a basis for this irrevocable communion which would anchor and dominate the pattern of their lives? Then he looked at Kamala's upturned face, serene and frightened and confident, and suddenly the weight of resignation fell across his shoulders, implacable but strangely sympathetic, compelling him into the prescient darkness, making him that which he was doomed to be.

CHAPTER TWO

The Demonstration

THE BEACH was long and beautiful and the city's pride when they acquired a sense of it. The sand went out flat for a hundred yards and nearly knee deep, before the shelving started to where the waters began. Sometimes the waves would splash up the slope, slapping gently toward the line of shells that was high-water mark. Today they steepened the shelving with their impact, coming in from beyond the galleons of cumulus on the brilliant horizon. The breakers rode in diagonally, so that the manes were long and wedge shaped, and the backs translucent green and glossy with the tension, before the explosion took place, or its frustrated force spent itself caressingly on the water. Above the shell line were the catamarans and the more substantial but still rickety boats, the nets hung over piles of rope to dry, and the smell of fish assailing the elite's delicate noses, as they paraded the five-mile drive in their cars or sat on the sand in rapacious clots of gossip.

Today there was little about which to gossip. Those whom continual acquiescence had made cautious, who felt they had more than their reputations to lose, who had decided that prudence was the better part of politics, had kept their imported cars away from the sea front, leaving the road free to the bare feet and the white caps scurrying breathlessly to their rendezvous with significance. The beach was filling slowly but convincingly with those who had still to learn, or preferred to forget.

Krishnan, Kamala and Vijayaraghavan had arrived early and had taken up their positions in front of the makeshift platform, before the sea of white expanded and swelled back almost as far as expectancy seemed to reach. Krishnan looked at the flotsam of faces, not all of them were young and vital, as imagination would have liked to see them, but some old, some tired, several apathetic, and many wearing that stark look of acceptance, as if to them rebellion itself were merely the most valid form of resignation. Some of them came because they liked processions; others because prison was four walls and a roof; and yet others because the calamitous years had struck them often and blindly, and this at least would be punishment with a reason. Why they came mattered less than what they hoped for from their coming. Assembled together, they would be a little more themselves, finding in the unison of protest a common chord and reminder of the truth, as if the sea of their sacrifice were the temple tank's clear waters, which they could gaze into, recovering the image of self-respect.

He wondered why he was there himself. His parents were unaware of his real whereabouts. Their impression was that he was at the latest sociological movie—a songful, sorrowful, and occasionally sinful exposé of gambling as the most deadly of vices. Perhaps it would have been better to have been truthful, since the logic of the situation was designed to flow into his and Kamala's arrest, and his deception meant that he would only have to face his family with the consequences when it was too late to retract the choice. Yet he knew that that was precisely why he had done it. He couldn't say no to his mother's twisting hands, his father's bludgeon of responsibility, the voices of resignation talking of practical politics. Nothing would change or somebody else would change it, the rains came or did not and the extra drop wouldn't matter, the work of constructive men was not reformation but learning to live with the essential facts. "Action," Kruger might have said. "It is basically a lower-caste privilege. A Brahmin is the intellect, the philosopher. He is not the king and even less the multitude." Well, this was a new fact, an essential one, and

they would have to live with it. It was a way to say no. It was
rebellion licensed. It was protest, the individual drop of protest,
merging and flowing in the collective sea, and a man's life was
given back in the tide of it, just as much as by the desolate land
over which the clouds of the monsoon gathered and the tryst of
the rain drew its advancing curtain.

The speaker was now taking his place on the platform. He was a
small, studious-looking man, his quiet face starved of everything
but the facts and the apologetic yet obstinate will to change them.
White-*dhotied* and white-capped, he seemed the natural extension
of the anonymous sea that had raised him to his accidental eminence, and the waves of which he would discipline with his teaching. He looked slowly around him, raised his hands for silence,
and ceremoniously flourished his spectacles, just like the lecturer
in the School of Economics. The British, he observed judiciously,
had ruined India politically, economically, physically, psychologi-
cally, socially and morally. This was the preliminary warming up
so that the audience would have time to collect its attention and
the police the opportunity to decide on countermeasures. Sadly,
the speaker proceeded to substantiate his case. There was no indignation in his voice, for he was attacking no one, not even re-
proaching a friend, but simply seeking to expose the circumstances
that ruined the ethics of even the best intentioned. The literacy
rate, he explained, was less than under Akbar. The expectation of
life was so low that half his audience was living on borrowed
time. A great maritime nation had been reduced to catamarans.
Instead of a network of canals which would felicitously provide
both irrigation and transport, the country had an inferior railway
system designed for the purpose of aggression rather than pilgrimage.

Vijayaraghavan nudged Krishnan's elbow. "Frightful rotters the
British. Absolutely satanic. Don't know what we would do without them. Who are we going to blame after they leave?"

The speaker was now entering the main stream of his discourse.
"We come now to the proposals before us. Let us not hold them
against their respected author." He paused. This was an important

point and proved his objectivity. One must never confuse the individual with the system. "But no less a person than Mr. Churchill himself has stated that he did not become Prime Minister to preside over the liquidation of the British Empire. Is it not true that the sponsor of these proposals, admirable in himself, is but the unwitting tool of these obsolescent forces of reaction?"

The picture came to Krishnan's mind of a mild-mannered man trying desperately to look like a screwdriver, while around him blared the stentorian tones of England's former Prime Minister: "Give us the tools and we will finish the job."

"It is true," continued the speaker, "that a Labor Government is now in power. But can we trust even the England of Laski, Attlee, and Gollancz? Traditions die hard. The engines of repression are not easily abandoned. Power corrupts and absolute power corrupts absolutely." He produced the maxim with an air of surprise at his own brilliance which almost convinced Krishnan that he had invented the phrase.

Vijayaraghavan groaned under his breath. "Time to get on with the business," he told Krishnan. "We'll lose enough of them through faintheartedness. We don't want to lose others through boredom."

"It doesn't bore me," Krishnan reassured him.

His colleague looked incredulous. "It's plain enough that you're new to it. When it's happened to you for the hundredth time you'll be more concerned with the essentials than with the verbiage."

But it wasn't verbiage at all, thought Krishnan. There was a point in the triteness which education missed. You had to come to it with your mind a *tabula rasa* to realize how right the man was in his total ordinariness, an extension of all of them, just anyone, only two inches higher, hanging on to everyone else's thoughts, diffidently, monotonously declaring the average strength. If he had been original he would have been set apart. He would have been their leader, not their expression, fishlike, hands flapping in gentle, irrelevant gestures, all the stubbed toes of everyone's mediocrity pushed back into the sudden capacity for resistance.

When Krishnan looked at Kamala he was conscious of how

much further her reaction went. It was not in what she said or what her silence said. There was an absorption about her too deep for protest or exhortation to animate her face, so that one might have thought that she was hardly listening, were it not for the constant, nearly commanding earnestness which made it plain that she heard some deeper reality. She had so much more penetration than he had—than the normal thrust which sympathy gave him—to reach the facts through the familiar phrases. Hers was a sense of identity with the occasion because for her, as Krishnan now understood, nonviolence was not simply a technique but an invoking of qualities instinctive in her nature. You did not oppose your enemy. You did not even consider him as such. You accepted him, but without surrender, completely without compromise, so that acceptance was a mirror pitiless and intact, held up remorselessly to the Gorgon's head.

"Nonviolence is a force and not an attitude," the speaker proclaimed, and watching Kamala, Krishnan knew that she felt something of the force exulting in her, joining her to the passive strength of millions in her country who, by the very depth of their resignation, were able to transform what was imposed upon them.

The speaker was exhorting them now to non-co-operation, the statement of freedom despite subjugation, the moral challenge like a lens focusing injustice. How it was to be done was not entirely clear; the crowd moved on to the road in masses and stood there with a crowd's uncertain strength.

The speaker himself appeared a little nonplused. He had accomplished his task, laid bare the logic and morality of protest, but it was as if his part in the common music was over, as if the feelings he had raised demanded a different instrument.

Vijayaraghavan stepped forward into the space of indecision.

"My friends," he said firmly and clearly, the deliberate lack of exhortation in his voice seeming to focus the expectancy around him. "My friends, let us stop both the traffic and the wheels of reaction. Peacefully but with maximum obstructiveness, let us march in the direction of the Governor's house."

A murmur of assent shook itself through the gathering. The

police stepped closer, fingering their *lathis*. Several who had come out of curiosity drifted away from the margins; others who wished to leave were pressed on by the crowd's momentum. The police set themselves in a line across the road and the crowd moved up with maddening slowness, unarmed, white-capped, the women in saris of ritualistic simplicity, as if seeking to prolong the tension of their helplessness. A few slogans were shouted. Then somebody began to chant in a thin, cracked voice Gandhiji's favorite song, and the refrain swelled into a muted, desperate murmur. Some of the police began to look uncomfortable, but the first line was up to them, and their clubs swung and swung again. Ten persons went down, bruised and bleeding. Two in the second row tried to run, but the police were moving in from the side, and both were caught, one with a crushing blow in the back that sent him writhing to the ground with a rasping scream of agony and terror.

Krishnan was sickened. "They're Indians, damn you," he shouted. "They're your own people, they're only doing what is right. Can't you see they're your countrymen even if you are police?"

He was surprised at how empty the words sounded. It should not have been so. Nonviolence was supposed to compel a man to his conscience, to purify the image of injustice, till he who created it could no longer endure it. But if that were the truth, the consequences were elsewhere. Perhaps somewhere in London an M.P. would rise to ask his questions, and a liberal don would write letters to the *Times*. But here on the road, with its potholes and its flower beds, the cemetery next to the examination hall, the morality was stripped away and there was only the conflict, the clarified forces moving as if in ritual, always the ritual that seemed his country's confession, whether in death or marriage or in protest. The crowd had its momentum, not simply that of courage, which here and there pulled taut an individual face, but of a fervent and triumphant submissiveness, every day's resignation wrapped around a purpose, the rock for the first time in the clay of their yielding. The police had their brutality because that was the only way to stop momentum; it was not an answer but simply a response, the iron-clad staves flailing away mechanically, mercilessly, devastatingly, at the advancing problem. They could see the end now beyond the faltering bodies. A crowd was no different from any man in a rice field, racked by malaria, laboring under the sun's lash, staying alive until he could stand it no longer. Give them a wall and they would kneel against it. Brutality was their wall now and their fate. The stones didn't matter as long as the structure was solid.

The crowd was wavering now, beginning to lose its cohesion. Many in the ruck were trying to turn back. There was the confused, spasmodic murmur of irresolution. A few more blows and it would rise to the pitch of panic.

Vijayaraghavan stepped jauntily out of the turmoil, striding up unhesitatingly to the nearest policeman. He swept off his Gandhi cap with an exaggerated gesture, as if it were a top hat at an Ascot gathering. The police stopped swinging and began to stare. The terror mounting in the crowd subsided into a ripple of expectant interest.

"Well, well," said Vijayaraghavan, his accent suitably mincing, "If it isn't Doraiswamy. You remember me, don't you? You cracked my skull in Virudhanagar once. I see you have been promoted, my dear fellow. How happy I am, in my own humble way, to have assisted you in your meteoric career."

The policeman stood there looking at him. He stood with his legs spread and his weight forward on the balls of his feet. He was a short, powerful man with pig's eyes and he was in his job because he liked it—particularly what happened at the other end of the *lathi*.

"Get out," he said to Vijayaraghavan thickly.

"Tut! Tut! Is that any way to speak to a colleague? Even a policeman needs a friend."

The crowd tittered a little. Humiliation was a danger that was past now. They knew it reassuringly and pulled themselves back, digging in the toes of their dignity a little, watching their fears

shrugged away in the self-deprecating gestures, the screwed-up
eyes behind the horn-rimmed glasses peering sardonically at the
officers of the law.

The policeman laughed but did not smile. He hadn't been told
about ridicule. But the book was an answer to many things not in
the book. He looked at Vijayaraghavan. Then his weight shifted
and the *lathi* swung viciously for the face.

Vijayaraghavan side-stepped hastily, but not far or fast enough.
The blow caught him close to his ear and he went down, blood
streaming from his nostrils. The policeman hit him in the chest
as he fell. He looked at the prostrate form contemptuously, raised
his leg, and twice deliberately kicked him in the groin. Vijayaraghavan's body clenched, twitched convulsively, rolled over and lay
still.

There was a hiss in the crowd, as if the pain were theirs too.
Then the reaction started, a murmur building up, but this time
with a somber, threatening overtone that oddly brought relief to
the faces of the policemen, stepping forward, fingering their iron-
clad sticks, ready once more to resume their assault on the problem.

It was anger at last and that was what they wanted.

"You bastard!" screamed Krishnan at the man still straddling
Vijayaraghavan's body. "You low-down, cowardly bastard!"

The policeman grinned happily. This was a language everyone
understood. He spat ostentatiously and hitched up his trousers.

Krishnan saw the blow coming and ducked under it. Then, as
the policeman swung around with the momentum of it Krishnan
drove hard into his solar plexus. The policeman grunted and
dropped his *lathi*. Krishnan straightened him up with a mild poke
in the face, jackknifed him with another jab in the belly and hit
his chin squarely with everything he had.

The policeman lost interest in the evening's proceedings.

Krishnan picked up the *lathi* and waved it over his head. "Come
on and get it," he shouted to the policeman.

The crowd roared and surged forward. They could always do
whatever the man in front did. Discipline was a tension they accepted, the way their lives stretched out into rebellion, but when

the dykes burst there was nothing to hold the barriers, and so they surged forward jubilantly, with an exultation that frustration had enriched. Krishnan felt the liberation welling in him also. It was the natural way to change a problem—the hammer of force and not the mirror of protest. If everyone did that, back beyond the beaches, into the hinterland and the four hundred million, if the hammers were multiplied those countless ordinary times, there could be salvation and dignity in that also.

He was up to the wall that they were going to break through, a man in khaki on a horse lunging toward him, and he swung from the toes up with an aggressive elation. The blow never reached its destination. Somebody chopped down with a *lathi,* a blinding bolt of pain shot through his arm, there was a crashing noise that splintered through his senses, and then the base of his skull seemed to break open. The red haze poured over him, roaring and burning. He saw the crowd an enormous distance off. Then the dark waters seized him, lashing his body against the avid rocks, down, down, everlastingly down, the pillar of pain pushing him down remorselessly, and then at last the black grotto of oblivion.

2

"Where am I?"

"Not in jail, thank goodness."

He wiggled his foot and noted with hazy satisfaction that it still seemed to bear an organic relationship to his body. Cautiously, he set out to find the missing part. The face seemed to be his own, notwithstanding the process of excavation that was going on behind it. The hands examining his face sent searing stabs up the arms to which they were painfully connected. Since the pain terminated wrenchingly in what he was prepared to recognize as his shoulders, it seemed to follow that the arms were his. He proceeded gingerly with his explorations. What should have been his chest was twice as large as before and peculiarly corrugated. A delicate tearing seemed to accompany every movement.

"Be careful," said somebody. "You're in a plaster cast."

He recognized the voice as that of his mother. With considerable effort he succeeded in focusing its context. When he had done so he wished that he hadn't begun.

His father, his uncle, and his father-in-law were there, and Kamala of course. Never since his wedding had he witnessed so formidable and united an array of talent.

His father, head of the phalanx, leaned forward aggressively. "I see that you have recovered consciousness. It is too much to hope, of course, that you have come to your senses."

"We mustn't be unkind to him," Mother protested. "We have to do everything possible to help him recover."

"Recover," snorted Father. "If he stays here for a month it'll be good riddance to addled brains."

"Think of the expenses," observed Mother innocently.

This seemed to unnerve Father, who turned promptly to the reserve strength of his phalanx. "You're much more temperate than I am, Sankaran. I leave it to you to handle this situation. Kindly inform my unfortunate son of the progress and consequences of his folly."

His father-in-law leaned forward, a spare, sad individual from the reproachful world beyond Krishnan's feet. He spoke levelly, precisely, giving to each word only that critical degree of emphasis which was necessary to display it in the mosaic.

"After you were disabled, the crowd surged over you. They were apparently excited by your belligerent example, and several laid violent hands on the officers of the law."

He was obviously proud of his carefully fashioned English, the periods meticulously balanced, in the silver-tongued tradition of South-Indian oratory. It was a pride that could have seemed empty, however, if his manners had not made it apparent that his sense of tidiness went deeper than his language, and that the world of the eighteenth century was a model to him in ways other than prose style.

"Several policemen were injured," he continued. "In the commotion certain people near you very wisely realized that having incited a crowd to riot and destruction, and having assaulted and injured, with deliberate intention, a police officer in the execution of his duties, you faced charges far more serious than simple disobedience of the law."

"In other words," explained Father, "you'd have landed a three-year sentence. As a common criminal, not a political offender, 'C' Class. Hard labor. That's what you'd have got, and don't tell me you wouldn't have deserved it."

"All men deserve damnation," pointed out Kruger. "It is a Calvinist plagiarism which the ancient pessimists of India first discovered. However, as the tale proceeds you will discern a fundamental divergence between the ideal and the actual."

Sankaran proceeded patiently to lay down his mosaic. "Your neighbors took measures to remove you from the scene. The crowd had passed well beyond the area of your assault, and you were able to leave by a side street. There was a policeman on duty, but he may have had a conscience; if so, it was assisted by the contents of Kamala's purse."

"How fortunate," said Mother excitedly, "that my daughter-in-law had such unexpected presence of mind."

She pursed her lip, realizing that she had picked the wrong word. "By unexpected I meant that she was so surprisingly modern. Happily so, of course. But in my day no one taught me to bribe policemen."

"It isn't a question of presence of mind," said Kruger, "but of certain marginal felicities in her horoscope. If she had been born even two hours later your only son would by now be a convict."

Mother shuddered and Father looked appropriately grim. Sankaran's face was somber also, but the reason in his case was largely chagrin at these unaesthetic interruptions of his discourse.

"You were taken to a house in the neighborhood," he resumed, with a noticeable acceleration of his tempo. "I was informed and removed you unobtrusively. You are now in a private hospital. The owner is a friend of mine who is not unaccustomed to dealing with political injuries. No questions will be asked. The nurse is completely reliable. I am not aware of any evidence likely to lead to your identification. You are, fortunately, unknown to the police. Your picture has appeared in the *Illustrated Weekly,* but those in search of suspects are unlikely to have seen the marriage pages of that estimable periodical. Once you have recovered from your injuries and from the mental aberrations of which they were the result, there is no reason why you cannot return to a normal, reasonable and constructive life."

The pattern was completed at last, despite interruptions, and he surveyed it with a craftsman's satisfaction. He looked at Krishnan intently but a little apprehensively, as if he were an inconvenient file, successfully disposed of but certain to return.

"You should be grateful to your father-in-law," said Krishnan's father. "Because of his discreet and able handling of the matter you have been saved from an onerous prison sentence, and your prospects for the civil service have not been materially prejudiced. If the blows of the *lathi* have hammered any sense into your fortunately thick skull, there may be some profit in this wretched affair."

"Let us leave him now," suggested Sankaran, "to the tender ministrations of his devoted wife." He smirked mechanically as he departed; it seemed the right accompaniment to so rotund a phrase.

The phalanx rose in unison to its feet, looking down with sedate satisfaction at the unnatural problem that had reared itself on the beach and was now reduced to its appropriate dimensions— V. S. Krishnan, with three cracked ribs in the plaster cast, collecting himself in the family strait jacket. It would be as it always had been, only more so. The best proof that it was over was that it could not have happened at all. The lava came down, the flood swept over the mud hut, and who was to know what impulse had been petrified on the threshold, where the door opened to the sky and the distant mountains.

They turned half about, Kruger swinging the door open as the pillars of society, gathered in single file, moved out of the room in an imperious colonnade. Kamala remained. The family juggernaut must have rolled over her too. But it had not changed her, had not even provoked in her expression the normal rejoinders of submission or defiance. It was as if she had let the facts flow over her and, when the tide had ebbed away, come back to herself.

She sat, not moving, at the foot of the bed, with what might have been mistaken for demureness. She said nothing. By now, however, he knew her well enough not to misunderstand her silence. He realized that it arose not out of any desire to be prudent but because she wanted him to find his own position, without seeking to direct his search or to fence it in with the barriers of an attitude.

He decided to start with what was on his mind. Perhaps it was too much to expect a citation for courage. Perhaps he hadn't been brave at all but only uninhibited. But coming back into responsibility, his beaten-up ego pinned on the hospital bed, he felt he had some right to an expression of sympathy, of moderate concern at least for the physical damage.

"They didn't even ask me how I felt," he said.

"I know how terrible it must be," she replied.

She was looking at him, not his injuries, as she said that, and his first reaction was a surge of relief that however much they might disagree they were able to speak the same language. Then he felt the prick of discontent because she hadn't joined his criticism of the family.

"They don't care," he insisted. "Not as long as their plans are not affected. Don't misunderstand me, I'm not trying to pretend I was a hero. But I wasn't a coward or a hooligan either."

"Of course not," she replied. "Of course you weren't a coward."

She was saying it only to him, and there was no lack of understanding or of sympathy in her voice, yet he couldn't avoid the uncomfortable feeling that she was prepared to say it of the entire human race. There was another standard in her mind, a different image of bravery. He knew what it was and, reflecting on it, decided to confront it.

"What happened to Vijayaraghavan?" he asked her almost curtly.

Her answer came as if the question were overdue. "He was badly hurt. The doctors say it will take him a month to recover.

When he does there's a prison sentence to follow. His having been injured isn't going to save him."

She couldn't keep the admiration wholly out of her voice, and he couldn't avoid feeling the implicit reproach which was its other side.

"I know," he said. "That's where I ought to be too."

"Remember what your father told you," she replied. "It would be several years and not as a political."

There was nothing insincere about her loyalty, yet he knew instinctively that that was not what she meant. She had wanted a different form of courage from him, the courage to go down like his colleague, unresisting. Now she took the consequences of his violence as the opportunity to forgive his failure.

He felt the anger working in him gently. It was the right course, the natural course, the only proper reaction to brutality, and he didn't need to be forgiven for it.

"Damn it, what was I supposed to do? Stand there and see him beaten into unconsciousness?"

"You did what you thought was right."

It was the sort of reassurance he least wanted.

"But what do you think?" he asked almost peremptorily. He would have it out of her even if it hurt him.

"In your position I would have done the same thing."

She wasn't saying that to be diplomatic. He knew her well enough, and at a deeper level of recognition, to realize that she was asking him only to be himself, and to let understanding come in its own way to him. But he couldn't sit down. He couldn't accept passivity, or maybe he hadn't the stamina for it. There was a nail in the wall, and he would hang the poster on it, even if the writing were to declare his guilt.

"That still doesn't make it the right thing, does it?"

"Please don't force me into criticizing you, Krishnan." She said his name deliberately, slowly, with no affectionate abbreviation, as if trying to make the fullest allowance for him. But the obstinacy was also there, unyielding in her voice. It was a time for understanding, not for judgment.

He tried for the first time to put his point of view to her.

"They were Indians, don't you see, that's what made it unbearable. Remember what Sundaresan said. Somebody has to apply the law, and we at least will apply it with humanity. That's their humanity. They enjoyed every minute of it. It was written all over them. They're the servants of the law for no other reason than what it lets them do."

It had sounded empty on the beach, but here at least he had expected it to sound meaningful. Brutality on the sands was a reflex action. Here it should have been something they could stand apart from and condemn.

She didn't condemn them. "They aren't like that," she said. "Not in the end. It's something in their hands. It isn't something they can always live with."

"It's their law," he told her. "They laid it down and they can suffer by it."

She shook her head. "It isn't that way, Krishnan. Only the truth is the law. It's in them too, the same truth. But it can't be torn out of them. You've got to bring them to it by letting them be themselves."

He tried another approach. "Maybe," he suggested, "you object to what I did because it went wrong. People got killed. There may be an excuse for more repression. I acted impulsively, out of anger, because I was sickened at what they did to Vijay. But don't let the blunder delude you. Most of the time—far more often than you think—when force is applied, force is the only answer."

She wouldn't give way. "It isn't a tactic, Krishnan. It's a way to the truth, and the truth is the same on both sides of the conflict."

She spoke of the large abstractions as if they belonged to her securely, without her having to raise her voice in order to reach up to their level.

He felt that her mind grew differently and from different origins. Or perhaps that was not so. Perhaps what surprised him was only her consistency, and how deep down the roots of consistency went. He couldn't tell. He only knew that he couldn't find out the shape of her character in this way by playing a flashlight casually on its edges. There had to be a different illumination, a recognition below the level of debate.

He wasn't ready even for the gentleness of her challenge. He could feel the tiredness closing in as he pondered, the aches in his body rising to heckle his thoughts.

The newspaper lay at her side, where the phalanx had left it in the course of its exit. He asked for it, grateful for the diversion.

"You shouldn't read it," she said. "There's nothing in it to amuse you. Only misinterpretations of your criminal misdeeds."

He welcomed the hint of the twinkle in her voice, coming as it did from her essential seriousness.

"It's safe enough," he assured her. "I'm ten minutes older now. It isn't going to hurt me as it might have."

She took him at his word, which pleased him also, and held the page up, since he could not do so himself.

He read the two-column headline: "HOOLIGAN ACTIVITIES BREAK UP PEACEFUL DEMONSTRATION." A grievous blow had been dealt, the report went on to say, to the forces of truth and nonviolence. What was to have been a disciplined march of protest had turned into a disorderly riot, with loss of life and wanton destruction of property. Such tendencies, if allowed to continue, might sound the death knell of the civil-disobedience movement. Their eruption on this occasion was obviously not the result of momentary impulse but the work of calculating forces determined to undermine Congress in its hour of triumph. Unfortunately, the provocateur could not be identified. Only fleeting glimpses had been caught of him. It appeared that he was unknown in the neighborhood, and this, combined with his brief appearance and obviously planned disappearance, lent credence to the theory that he had been imported for the occasion. The police were investigating intensively, on the assumption that the young man was a Communist.

Krishnan chuckled quietly. "It's just as Vijay said, we need a scapegoat. The British were fine, and now it'll be the Communists. We'll hang failure on them any time things go wrong."

"I don't know much about scapegoats," said Kamala disconcertingly. "As a matter of fact, it was Father who had the idea circulated. He thought that if the police were fed this kind of suspicion, they would waste their time to our benefit in raiding bazaars and excavating godowns. The last place they would dream of looking for you would be in a private hospital run by an eminent liberal."

It would have distressed him earlier, this new evidence of his father-in-law's farsightedness, the perfect maneuver executed by the phalanx, wiping fact out and now creating fiction. But lying there in the room, with Kamala by him, the family pressures seemed less intimidating, at least to the extent that he no longer felt the failure of his rebellion as an assault on his sense of self-respect. Looking up at Kamala's calm, he could not share it; but he could at least visualize, mirrored in its conviction, a more secure way to find and be himself.

He began his inquiry again, wanting at least to feel the surface of her serenity. "You're so much more Indian than I am, Kamala, and maybe for you nonviolence isn't just a philosophy but something in the blood—"

She cut him short, still trying to be fair to him. "It isn't like that. You mustn't feel a difference. You acted bravely and decently. He was stronger than you, and you had only your hands. Still, if you could recognize the existence of a higher form of courage, not as a criticism of you but as something you might develop into . . ."

She paused, pursing her lips. She hadn't meant to be patronizing, but it had happened that way out of the stubbornness of language. In her eyes he could see the wish for a more adequate form of sincerity and the flicker of gratitude when his response forgave her.

"I can vaguely understand that," he said, shifting the argument from the personal to the political. "Still, both you and I share an ordinary patriotism. We want our country to be free. What if nonviolence cannot achieve that?"

"It will achieve it," she insisted gently, "and if it doesn't, nothing can. Yes, I know you'll argue that it's never happened before. But all of a sudden things do happen in history, and then all history after that is different. Like fire. Like the wheel. Can't you have a moral discovery like those physical discoveries?"

He looked at her, taken aback a little at her intensity, as she continued eagerly, unconcious of his surprise.

"When a country is poor it must build its strength on its poverty. Nonviolence is like water falling, forever falling. Each little drop of protest doesn't matter, but if it keeps on eternally, unceasingly, it wears down injustice to the very stones of conscience."

It wasn't the argument that impressed him so much as the way she said it, as if it were part of herself, like the glint of moonlight fingering her hair's luster, or sloping down the trim contours of the unaffected body, so gently given and so completely retained. It didn't matter how remote the argument was, how desiccated the slogan. She would pull it back to experience, to wave and curve and origin, the force of engagement, the challenge of recognition.

He made his objection as firmly as he could. "It's all very well, this reaching down to conscience, but what if it isn't there? There are tyrannies enough that have managed to do without it. You can hold up the mirror as much as you want to, Kamala, but there's no law obliging one to look at the image."

"There always is a conscience," she replied. "Always, if the water washes away enough."

She didn't say it with the fervor of persuasion, or half-rhapsodically, as a statement of faith. It was fact to her, not belief, not even conviction, but fact as indisputable as the color of the white wall or the length of the hospital bed in which he lay. He couldn't change it unless he was able to change her.

He said, "It's no use my disagreeing. I wouldn't want you to be different. It's the way you're built, the way you breathe. Only take care that being it doesn't break you."

He had come a long way in understanding to say that, and she took the warning like a hand held out in friendship, the fondness animating all her face for the first time, relaxing the fine mouth with its sensitive severity.

She moved closer, close enough for him to touch her and to let his fingers roam quietly in the turbulence of her hair. Her face was still serious, though gently so. Perhaps it would never be reconciled to happiness, but coming in on the far side of that feeling, he knew it would inhabit a more secure contentment.

He wasn't happy but he was more at peace with himself as he looked at the bare walls and up at the high white ceiling, with the suspended fan spinning slowly from it. The rebellion had failed. Others had paid for it with their lives, but his own life would flow down the prescribed course unaltered. Indeed, measured by the consequences, there had been no rebellion. It was a mirage, an imagined exclamation mark. Undoubtedly Kruger would have called it *Maya*. But the family, the career, the forward look, all that was reality could never be brought to admit it.

He should have felt frustrated in such a situation. He didn't, partly because of Kamala's presence but also because, working in him, achieving the first forms of definition, was a realization of the validity of failure. There was something happening he could lean against and fight with, a chain of events, a pattern of confinement. The land was his now, the stake was driven into it, he could probe to its nature and react to its enmity. The plant had taken root, and even if the roots were bitter he could still learn enough to win something from their bitterness. At least the fingers were still there and alive, stretching, clutching, at the reluctant soil, forcing it into fertility, till the green blades burst defiantly forth, through the cracked earth, into the rainless eternity. The battle would come whether or not he chose it, and what was understanding but the lightning flash of insight, the uneasy truce before the darknesses joined.

CHAPTER THREE

Seventy-three Days to Freedom

THE HILLMAN labored up the ramp toward the Secretariat. On either side the office buildings rose, sandstone and gray, in orderly perspectives, flanking the impressive mass of Government House. Behind, the geometry of the approach stretched along Kingsway to the triumphal arch, trim pools, disciplined trees and regimented fountains. The brightest jewel in the imperial crown, and Delhi was the center of its radiance, a well-mannered city with the suffering look of a fat man perpetually dressed for dinner. The approach of independence had not yet removed this fatalistic decorum, and the expertly drilled clouds still marched across the horizon at rates appropriate to Elgar's music.

At the head of the incline, the guard was being changed. Krishnan pulled to one side and watched the elaborate maneuver, the marching exactly rehearsed, the horsemanship almost casual in its perfection, everything done with an *élan* and a precision that oddly commemorated the triumph of nonviolence. Below, at the entrance to Kingsway, a citizen of India watched the proceedings stonily as he washed his shirt in a convenient fountain. It was not quite, in the words of Krishnan's favorite poet, "an easy commerce of the old and new," but the juxtaposition nevertheless had vivid possibilities.

The spaces beneath the trees were already occupied. He pulled the car up as close to a tree as possible and walked toward one of the formidable entrances. Now that he was close to it he liked it even less. The pomposity dismayed him. It was his family written large, memorialized in stone. He looked at the cliffs of masonry on either side, the doors like cracks through which the streams of diligence trickled, those who went in because survival said so, in the way the past and good behavior walked, brilliant men, resigned men, and men with no alternative.

He was surprised at how easily he had come to this. It was, he recollected, not so far back in time, although it seemed so distantly behind him in terms of submission, that his second rebellion had been stubbed out, the flame of it not even bright enough to light his retreat with the lucidity of failure. They hadn't even had the momentary vitality of the first revolt, those few weeks spent in the decrepit lecture room, with the truth flowing down from the anxious faces that they wanted to succeed and not to learn. "Don't be too hard on them," the head of the department had said. "Remember, it isn't only for themselves." He remembered it, conjuring the ghosts of their involvement, the unborn sons and the unmarried sisters huddling behind the already constricted shoulders, the fever of their responsibility burning haggardly in the still-young faces. What could he give them to grow into? What use was the power to find and be themselves when all that the illness, the obsessive malady, coveted was to inch over the line between acceptance and rejection. Sixty-one or better in the examination lists, sixty-one in the long roll of ten thousand. That was all that all the effort led to, the last spasm that pulled them over the barrier, and on the other side was freedom, whatever it meant, and self-expression, a flame for a burned candle.

"I was like you," the Professor had said gently. "I wanted to teach them the truth too, but the truth is in the results. You've got to have your quota of successes, and if you don't nobody wants you, neither the missionaries nor the students, and after you've seen the faces of failure you'll end up as I did, not even wanting yourself."

Krishnan had protested vigorously, putting in his claim for higher standards, do as you should and to blazes with the subsidy. But the logic of it, always requiring to be held at arm's length, was clear and implacable in the examination hall, with the cemetery so appropriately beside it, and the lines of his duty drawn in the desperate faces—third row down, fourth from the right, with a hundred and four in his bloodstream, and the man with malaria trying to hold his pen straight.

He had left when the end was obvious, before those he had tried to help disowned him, those to whom he had given the emptiness of knowledge. Be yourself, he had told them, robust and individual; but by what title could he ask for honesty, the rootlessness wavering beneath the floor of success. He had come out through the chemistry labs, with the leper standing as he always did at the exit, peering in apathetically at the bubbling retorts, waiting forever for the explosion of hope. He gave him half a month's pay. Maybe he could shock someone into significance. He had nothing to give with his own mind, but the money was different; it was supposed to buy something, it was at the very least a superior form of scandal. He had watched the beggar counting and recounting it, waiting for the realization, the numbing of years to work off, the joyous awakening into a different dimension.

When it came, he had gone away, unable to stand it. He had hardly heard the whine of the man's gratitude, struck only by the impact of the unnatural fear in his eyes. In retrospect, he had tried to make it logical, putting the consolation of the road's distance behind him, walking away down the perspective of bitterness. The man had to see himself, he insisted. He had to see himself before he could change himself, and so hope couldn't be reached except over the threshold of horror. The reasoning had helped to arrange his frustrations for him, but it couldn't remove them from the sharpening knowledge that something else was needed to help the man over the threshold, something he couldn't teach and couldn't give.

He had to come home because his failures led home. Home was wherever the defeats became significant, not because he could derive any dignity from them, but because the alternatives had been exhausted, because he could live now as his family did. His father had taken the news of his extravagance with a philosophic calm that seemed almost foreign in him. "Half a month's pay may be a small price for wisdom." Perhaps he should have congratulated himself that his dissent had achieved a monetary value, since in his father's eyes that must have been evidence of progress. But he had decided against the momentary flattery. They knew and the gods knew what would happen, and the money was simply part of the ceremony, the price paid for the prodigal to return.

Kamala's silence had disturbed him more. He realized that he had wanted her to protest, to tell him he had given in too easily, that it was his vocation and that he ought not to have deserted it. Maybe she didn't believe it, didn't believe in him. Was she like everyone else: quietly convinced that he could fit into anything? Clothes didn't make the man, the real man, the interior *sadhu* on his private nail bed.

If she felt that way, why didn't she tell him that? Why didn't she tell him to stop nursing his adjustments? There were three hundred and sixty-six thousand gods in the Hindu pantheon, each of them representing ways for the exceptional to die, and the way didn't matter, provided that he did it. He had two cheeks and was prepared to be slapped on either. But it was time for a solid reaction, loyalty or, failing that, indignation. Love wasn't real if the bloom of it didn't come out of prejudice, something to lean on, something to push away from.

She never rose to the reach of his desire. For the first time he began to question her tolerance, the tolerance which seemed to assume that any failure was a fraction of wisdom as long as one survived it. It was too close to complacency, this tranquil teaching of the impregnable self which circumstances flowed over. One day the current might grow dangerous, and the gathering waters might rip her convictions away instead of tautening her skin or giving her philosophy gooseflesh. What would happen if his rebellions really involved her, if his failures were nicked on her flesh instead of on his ego? Would her beliefs still have the shape of her womanhood, the contours of her mind's body, or would she step out of them into a different protection? Did they live in her or did they live because of her?

He didn't know the answer. But he did know that he was beginning to ask a question which had not formed in his unhappiness before, that there was a misgiving, even if the other side of
it was respect for her position and for the fidelity with which she
had so far held it. Perhaps it was not so much her integrity that
he doubted as whether her integrity could assist him. She would
leave him alone, and in a sense it was proper that she should, since
the deepest sincerity came only out of solitude. But he wanted
something else on which to fall back, a cause to which he could
dedicate himself, her happiness, the prospering of their marriage,
or, failing that, a reason for rebellion.

She didn't give him the pretenses that he needed. She made him
realize that the only way was through him, and so he looked now
at his future, at the ramp, the curve of the car tracks ending beside the tree, the trajectory leading to the eternal entrance. It was
the line he would follow again and over again, the shape which
only repetition could hope to make significant.

He had asked for a pattern and would compromise on a routine.

He had come to the uniformed man at the door of insignificance,
an individual like a *diminuendo*. He was too small to be noticed
by anyone coming out but he could deal with those who had no
right to go in. He guarded emptiness as if it were infinity. Undoubtedly he had never been out of Delhi, but he looked at Krishnan with an habitual contempt that yielded nothing to the con-
cierge at the Savoy.

"I have just joined Government Service," explained Krishnan. "I
am to work here."

"Where is your pass?"

"I have no pass as yet. No doubt I shall be given one."

"Nobody can go in without a pass." He said it looking ostentatiously the other way. Men without passes were unfit to be noticed.

Krishnan decided to keep on being pleasant. He knew that the
proper course was to expose succinctly the cumulative deficiencies
of the man's ancestors, the resultant meanness of his present station,
and the desirability of not annoying innocuous-looking officers who

were in reality possessed of devastating influence. But invective had
never been his strong point. He wasn't able to utilize it now. He
kept his voice down and as urbane as he could, hoping it wouldn't
show the beginnings of nervousness.

"How am I to secure a pass if I can't go in to get one?"

The functionary shrugged the illusion of his shoulders. He could
not fill his uniform with his physique but he had no difficulty in
filling in with his authority.

"Undersecretary Sahib will give you a pass."

"Then may I see Undersecretary Sahib?"

"Certainly, if you can show me your pass."

There was a limit to reasonableness, thought Krishnan, and this
was passing beyond it. Even if the higher reaches of sarcasm were
beyond him, he could at least tread the foothills of simple abuse.
But he managed to fight his exasperation down. It was the era of
nonviolence, he told himself, and the man represented the inarticulate millions of India, even though in the present circumstances he
seemed much more articulate than V. S. Krishnan himself, the man
without a pass, without a pretense, standing there, his self-confi-
dence waning in the hot sun.

"Could you please telephone the Undersecretary and tell him that
Mr. V. S. Krishnan would like to see him?"

It was the right approach at last. The man nodded his head as
if he had no option but to do so, laboriously made several entries
in a book, lifted the telephone as if it were an unfair physical effort and proceeded with heavily advertised reluctance to establish
his visitor's credentials. Krishnan stood there uncomfortably and
more than a little uncertain, while the seemingly interminable inquiries were pursued. "Mukerji Sahib will see you," the man announced eventually, and Krishnan felt a slight relaxation of arrogance. He had achieved the beginnings of recognition. "Second
door on the left after you reach the corner." The man said it with
a smile of supercilious benignity, satisfied to have hammered some
rudiments of protocol into the dense skull of this parvenu.

Krishnan walked down the corridor. The walls were lined with
notices forbidding Class IV Government Servants to spit on the

floor or sit in slovenly attitudes. Under each notice was a bench on which one or more Class IV Servants were draped in poses of defiant indolence. Krishnan approached the particular individual he had to deal with and, after some coughing, succeeded in distracting him from the lethargic manicuring of his toenails.

"My name is Krishnan. I have an appointment with Mukerji Sahib."

"Mukerji Sahib is busy," said the *chaprassi* without bothering to look at Krishnan. He conducted a further operation on his toe and then decided that the excavation of his nose would be more indicative of his contempt for his visitor.

Krishnan watched him, his irritation mounting. The Government had unfortunately provided no benches on which Class I and Class II Government Servants could recline in poses of intimidating mastery. Consequently, he was obliged to stand and perspire. The air was stifling, but it was also still enough to convey any sound of business being transacted, and Krishnan, listening intently, could hear neither voices nor the rustling of files. Losing patience with the situation, he pushed brusquely past the *chaprassi* into the room.

Mukerji sat behind the rather battered desk, typical of Government offices the world over. Trays of files on a side table gave evidence of his industry, and the two telephones were prominently displayed, a gentle indication that here was a man who sat at the nerve center of something and who wielded influence in excess of his position. At the moment he was not using either. In fact, he was doing nothing and gave the impression that he was not entirely unfamiliar with that state.

"My name is Krishnan." He sat down without waiting to be invited. "I've just joined the Ministry."

"Why, of course, my dear chap," said Mukerji cordially. "I've been expecting you. I'm delighted to meet you."

"There's a Class Four manicurist on your bench outside. Perhaps you should have told him you were expecting me."

"Manicurist?" said the Undersecretary, bewildered. Then his face broke into a smile of understanding. "I see what you mean.

You're referring to my *chaprassi*. He probably told you I was busy. They always do that on principle, you know. But once you have a *chaprassi* yourself, then yours and mine can negotiate our appointments, and I'm sure there won't be any further trouble."

"Pretty cumbersome, isn't it?" said Krishnan curtly, still resentful of the treatment he had received. "Why can't we deal directly with each other? It saves manpower and it saves misunderstanding. I'm told the first at least is considered important around here."

Mukerji put his hands together and leaned back. He did so partly to put Krishnan more at his ease but also to indicate that he possessed a swivel chair, which was not part of an Undersecretary's normal office equipment.

"It's only a matter of etiquette, my dear fellow, and, as you know, India invented diplomacy. Besides, you might as well give the poor devils some small responsibilities; they've precious little else. Now I take it that you want your pass. I'm afraid it won't be ready for two days. Formalities, you know. References have to be made to other departments. It takes time for the percolation of initiative."

He saw the expression on Krishnan's face and hastened to reassure him.

"Interim arrangements will be made, of course. Your temporary pass will be ready in two hours. Not the real thing, naturally, but it will serve to pacify Pluto at the entrance."

"Eternal thanks," said Krishnan with a sarcasm that was lost on his colleague. "Now that I've acquired my right of entry could you tell me where I'm supposed to work?"

Mukerji tapped his forehead with a pencil. "That's difficult, my friend. That's very much more difficult."

"Don't mind me," suggested Krishnan. "I can always live in the corridor."

Mukerji looked at him reflectively. "An interesting suggestion, and in fact there's nothing against it in the rules. But it wouldn't be practical. It would seriously obstruct the traffic of *chaprassis*. An orthodox solution will have to be found. Immediately, of course. I shall investigate myself. You have fortunately come to an officer of resourcefulness."

He wandered over to a large chart on which several flags were pinned. "It will have to be one hundred and two," he said, after surveying the position. "You'll share with Pratap Singh. Of course, one hundred and sixty square feet would be your normal entitlement, but accommodation is scarce, as you've no doubt realized, and a hundred and forty is the best we can do."

He took Krishnan down the corridor. One hundred and two was ten doors farther on, a walk from the entrance which could be exhausting in summer, and it faced on an abandoned pile of furniture instead of on the splendors of the approach to Government House. Pratap Singh, rotund and chubby, greeted them with a perspiring smile.

"Ah, yes, V. S. Krishnan. I've heard of you. My cousin was sent down from Balliol, you know."

"I'm afraid I have to leave," said Mukerji, having completed the introductions. "One of the assistants is demanding an increment and is unable to produce his birth certificate. The superintendent says he is technically not alive."

"Sit down," said Pratap Singh hospitably to Krishnan. "Please let me know your age and seniority, the occupation and salaries of your father and father-in-law and whom your sisters, if any, may have married."

Krishnan provided him with the information, which Pratap Singh digested with evident approval.

"You are apparently a professional Government Servant. Splendid. In these days of deteriorating standards the Service needs the stiffening of tradition." He spoke English with a singsong intonation, rolling the words on his tongue, like an unsuccessful imitation of a Welshman.

Krishnan intervened, anxious to have the correct impression established. "As a matter of fact, I've no real interest in Government Service as such. I wanted to be a teacher and was one for some weeks, but apparently a teacher is a teacher only because he has failed to be something better. Now that independence is more or less around the corner public service becomes a different thing and perhaps the approach to it will be different also."

"I understand fully," said Pratap Singh imperturbably. "You are a member of the political elite. Even more splendid. In these days of hidebound traditionalism the Service needs initiative and a dynamic sense of enterprise. You are a graduate of Yerwada, are you not?"

"I regret to say, no."

"A pity. A very fine jail, Yerwada. All the best people went there. Eton, Trinity and Yerwada—it's the accepted lineage. Still, I forgot, you're a Southerner and I'm sure the South has jails just as exclusive as Yerwada, even if we ignorant Northerners don't happen to have heard of them."

"I'm sorry to disappoint you," said Krishnan. "I've never been to jail."

"Never been to jail! My dear man, what have you been doing all your life? This is a serious matter; it calls for *lussie*. Two *lussies*," he yelled in a stentorian voice, and feet were heard hurriedly scampering down the corridor. Pratap Singh looked at the second hand of his watch and beamed. "This isn't much of a room. All you can see from the window is that pile of P.W.D. junk. The Deputy Secretary's place is nearly a hundred yards off, and you'll have to trudge it five or six times a day. But if you ever want something to drink, or a *rasgoola*, a *chaprassi* in good condition can get it in two minutes."

The feet were heard in a returning crescendo, and the *chaprassi* burst in, panting and disheveled, carrying two tall glasses of cool-looking buttermilk.

"One-forty-seven flat," said Pratap Singh approvingly. "This man is, of course, the champion. I picked him after observing his performance in the Class IV Government Servants' egg and spoon race. You are not," he inquired a little despairingly of Krishnan, "a member of the I.N.A.? Splendid chaps they are, like everybody else. And who is to presume that they were mistaken? After all, I myself once worked in Netaji's part of the country."

"I haven't been in the I.N.A. either. As you can see, I'm a man of no distinction."

Pratap Singh looked disappointed. For the first time there was a hint of reproof in his voice. "Most unfortunate. If you fought the Japanese, your services would be considered in determining your future. And if you fought the British instead of the Japanese, your sterling services would be considered also. If you fought nobody at all, but non-co-operated nonviolently, that too could powerfully influence your progress. Our *Raj* is a liberal one and will take into account all forms of enlightenment or misguidedness provided they seem to contain dynamic tendencies. But you have done nothing, my dear friend; you have neither been in jail nor put anybody into it."

"Oh come," protested Krishnan. "It's not as bad as all that. I got three ribs fractured in a civil-disobedience demonstration."

"Fractured ribs, my dear fellow," observed Pratap Singh scornfully, "are no substitute whatever for a jail sentence. What do they prove? That you drive a motorcar rashly. That you are too free with intoxicating liquors. That in using your spare time to ransack godowns you're too clumsy to avoid detection by the police. In the absence of a conviction duly enshrined in the judicial records, fractured ribs only prove that you're a *goonda* instead of a patriot."

"In that case I shall have no alternative but to succeed on my merits." Krishnan, who had originally accepted the interrogation with good humor, was becoming impatient of the snobbery it revealed. He had met the type. He recognized the sarcastic approbation, the indiscriminate approval of career men, jailbirds and political agitators as concealing a reality more servile than sarcastic. It was like a tipsy man asking you to admire his excellent imitation of a drunkard, and he couldn't help feeling that he preferred the vice to the camouflage.

"That's an important-looking note that you are writing," he told Pratap Singh, endeavoring to change the subject. "Momentous issues must depend upon it."

"To be sure they do," the Sikh responded eagerly. "It relates to the settlement of war claims. Basic questions of principle are involved and I am trying to expose them with lucidity. D.S. will see it, and probably J.S. It might even require the attention of the Secretary himself."

"How inconsiderate of me," apologized Krishnan. "I have detained you from the completion of a masterpiece and one which I am confident will put the work of the section on a more rational footing."

Pratap Singh beamed. He knew very well that Krishnan was pulling his leg, but even leg-pulling presumed a certain importance, and he was happy to bask in this accession of glory.

Krishnan went over to his own desk. He dickered with the office pen, trying to persuade it to write. Pratap Singh, now that the epoch-making character of his work had been established, had no alternative but to engross himself in it.

Krishnan picked up the telephone and dialed a Secretariat number. When he heard Vijayaraghavan's voice he was more relieved than he had expected to be. Not that it wasn't affected in its own way, but at least the affectation seemed to bring a sense of reality into the organized emptiness.

"This is the Officer on Special Duty speaking."

"Come off it. This is Krishnan."

"Ah, my comrade with the cracked ribs. What brings you, my friend, into these imperial catacombs?"

"Money, of course." At least it was a positive reason, Krishnan thought, and more convincing than lack of an alternative.

Vijayaraghavan was completely unconvinced. "Money indeed! You can make ten times more money in Chandni Chowk selling antiques to gullible Americans."

"I didn't mean money literally," Krishnan explained. "I meant it symbolically, as a failure of conscience."

"Interesting," said Vijayaraghavan. "Much more interesting. The Secretariat is, of course, the best place for resolving inner conflicts. Some prefer the Himalayas, but they misunderstand the nature of privation."

"When can we meet?" asked Krishnan.

"As soon as it can be arranged. I have soul-stirring tidings to impart to you and Kamala."

"You can come to our place this evening if you care to. I've borrowed a house from someone on vacation."

Vijayaraghavan pretended to ponder the invitation. "Your house, my friend, suffers from two serious deficiencies. There are no beautiful women in it, apart from Kamala and the goddess Saraswathi; and there is no alcohol to console one for the lack of beautiful women. Why not be my guest at the club, where the Scotch is so cheap it almost atones for the people."

"Meet you at the club then."

"No, pick me up on the South Block. It's the twenty-ninth of the month, you know, and since I was seized by a sudden desire to observe sunset on the Jumna, I have squandered my month's petrol ration."

"Very well then, South Block about five-thirty."

He put the receiver down.

"Did you say *the* club?" inquired Pratap Singh admiringly.

"What of it?"

"It's extremely exclusive, you know. There was a time when natives weren't admitted."

Krishnan winced at the phrase, but Pratap Singh seemed to use it without resentment and without being too aware of whom the word included. A snob could be reconciled to someone else's snobbery.

"It's open to Indians now, of course," he went on, "but only to the *Onlooker* set. It took me weeks to get in even as a guest, so you've every reason to congratulate yourself on being invited on your first day."

"I have secret sources of power," declared Krishnan, "which I refrained from revealing to you."

Pratap Singh began to look uncomfortable.

"This is strictly confidential," continued Krishnan, "but the truth is that I am here on a Special Mission. Now that the new era is beginning, it is necessary to assess the attitudes of Government Servants to their work and to their colleagues. For this purpose, I had to pretend that I was wholly without patronage or special qualifications. I regret to say that your response was extremely unconstructive and revealed no grasp of the conception that merit is all that matters."

"But I wasn't being serious," said Pratap Singh a little anxiously. "Surely you were aware of that."

"I might have been able to overlook your distorted notions of privilege. But it is necessary to say emphatically that your patronizing treatment of Class IV Government Servants is not compatible with a democratic order."

Pratap Singh was now obviously unsettled, and Krishnan felt that it would assist the pretense if he were to appear to relent a little. "If your noting shows evidence of a sense of proportion, I am, of course, prepared to reconsider my estimate."

"I very much hope you can do so," said Pratap Singh eagerly. "And I would be very grateful if you could ask D.S. for his opinion. I have been in the section for several years. I am well known to my superiors for my conscientious work."

"You seem to forget," pointed out Krishnan sternly, "that D.S. and J.S. are also under scrutiny." Pratap Singh gasped. "I must, of course, demand that you say nothing of this to them. You will appreciate how adversely the smallest leakage will prejudice my inquiry."

"Of course, of course. You can rely on my discretion."

Krishnan picked up the receiver and dialed Kamala's number. "I'm afraid that the dinner for the Vice-Chancellor will have to be on Thursday instead of Tuesday. I shall explain everything when I return."

He looked at Pratap Singh as loftily as he could and pretended ostentatiously to engross himself in a file.

2

"That's the idea, you see. The punishment must be made to fit the Ministry. The Minister for Works must go to the bottom of the housing queue. And the Minister for Food must be made to live entirely on the ration."

"What about the Minister for Communications?"

"He should travel third class from Amritsar to Cape Cormorin."

Vijayaraghavan pulled at his lime juice and soda. His remarks on the consolations of Scotch were largely rhetorical. He could do without it and carry the white man's burden.

He stuck his thumb out at a paunchy individual waddling past in jodhpurs.

"See that man? He's supposed to increase production, so he increases his waistline."

"My dear chap," protested Krishnan, "give the poor blighter time. Why don't you acquire some Oriental patience? The British took two hundred years to ruin us. Now we'll need fifty to pull the pieces together."

"Jelly," said Vijayaraghavan. "There's no way known of pulling that together. It is necessary to discover a spine. Spines should be given first priority in our imports."

"You're not being fair to the figures," pointed out Kamala. "Statistics show our production is slowly increasing."

"Statistics my eye!" said Vijayaraghavan scathingly. "You're being bamboozled by the over-all index. But what do you see when you look at the details? Food is down. Textiles are up by one and a half per cent. The only *real* increase is in the output of cement. And that's only because of the increased production of blockheads."

He took a cutting from *Blitz* out of his pocket. "I advise you to read this. Appalling revelations. Ninety per cent of Government employees are sons-in-law of somebody."

"Doesn't that only mean that ninety per cent are married?"

"I wish you wouldn't make such shattering deductions, Kamala. Turn your innocent eyes instead to the spectacle of frivolity that surrounds you. You are a serious girl from a conservative Brahmin family. Does not such behavior wound you to the core?"

"If I knew how to waltz," said Kamala demurely, "I could be so much more objective about the evils of waltzing."

"Ah, I see. An empiricist. May I remind you that you don't have to be a hen to identify rotten eggs. Tell me, Krishnan, since you are the embodiment of Western man, what is the point of this dancing where two individuals rotate strenuously on their collective axis and continue with much exertion to remain in the same place?"

"Well, it's pleasant, it's difficult to do well but not difficult to do, it's a moderate form of exercise, and it helps one to become acquainted with people."

"A poor set of reasons, and only the last has practical validity." He paused to scowl at a good-looking girl in a diaphanous green sari, with a generous expanse of trim, bare flesh between her waist and her bodice.

"That girl is a Communist. She is determined to give everything to the State." He turned to Krishnan belligerently. "I see you do not agree. You have doubtless a more basic definition."

But Krishnan's thoughts were not on the girl in green. He was hardly aware of what Vijayaraghavan was saying or of his demand for a retort. He was looking across the sprung wood floor upon which the couples swayed and circled, trying to dismiss the memory as it came back. It couldn't be Cynthia, he assured himself. The girl in the black gown, on the other side of the dance floor, wasn't Cynthia. She merely had Cynthia's height and Cynthia's hair, but she wasn't the intense, gauche person he had known at Cambridge and for whom he had felt the pull of more than fondness. It had ended long ago anyway, and the snubbed feelings had died their natural death. The book had been closed and couldn't again be opened. This was a different world and she had no right to come into it.

Yet why shouldn't it be she, why did it have to be otherwise? She had often spoken of India as her country. He had discounted what she said then as an attempt to justify her eager, almost avid enthusiasm for things Indian. It was the sort of enthusiasm one encountered only in foreigners—the claim of a curiosity without a tangible sustenance. Was it unreasonable that she should want to make it real, that she should want to see what she had so often discussed? He remembered how often and vehemently she had defended his country's right to and fitness for independence. Was it wrong that she should be here when that right was about to be realized?

Finally, he told himself, no one but Cynthia, with her disdain
for conventions, would have had the nerve to enter the club without an escort.

Wasn't this the place and the eve of independence the time?

She turned, and it was Cynthia, but not as he had known her;
she was more svelte and more self-possessed, even as she stood
there, her face lighting up with the surprise of recognition.

She came toward them with a grace he had not previously asso-
ciated with her body.

It was amazing, he thought, what five years could do to Girton.

When she was with them he noticed the details, the slouch that
wasn't there, the different hair style that made the face seem different, the string of pearls, even if out of Ciro's, which she wore now
and would not have worn earlier. "Not when the people starve,"
she might have said. He realized that he was disturbed not by the
jewelry itself but by the knowledge that it suited her better than
the slogan.

He remembered the introductions and mumbled through them.
"Cynthia Bainbridge, an old friend from my university days."

The expected tension did not materialize. "Won't you sit down?"
said Kamala a little guardedly, but the cutting edge that might
have been there was absent.

Cynthia switched the smile on, but when she said, "I do hope
we'll get to know each other better," it was not with detectable insincerity.

He was glad that it hadn't been worse, until it struck him that
there was no reason for it to be otherwise. It could happen to anyone, even if it didn't, and a man needn't change because his
remembrance had altered. The sky was different every day and
every minute. But year after year the earth remained the same earth.
It would be the same with his pattern of commitment.

"Krishnan taught me so much about India," he heard Cynthia
explaining. "If it hadn't been for him I mightn't be here at all."

He wondered how deliberate the ambiguity was.

"My dear lady," Vijayaraghavan protested. "You have chosen the
wrong *guru*. He left India too early to know what he was talking

about; and he has returned too late to do anything about it. Now if you had selected me—"

"And who may you be?" asked Cynthia without curiosity.

"I am the inventor of the principles of geometry."

"How exciting! I've always wanted to know somebody called Euclid."

It hadn't been that way at all, Krishnan remembered. In a sense it was she who had taught him. He had met her after a lecture on the economic impact of industrialization in the Far East. She had walked up to him, probably because he was the only Indian in sight, her stride long and inelegant in her flat-bottomed shoes. "I can never forgive my countrymen for Jallianwalla." Her face had flushed, and anger as well as shame had flared up in her green eyes. Since he did not know where Jallianwalla was or what had happened there, the blood had come in embarrassment to his face too, and she had fortunately mistaken it for a kindred emotion. "A terrible thing," he had retorted angrily, and she had held her hand out in sympathy. "The world marches forward. It must not happen again." That night he had sat poring over the history of the Indian National Congress, first shocked, then bitter, and finally excited, both by his confinement in the family rose garden and by the tragedy of the events outside it, futile at first against the force of authority but, in the very process of resistance to that pressure, slowly discovering its inner strength and destiny. Next morning his indignation was at least not illiterate. "Jallianwalla is the first nail in the coffin of imperialism." He winced when he recollected the phrase, but they had thought it excellent then, and he had welcomed her smile, even with the untidy lipstick. They had been to many meetings after that, in the absorbed fashion of their age and generation, reciting the statistics of poverty and oppression, licking envelopes tirelessly in noble causes, he never quite realizing the extent to which the tall figure in ill-chosen tweeds, the faintly aggressive voice awaiting the heckler, had become part of his background of reassurance. Now she was here, modulated to a different universe, with a shrewd detachment he would have thought impossible.

The band struck up and she looked directly at him. "Aren't any of you going to ask me to dance?"

There was no alternative; he was the only one who could. She was slimmer now, and he began to wish that were the only difference. He tried to remember her in the disheveled days when her principal diet was crumpets and good works. Her figure then was as haphazard as the rest of her, clad in the sackcloth which serious undergraduates wore instead of skirts. She was a plump girl, teetering on the edge of flabbiness. Now she had retreated to a controlled voluptuousness which Krishnan found disconcerting, since, without being aware of it, he was inclined to believe that any organized woman was a conspiracy against him. He piloted her onto the floor. In high heels she was fractionally the taller of the two, a discovery which unsettled him the more. He held her stiffly and as far away as possible, trying not to be too aware of her. She made no attempt to alter the situation. He was relieved at first and then concerned, lest this indicated some more elaborate and less detectable strategy. His mind ran through and rejected various conversational gambits. He decided to say nothing. He concentrated with ferocity on the vacant area to the left of her right ear.

"Why don't you tell me I'm good looking?" she suggested. "It's true, and anyway it would help to break the ice."

He managed to smile, but not with too much assurance. "I didn't mean to be boorish. It's just that meeting you was so unexpected. And you're so different. The other image I could have put away."

"Well, if you add something, something usually gets subtracted. Figure it all out," she said a little acidly, "and I'm sure you'll be able to find the right shelf."

"You don't understand," he told her, doing it cautiously, looking for the words to fence in an apprehension that he couldn't entirely state. "You don't understand because you haven't lived here. It takes time to get used to any change."

"I see," she said. "Like independence, for instance."

It was a piece of the old Cynthia, the debating-society technique, and he found himself relaxed by the knowledge that it was still there. As long as they argued there was nothing to worry about.

The trouble would start when she started to understand him.

"Yes," he said pugnaciously, "like independence also."

She came back with icy commiseration. "Poor Krish, it must be awful. Haven't they allowed you to become free yet?"

"I run my own show," he answered.

"Then run it in your own way. I wasn't looking for you, I just happened to meet you, but I was glad, ever so glad, that it happened. But if that isn't the way you feel, or want to feel, there are other things I can be happy about."

He felt he owed her a degree of explanation. "This isn't my most successful night. I'd probably put it wrong, however I tried, but meeting you *has* made a tremendous difference, and it isn't one that I would want to undo."

It wasn't meant to be much of a concession, but she disarmed him by taking it at its maximum value, smiling at him and moving a little closer.

"You don't have to act as if you were guarding Government House."

He didn't like it entirely but felt some of the stiffness going out of him.

He became aware for the first time of the music. The band was playing a slow fox trot, in time, in pitch, but with no sense of purpose beyond the weary recognition that the show had to go on until it was time to pack up.

She didn't dance it that way, though. She was light on her feet and responsive to his hesitant leading, giving his intentions a firmness they hadn't possessed. She had dignity but she combined it with *élan*.

That was part of the change too. Five years ago she would have done a slow fox trot reluctantly, defensively, like an army retreating under superior odds.

"What brings you here?" he asked her.

"Field work on a book I'm writing. I was fortunate enough to receive a foundation award."

"I must say the club is an unusual place for field work."

He was sorry as soon as he had said it, not so much for his

rudeness as for the sense of insecurity which his rudeness had made evident. He half hoped that she would react with indignation, but her response was civilized, as he feared it would be.

"Krish, I could make the obvious reply and say that one comes here for fun and not for work. But even if it were the other way, for argument's sake, don't think that you can't learn a good deal from this place. Just look around you. It's a sociological cauldron."

"It may be motley," he said, "but at least it isn't monotonous."

He was speaking defensively, like many of his countrymen, suspecting the overtones of criticism and in her case particularly of English condescension, in everything that wasn't blatant praise. Her reply made him realize that she might be really on his side.

"That isn't the point, Krish," she explained. "It's much more than simply a mixture. Don't you feel something else in the mingling and flowing? The promise and strength of your country? And the threat of it too if it should take the wrong path?"

Five years before she would have been too busy watching her feet to say that, and if she had said it, it would not have been in the same way. He was aware of the difference in everything she did, but he decided to seem imperceptive about it, trying to treat the changes as external, new clothes for the mind, a different kind of hairdo, but not that embarrassing growth of understanding that would search his honesty every time he faced it.

He said, "You haven't changed too much, after all, have you, Cynthia?" It sounded even worse than he had thought it would, but at least it passed the responsibility to her.

"Yes, I have and you know it," she replied. "I'm trying to see the truth instead of the slogans. The facts about myself and about the way I am, and then about this country and what is to become of it."

"That's easy enough," he said. "What'll happen to us, I mean. Independence, with or without partition. We're going to be a free nation, or maybe two free nations. It doesn't matter so long as we run our own lives."

"Don't pretend, Krish," she reproved him gently. "It isn't as simple as that. A plan isn't drawn on paper. It's drawn by the difference it makes to millions of people."

"It's what it costs us," he asserted brusquely. "If it's the price of freedom, freedom is worth any price."

It was he who was now back in the debating society and he even said it truculently, in the manner of years ago, his hold on her tightening before he became aware of it.

She was still reasonable, determined to be fair to the argument. "Maybe it's worth the price," she said. "If you're sure of what you'll get for what you pay. But is it as certain as that? Set up a commission and carve out a country. Only, will the facts—four hundred and fifty-two million and a few miscellaneous facts—march like tin soldiers down the roads of their future just as we want them to in the tidy blueprints?"

He was trying to think of an answer when the music stopped. They threaded their way back to the table. He was relieved, not only because he had been spared a difficult argument but because he felt that his sense of vigilance was giving way to her friendliness. He was afraid she was beginning to understand him.

He took the chair next to Kamala, with Cynthia at his left. She looked at the gathering as if she were giving him back. "He dances well," she said, looking directly at Kamala. "You ought to make him teach you. Don't let him sink himself in being Indian."

"I'm sure he'll never drown," said Kamala sweetly, "with so many kind souls concerned about his salvation."

Vijayaraghavan intervened. "My dear lady," he said, addressing Cynthia, "dancing gives Krishnan an unfortunate monopoly. Can we not have a more democratic diversion?"

They decided to play bridge, roping in one of Vijayaraghavan's acquaintances. Kamala could not play, and Krishnan played Culbertson indifferently. Vijayaraghavan drew Cynthia as his partner. He had the memory and she the cards, as well as a certain flair for succeeding with calculated risks. After the second rubber had ended in a little slam, doubled and made by a finesse against the odds, Krishnan concluded that this might not be his night.

"Now that you have made me penniless, do you mind if I jump in the pool?"

"I shall be happy to push you in personally," said Vijayaraghavan. "What does it profit me to win a card game and to lose the peerless Cynthia!"

"Don't mind him," said Cynthia. "He's drunk with his success."

They wandered out into the grounds. The night was beginning to look ominous and the moon dodged fitfully in and out of the thickening clouds. Krishnan unlocked his car and switched on the radio.

"Bought it from a planter," he explained a little proudly. "It's probably the only ten in Delhi with these extras."

Then they heard of Rawalpindi, and the mounting carnage, and the faces in the faint light grew suddenly concerned. The voice on the radio was impersonal, with a close-to-Oxford accent, talking of death and the frenzy of communal rioting in the same calm way that it always talked of the weather. Somehow the neutrality of it, the studied absence of passion, made what it narrated the more shocking.

"You see," said Cynthia. "Four hundred and fifty million facts."

She hadn't said it complacently, but the very fact of her saying it made Krishnan want to lash out.

"I told you so," he said, mimicking bitterly. "That's all you sociologists are capable of saying. My, my, oh my, and fancy all that violence. It's something that comes out of what you did, remember, out of two hundred years of occupation."

He was getting ruder as the night went on. He told himself that he didn't have to act scared. She was different, of course, but why should that make any difference? It could happen to anyone, happen even in Delhi; it was simply the normal, recognized way to grow up.

All he had to do was to look her straight in her green eyes and go home.

Then he heard Kamala rallying to her side. "It isn't really in anything that your people did. You couldn't have brought it out if it wasn't in us. It's all in us, in the many, many years of occupation, submission to the State, obedience to the family, every inch of our lives completely calculated, every step, down to the relief of the grave. And if we wanted to protest, there was only the pitiless

discipline of nonviolence. Then all of a sudden the garden belongs
to us, and we reach up into the blossoming tree to pluck the
ashes."

"We're going to be free," said Vijayaraghavan. "We're going to be
responsible for ourselves. Who knows what it will cost us and how
much blood will flow, perhaps as never in half a century's struggle."

Krishnan looked back at the club. The lights were brilliant
through the open windows. Beneath them the band was playing a
Viennese waltz, and the oblivious couples were swirling, *achkans*
and suave dinner jackets, thin legs in *churidars,* pampered women
in Directoire gowns, the richness of Delhi in satin, silk and brocade. Swirling the sleek hips and the jeweled faces, beard pomaded
and elaborate turban, lift and click of glittering golden scandals, a
tarantella danced upon the crumbling edge of disaster. All of a
sudden the crowd became remote. The night had gone dark and
a warning bolt of lightning shot through the sky. The first few
drops of rain fell, thick and heavy. The lawns were still green,
trimmed with devoted industry, bordered by meticulously kept
flower beds, but under his feet he could feel them sullen and trembling.

3

Next morning Pratap Singh was not his urbane self. As far as it
could be, his rotund face was set and haggard, and he shuffled dis-
tractedly through his papers, as his eyes kept wandering to the
whiplash of the headline.

"Don't tell me it had to happen. The police could have stopped
them, and what did they do? Stood there and let them kill us.
You can preach nonviolence and turn the other cheek, but sure as
the sun sets there will be a night of reckoning."

"And what then? When does it stop?"

"When they've had enough."

"There are sixty million of them."

"I've never been good at statistics. My father and mother are probably dead. Their home was in the heart of it. I'm a Government servant, I've a discipline to keep, and even if I hadn't, it wouldn't be in me to go out and level the score. But there are plenty to whom pulling a knife comes easier. You wouldn't guess it from all the mass marches and pacific protests, but down in many of us there's a core of desperation waiting to explode whenever the pressure is turned off.

"I know," said Krishnan. "I've felt some of it myself."

Pratap Singh looked unbelieving. "Thanks for sympathizing, but you don't know. You couldn't possibly, unless it happened to you. You're a South Indian, you're two thousand miles away from it, your people aren't on the invasion route, your land isn't torn by this kind of dissension."

"It's our country," Krishnan reminded him gently. "It doesn't matter how far away the corners are. What happens in the room happens to us."

"You're trying to soothe it away," Pratap Singh said. "It'll die down eventually. Die down in me, that is. But outside it's only just beginning."

"It's our business to see that it doesn't begin."

The Sikh played with the paper knife, his lips curling.

"It's our business perhaps, but don't even try to stop it. Nobody argues with an avalanche. If you're lucky you get out of its way. Maybe you remember Calcutta and Naokhali. It seemed the end then; it seemed impossible that insanity could go further. Now it's starting again. Last year was only the prelude."

Krishnan looked at him, uncertain what to do next. He couldn't reason him out of a pessimism which he was not beyond sharing. He too was aware of the core of desperation, the violent flood beneath the disciplined surface. The skin had torn loose, and the anger started to thrust through. Who was to tell where the beginning would end?

But they were civilized men; they lived in a conspiracy—the job, the pretense, the routine, the *esprit de corps*. He would speak to him as to a civil servant. It was meaningless, but it would be understood. It would involve the right gestures, push away the evil.

"I don't want to seem unfeeling, Pratap," he said, "but it might help you if you were to give your mind to something different. The disposals question, for instance. You could take it up with D.S. I suppose it's a merit of his, at least in this situation, that he discusses nothing but business during office hours."

"I dare say you're right," Pratap Singh replied. He said it indifferently, mechanically, collecting his papers and shuffling off without even telephoning for an appointment.

Krishnan tried to suppress his feeling of guilt. He *had* felt the shock of sympathy for his colleague, the sense of identity, the sharing of a tragedy. He had done what he could to help him and himself. But now, with the Sikh gone, he was conscious only of the vacant room and the opportunity it gave him. He realized with chagrin that he had been waiting all morning. Was sympathy only a cloak for his impatience?

He reached for the telephone indecisively, jerking his hand back as the door opened. It was only a *chaprassi* with a *Most Immediate*. He went to work on the problem, taking his time, hoping that Pratap Singh would come back. He threw it into the OUT tray only when there was plainly nothing more that he could do with it. His fingers found the receiver. It was a question of good manners, he reassured himself. He had been rude yesterday, and it was only decent to say that he was sorry.

He dialed the Imperial. It was beyond the purses of all except top-ranking Government servants, but a foundation scholar could afford the price of plumbing. A sudden hope seized him that she might not be registered. She could be somewhere else, with friends, without a telephone, and then he could give up the club, concentrate on his work and put the memory down where everything else would cover it. But he had guessed right and got her extension, though he wished that he had not, hoped that she wouldn't answer, and then was angry at his happiness when the warm voice came through.

"Krish, how nice of you to remember me."

"I wanted to apologize," he explained to her lamely. "I was terribly rude last night."

"If you're really sorry, then you can buy me lunch."

"Later on," he said, evading her, snatching at the excuse. "The bridge game cleaned me out. I'll stick to my brass tiffin carrier with the moat around it to keep out the ants."

"Oh, no, you won't," she told him. "I'll buy you lunch instead. Out of last night's ill-gotten earnings."

He squirmed a little. "I couldn't possibly accept that."

"You can pay it back when you receive your increment."

It was no use protesting; he was only going through the motions. He left ten minutes early and drove the Hillman down, swinging it around the roundabouts a little more carelessly than he normally did, chiding himself when he found his foot nudging the accelerator, but not getting there any the later for that.

She met him in the corridor. Her dress was summery, and the heat made it cling to her. The pattern was a fussy one, and she did not look particularly well groomed. She wasn't everything she had seemed to be, and he found himself noting the debits: her rather too sturdy legs, for example, and her wrists, which were thickset even for the strong-looking hands. It reassured him that he was able to point out these shortcomings to himself until he realized that his insistence on them did not change his reaction.

Since they had been old acquaintances and had shared common loyalties, it seemed natural to talk of the changes brought about by the intervening years. He told his story first, since it was so much simpler. The tide of war had left him high and dry in England, and his parents had preferred that he stay on at Cambridge, where he would remain relatively safe and possibly grow wiser, rather than risk the long voyage around the Cape. His accumulation of degrees had qualified him to claim an ampler dowry, while at the same time ensuring that the larger benefactions would be spent intelligently. He had come home in his middle twenties, at the point of diminishing returns, when the advancing years began to take away more from his eligibility than the academic ornaments were capable of adding.

Hers was the typical story, up to a point. He remembered that when her shortened term at college was over she had joined a Lancashire munitions factory. They had written to each other regularly at first—long, polemic and crusadingly indignant letters that generously discussed everything but themselves. Gradually the issues became less flaming, and the correspondence briefer and more sporadic. When in the end they had to write to each other, and not simply to each other's addresses, they had little to say and could only say it awkwardly. There had been more than they had realized in their liking for each other and, discovering that uncomfortable fact, they could do no better than let the distance hide it. It was the typical stammering end of an undergraduate friendship, tapering off into an embarrassed, mutually sustained disuse.

After that, she told him, she had spent two years in uniform. She was laconic about the experience, she was born to be a sergeant, she alleged, her only defect being that she bruised a little too easily. At any rate, having helped to make munitions, she found it progress of a kind to assist in their delivery. She ought to have been accustomed to disaster by the time the doodlebug hit her London home, but it was a shock nevertheless, to go home expectantly on the night of her leave and to find herself staring at the gutted shell and the still-smoking debris and at the broken bodies of her parents, disinterred eventually from the ruins. They had more than enough money to leave, and several among their friends had left for safer places, but, though they had no particular affection for the house, there was still a pride in them that compelled them to remain.

After the death duties, she was reasonably well off. The war ended ten months later. There was only a younger sister to think about, and she married into diplomacy the following summer. Having stood for several years in rationing queues she had appropriate talents to apply to cocktail parties and to seeming serene in an elegance of olives. So there she was alone, Cynthia concluded, the tone of her voice indicating that she was putting the book back on the shelf, with nothing ahead of her but understanding and no attachments behind her but her memories.

She wouldn't speak further of what the memories were, having provided her accounting as far as she deemed fit, but he himself had known Keith, tousle-headed and slim-hipped, declaiming advanced verse in a languid falsetto, a Byronic wing-three who was unexpectedly easy to tackle and who always looked his handsomest when falling. When he mentioned him casually it was impossible to miss the tightening of her mouth or the way the indifference slammed into her manner, as if her foot were pushing down a trapdoor. A girl had to become used to herself, she said a little later, apropos of something deliberately different, and though she spoke the words blandly enough, there was no question of how she regarded her femininity. It was another examination that she had decided to pass, another debate she wanted to control, it was the application of taste and intelligence to her undoubted natural assets with her typical, methodical, almost meticulous thoroughness. The effect was formidable, as it had to be, until one realized that it was not in the least spontaneous. After that, one was less hemmed in by her smartness, and by her carefully directed stabs of conversation. In a sense, one began to play her at her game; it was perhaps a safer, certainly an easier procedure than making contact with the loneliness underneath.

He threw in his apology, deciding to return to the conventions. He felt like a girl at a street corner dropping a handkerchief.

"I can't imagine what came over me," he said.

Her face relaxed. She too was not at all unhappy about going back with him to the verbal dance floor.

"Don't worry," she reassured him. "You can be as rude as you like. It just shows how badly your subconscious wants me."

He couldn't help smiling but he had to remind her. "Aren't you forgetting that Kamala is my wife?"

She got to the crux of it with her usual directness. "Why did you marry her?"

"In order to get married."

"If I weren't so perceptive, I'd call that an unintelligent answer."

"If you were perceptive, you'd realize that it wasn't meant to be intelligent. It was supposed to be adequate."

Her eyes started glinting. She still looked for the opening, still couldn't resist the barb.

"Oh, Krish, after ten years of living in England, don't tell me that the ancestral customs got you."

He always flushed easily and this time she had struck deep. Ancestral customs. What did she know of it, of the pull of belonging, the pressures of conformity, the knowledge that without acceptance, without a soil for significance, homecoming was only a harsher kind of exile, the fruit forever beyond the clutching fingers. She wasn't Indian, she couldn't understand. Ancestral customs. That was all it was to her. Not just giving in, but giving in to barbarism. But he counted ten, which was just as well with Cynthia, and then realized that she had said it precisely to provoke him, either into a kindred condescension or into a defense too emotional for even him to consider it valid.

"Those ten years," he said slowly. "They're the years of my education and of course I'm grateful for them. But there are things you learn only after the learning has stopped. Some things a man only comes to with his fingers. He has to feel them, put his convictions around them."

"That's love," she cut in unexpectedly. "A fancy philosophy for a four-letter word. If you love Kamala why can't you be simple and say so? Or maybe you only *want* to love her."

She had put the question in such a way that he found it difficult to answer. He had to go back to his train of thought, but he was beginning to feel it to be more and more of an artifice.

"Somewhere, somehow, my life has got to grow up, it has to live with the problems of my soil and people. Kamala's Indian, intensely so, not simply in what she knows and does, but deep down, in ways that I can only sense and don't even want to understand."

Cynthia smiled benevolently. "She's a nice girl, I'm not denying that. Perhaps I like her because I can break her in two. But now that we're trying to be honest, does she really have all that remarkable depth of character?"

He nodded. "It takes time to get beyond her gentleness. When you do, you find her receptive but not passive. She doesn't have smart answers, most of the time she doesn't have them at all, but more than anyone else she helps me to see how to begin."

"You're sure she's really like that, and that you haven't cast her that way in a play you want to finish?"

"You may be right but I don't think you are."

"Hmm," said Cynthia dubiously. She swung her stool around, dangled her legs, and then recrossed them. "Krish, I've thought about you a lot since I went away and I probably know you better than most people. You have a streak of resignation in you that's a mile wide. That's why I'm not happy about this business, building a cage around yourself and calling it belonging."

"Believe me," he insisted, trying to be firm because he was feeling the prick of it. "Believe me, it isn't that way at all."

"Anyway," said Cynthia flippantly, "if you must sit in a cage, do let me have the keys to it."

"Lunch is ready," announced Krishnan. "Which do you prefer, mutton stewed or mutton curried?"

She sighed. "It's been that way for weeks now. I do wish they could think of something different."

"Why don't we go somewhere else? If you're still a Roman, there are ways of testing your fortitude."

"My mother taught me to stand anything once."

He took her to a place off Connaught Circus. It was murky, smoky, with blobs of *pan* on the floor, bare benches and rickety tables. The clientele was miscellaneous, with students the most easily identifiable element. Nothing like Cynthia had ever crossed the portals, and curious glances followed her minutely, punctuated by whistles of approval.

"Don't mind them," said Krishnan. "They read *Esquire* in the information center. They wouldn't do it if you weren't like the pin-ups."

"At last you're beginning to appreciate me," she murmured. "If I hadn't sneezed at the wrong time, I might have been chosen as Miss Chipping Todbury."

The *iddalis* and *sambhar* arrived, succulent and steaming.

Krishnan was glad that she looked at them with interest and not with apprehension, as so many others of her kind might have done.

"The *iddalis*," he informed her, "are made of black gram and parboiled rice. They are soaked for several hours. Then the cook's assistant develops his muscles grinding them in the stone mortar, which you must have seen if you've been to one of our houses. The gram in particular has to be the texture of whipped cream. After that you mix them, take a well-earned rest, and the next morning make them into pancakes and steam them."

Her eyes widened. "Krish, you never told me you were a cook as well as a scholar. Isn't Kamala lucky to have landed you for a catch?"

He laughed. "When I was a little boy I used to read the cookery book because the only alternative was Hall and Anderson's catalogue. But the craft is inherited, like any craft in India. It isn't in any book. When Mother was at the sewing machine I used to stand in the kitchen and watch Vaidyanathan do it. They're great people, the Vaidyanathans. For six generations they've been cooks to our family."

"Now tell me how Vaidyanathan made the *sambhar*."

"He'd boil red lentils in salted water. Then he'd fry a multitude of spices, fenugreek, turmeric, coriander and the rest, each separately, the only way it should be. Then the assistant would go to work with the grinder, and when it was fine enough to powder your face with, it would all be thrown into tamarind sauce, half boiled over a slow fire and cooked till the full flavor was brought out."

"It sounds delicious," she said.

"Don't be impatient," he admonished her. "There are still green peppers, eggplant and white onions to be added, not to mention asafoetida juice and Chinese parsley."

She took a mouthful and did not wince at the chilis. "It doesn't taste quite as good as all that, of course. But then I don't suppose anything can."

"Vaidyanathan's does," he assured her. "He's an artist. Escoffier is not even in the same league."

"I like it though, even with the compromises."

"Enjoy it by all means," said Krishnan, "but don't believe it if these Northerners tell you that it's the principal contribution the South has made to India."

"Go on," she said, "go on and tell me what else."

"There was Sankara, who died early but late enough to make Aquinas look like a schoolboy. There are temples, huge temples carved to the last square inch of stone and no two square inches are alike. When you walk through them you begin for the first time to understand the meaning of unity in diversity. There is the great Nataraja at Chidambaram, infinite energy and infinite repose; you may not think that such a fusion is possible, but there it is and maybe more than anything else it's India."

"When you talk like that you remind me you are a Government Servant and not the teacher you were going to be. Is that another bar in the charming cage you are building?"

"A man has to live."

"You make it sound like the second oldest profession."

"I don't think the state is quite as old as all that." It sounded feeble, so he tacked on his formula. "If you're a teacher it's only because you've failed to be anything better. That's what they all think, right or wrong. And how can you respect yourself if others don't respect you?"

"Nonsense," said Cynthia decisively. "I'd respect you and so, I imagine, would Kamala. Respect has nothing to do with it and you know that. You can't stand up to social and family pressures, so you've invented this high-class fib about belonging, and there you sit tying yourself up and trying to make your frustration look significant."

"You're very rude, Cynthia. But you'll find you aren't right."

"Krish dear, where you're concerned I know the score so well, and poor Kamala simply doesn't. So she trots along behind you like an obedient Hindu wife trying to fit in, and of course the family solution is the easiest one to fit. She's receptive, not passive, to use your delightful description. But I don't fit in, do I? I move around and threaten to bowl you over."

Krishnan took a long hard look at her. That, he decided, was just about what she did.

4

The work wasn't the anodyne it was supposed to be, and the sense of responsibility came shouldering through the routine. It was oppressively hot; if the fan was turned up enough to move the air significantly it also blew the papers off the table. A paper streamer hung impotently over the grille near the ceiling, where the air conditioning was alleged to function. Home-made *khus-khus* would have been more effective.

He looked at the P.W.D. pile outside the window, junk accumulated like the wasted years, odds and ends, frustrations and blind alleys. He would go through all the motions and promotions, down the Jumna with the handful of his ashes, down past Triveni in the Brahmin's orderly progress.

His eye fell upon the inside wall. It seemed almost a yard thick. The bars in the window were massive in proportion to the masonry.

A cage, she had said, an interesting cage.

The map hung canted from the rusty nail, a red hole to indicate Calcutta, the starting point of frenzy, the scene of the great killing, second-largest city of the ebbing Empire.

Maybe she was more right than she knew. The cage had always been there, always around them with its solacing confinements, the cage of discipline proof against hysteria, and now they were all in it together with the wild beast.

The minutes slipped by into the junk pile and he drove the car home much slower than he had to. The voice on the radio advanced the line of disaster.

Dinner was tasteless, interminable. She knew he wasn't quite himself so she served it to him on the silver *thalis* that sometimes made him happy because of their workmanship. The cook had left, she said, and the emergency help didn't know much about it. The cook had gone, last of a long line of nomads, the stray cooks of Delhi forever wandering, house to house, in search of the perfect formula.

Kamala looked tired. Her hair had lost some of its customary gloss, her eyes were clear but not luminous, as they usually were. Tired doing nothing, he thought, tired just waiting, waiting without expectancy, waiting as the minutes tick by to the bomb burst.

You were right the first time, he reassured himself angrily. Her loyalty isn't a chain, it's a challenge. Pull of the earth, it gives your resistance a purpose, it's the condition of your strength, it's the problem you live in, go down and love the stones in it, don't pity it, don't regret it, but make it change with the strength of dedication.

He wriggled his feet uncomfortably on the cement floor. He looked out of the barred windows at the voluptuous blue of the sky.

"How long have you known her?" she asked him.

She had that capacity to stand among his thoughts, but he was surprised that what he was trying to hide from himself could be so transparent in its implications to her.

"For several years. When she and I were students. Of course," he added hastily, "she wasn't at all the same then."

He had meant to reassure her about the past but he had done it at the cost of unsettling the present. It must have gone down deep, it must have taken root in him, for it to come out that way in the nuances.

"She's very attractive now." She said it to him completely matter-of-factly, without envy, without attempting to be complimented, without even seeking the insincere denial.

"Some people think she's too tall." He threw in the criticism to show he was still impartial. But it was a token objection, the one that mattered least. All it now seemed to expose was his reluctance to be honestly critical at any significant level. He wasn't even sure that he agreed with it himself.

If he had betrayed anything she was still too gentle to notice it. "I didn't mean it," she said thoughtfully, "in that superficial sense. Not that she hasn't a face and a figure. But what I wanted to say was that, at least from the outside, what you can see or sense is all pulled together. That's why she doesn't lack repose even though she's such a vital person."

It was remarkable, thought Krishnan, the two of them hadn't

exchanged more than half a dozen sentences and yet she was able
to make a statement like that, perceptive to a degree that implied
a long acquaintance. So she wasn't quite as matter-of-fact as she
seemed. Without a radical concern for their relationship there
wouldn't be this penetrating interest.

"Why don't you ask her to dinner?" she continued. "If she's an
old friend it would be no more than courteous."

So that was the logic: make her eat your salt, put her conscience
on your side, even if you couldn't do it with her emotions.

"I was thinking of that," he replied, "but I don't know where
she lives."

The lie had come without his having planned it. Now it had
sprung up between them and could not be retracted. He had willed
it this way, he knew. It could not have happened if he had not
desired it, but reason and loyalty might have curbed him and had
not. So it would be concealed, guilt would become its undertone.
Even if they were to wish it otherwise, the two worlds would
grow up separate and secret, and one or the other would have to
claim his life. A choice on those terms. What could it do but injure? He did not want it, yet he had demanded it, and now he
would move to it down the slide of his acts.

"You can find out," he heard her saying. "One of the hotels, most
probably. Or if not, somebody at the club should know."

"Surely it isn't as important as all that."

The second lie was easier, so much easier, that he was angry
with himself. He had half hoped the deception would show
somewhere. But it did not, at least not to the extent that he could
observe it reflected in her reaction.

Perhaps he was a better actor than he thought. Or perhaps he
wasn't acting. Perhaps the lie was becoming him, growing into
his shape, the protective mask he would always have to wear whenever he looked into the mirror of her fidelity.

5

At lunch next day he took Pratap Singh with him. It was a
pointless thing to do, but in the immediate aftermath, he felt that

a witness would lessen his sense of betrayal. Perhaps the lie could
be retraced, or the tracks covered, so that no one would suspect
the existence of the animal. He could tell her that he had acted
on her suggestion, rung up the hotel, and of course there she had
been; wasn't Kamala's deduction intelligent? Then he had to ask
her to lunch. The second man would show that everything was
innocent. They would have the dinner just as Kamala planned it,
and sit around the table partitioning the future, neatly mortgaging
it to the correct emotions.

It would take time, he admitted to himself, to subdue his reac-
tions to the physical difference, and there was the danger of the
more subtle changes which he was aware of, though not sufficiently
to assess. But he could contrive against the possible opportunities.
There were ways to protect himself—the company of others, a more
outgoing response to his colleagues. Perhaps, too, the gathering
storm of his country's future might help to divert him from the
unrest in himself.

If it was infatuation, that would be painful but easy. He would
snub it systematically or, better still, would starve it. The loss of her
would leave some sense of emptiness, but the ache could be disciplined, he would surround it with responsibilities, dilute the pain
by diversifying his interests, and the blue image would steadily
lose its outlines and become part of the intense, anonymous sky.

When he saw Cynthia he knew that it was an illusion and that
he wanted the lie because it told the truth. He was still concerned
about where the lie would lead him. But life, he was able to reassure himself, was not so pitilessly logical, and perhaps when the
time came to choose, their own feelings would have already made
the choice or arranged in advance for the shock of it. He was
anxious chiefly that there should be no injury. If no one was hurt,
he told himself, then no one had done wrong. Know the inevitable,
see it clearly, and one could accept it gently. As long as one didn't
have the collapse of the expected, the express screaming over the
dynamited bridge.

If Cynthia was surprised at Pratap Singh's appearance it did not
show in her face. She preferred to express her disapproval indi-

rectly, by concentrating her charm on the delighted Sikh. "I've always admired your people for their solid virtues. I've never thought them simply picturesque."

Before Pratap Singh knew what was happening she had coaxed him into a dissertation on his beard to which she listened intently, her face cupped in her hands, her eyes flickering with an admiration so convincing that even Krishnan was left doubtful after some minutes of the exercise. "I hope you don't think I'm being vulgar or inquisitive. But it seems to me that beards have always exerted the most profound influence on history. Someday I plan to write a book about it. Not sensational, you understand, but a temperate, objective work of scholarship."

Pratap Singh had nodded enthusiastic approval. "A splendid idea. It will be a truly distinguished contribution to knowledge."

Krishnan was telling himself that he had never suspected the man of being so fatuous when Cynthia dexterously steered the conversation, first to the martial traditions of the Sikhs, then to their political future. With his confidence won, Pratap Singh did not attempt to be evasive, and his response revealed a sense of perspective which, to Krishnan, was as unfamiliar as his previous inanity.

"The Hindus want independence. The Moslems want their theological state. We'll have to pay the price between the millstones."

"But is there no hope of a third way for you?" she asked.

He shook his head. "It's a sentimentality. Your heart asks for it and then your head tells you it isn't practical politics. There are only six million of us, but we straddle the great rivers, the highways of commerce, the traditional routes of conquest. Our land is the watershed of destinies which are so much larger than our people."

Cynthia listened with what seemed genuine sympathy. "It's a tragedy," she said gently, "and doesn't cease to be so by being called practical politics."

Pratap Singh nodded his head in appreciation of the proffered understanding, while Krishnan, left out of the conversation, tried to occupy himself by working out the significance of the interchange. His self-esteem, pricked by her neglect, reacted by assuming that the operation must have been conducted at least partially for his benefit. On that basis, what could be her motives? If she was trying to say that people were as one found them, that was a sensible conclusion certainly, but hardly one that justified these maneuvers. Surely there must be a more threatening moral to this artful contrast of asininity with intelligence. Was she trying to tell him bluntly that she could do more or less as she chose to with most people? That was the obvious conclusion, which immediately made it the most unlikely, since Cynthia (at any rate this Cynthia), for all her directness, never leaned to the obvious, particularly if the obvious happened also to be vulgar.

She was telling him that she would play it her way, he concluded. He had come here armed with a certain strategy. She was saying politely that she wouldn't accept the plan, that she had certain rights, that he couldn't just work out a part for her and unilaterally proceed to cast her in it. The conclusion made him feel a trifle happier, which was probably the main reason why he reached it. A very reasonable objection. Of course, it would have to be done gently, with due consideration for everybody's feelings.

He looked at her face, which was in half profile to him, as she questioned Pratap Singh on the beginnings of his religion. "It was essentially a movement of protest, wasn't it? Reform always has a nonconformist basis."

Her features, he assured himself, were undoubtedly handsome but a little immobile. And chestnut was not the happiest of colors for her hair. Didn't she admit it tacitly in the way she wore it off her face?

Analyze it, he thought, and the alchemy goes, the lightning strikes but the storm is as suddenly over and the earth is as it was, only more verdant.

In the end it hadn't been such a frustrating afternoon. He was able to leave, looking her in the eyes, did not wince at her effusiveness to Pratap Singh and watched without significant regret the elegant figure diminishing down the corridor.

Pratap Singh waited till she was safely out of earshot. "Never realized you were such a dog," he said admiringly.

"Is she as unusual as all that?"

"When I go to a movie that's what I go to see. Why wasn't I told it was walking around in Delhi?"

He made a determined attempt to look lecherous and failed miserably because of his chubby face. At another time Krishnan might have resented the innuendo. Now he had almost persuaded himself to applaud it. She had done her best, she had played on his self-esteem, she had given him all that intelligent, winning sympathy, and in the end this was all that he thought of her. Why should he value her more highly? Reduced to realities, what did the spell amount to, a glossy absorption, just something in a magazine, leer at it, put it away in the top office drawer, and they would all go eventually—the clippings and the daydreams—into the trash basket with the forgotten years.

He went home more happily. Kamala was on the lawn. She was dressed in green, but cooler than the panting grass, brighter than the tall trees that stirred casually in the breathless air. A squirrel sat at her feet and a myna in the branch above her.

He took her hands and felt something more than gratitude flow into him. He could still be the whole man, the capable officer, the devoted husband, cultivating his mind privately, like a rich garden, before the cruelty of summer seized it. What madness had been in him, urging him to abandon the accepted ways of contentment?

He called for coffee, and the bearer brought it in brass tumblers and she poured it for him, back and forth, forth and back, in that perpetual concertina motion, till the steaming fluid was completely aerated and he could drink it foaming, his head against her lap, looking up into the gentle eyes of welcome.

The night was close and warm. They sloshed buckets of water over the *khuskhus* and on the cement floor, which drank it all up thirstily. "Let's sleep in the open," he said. Kamala protested that it was dangerous, but he scoffed at her affectionately. The air was still out of doors also, as if reluctant to leave the oasis, but it was fresher as it moved almost imperceptibly against the tired limbs. He fell asleep in a mood approaching contentment, counting the stars in a sky of darkness so deep and so immaculate that it seemed washed clean of everything, even frustration.

It was still night when he awoke. His first awareness was of a sinister shape above him. With nightmares of dacoity burning into his consciousness, he rose unarmed but ready to fight and perish.

"It's only Mehta's cow," Kamala reassured him sleepily. "It keeps wandering over the broken wall. Tell it to go away."

"That would be improper," he reproved her. "A cow stands higher than a woman in the Hindu hierarchy. If you behave yourself and dedicate your life to pleasing your husband it is entirely possible that you may be a cow in your next birth."

She looked mischievously at him. Her arms went around his shoulders, pulling him gently down. "I promise to try. I promise I'll never stop trying."

6

"What was the chaperon for?" asked Cynthia. "I never eat anyone except in self-defense."

He had waited a while before asking her. He had even thought of dropping it completely, though not seriously enough to alarm himself with the prospect. When the desire to see her became difficult to frustrate, he was able to tell himself that it was a matter of civility, he shouldn't be too abrupt, the temperature had to be brought down slowly, and, in any case, until he was able to face her, he couldn't be certain that it was really ending.

She had replied to his invitation with disconcerting naturalness, not asking any questions about the hiatus, and with none of the resentment in her manner which might have persuaded him that her hold on him was weakening.

With the thermometer up to a hundred and ten, she had wanted a brief swim before lunch. Since he was not yet a member of the

club, his use of the pool was restricted, and that was a good enough
reason to sit on the sidelines and watch her.

She swam a six-beat crawl much as she did anything else—
lazily, fluently and a little better than she should. She used the
high recovery, which was going out of style, largely, he suspected,
because it made her look more graceful. He admired her in the
water with what he hoped and didn't believe was detachment;
she was sleek, trim and yet voluptuous, the long line flowing
supplely from hip to toe.

She had come out after ten quite strenuous minutes, breathing
only a little harder than usual, walking toward him on the balls of
her feet, not ostentatious about her body, but not forgetting that
she had it.

"Dry my back," she said, throwing him the towel.

It was pleasant and nothing more, he reassured himself, to feel
her flesh under his fingers, live and firm and as trained as an
athlete's.

"I'm scared of you," he said. "That's why I need protection."

Maybe the half-truth would melt away if he put it like that and
both of them made fun of it.

"But, Krish, I've done nothing," she protested with mock concern. "Cross my heart. What have I ever done but what you asked
me?"

He seized her neck in the towel.

"Don't forget to rub behind the ears," she reminded him. "I'm
telling you now, in case you are blessed with a daughter and have
to manage without domestic service."

"I'm scared," he repeated. "You have Helen's face and Miss
America's bust."

"I'll put the twelve pounds back if you insist, dear. I'll dress in
saffron and sackcloth, and you and I can go to Badrinath, if you
promise to hold my hand when I haven't the head for the heights."

"What good will that do," he grumbled, "if you insist on making
me dizzy?"

"But if it's only the physical part that worries you, why should
I? That was all you mentioned, wasn't it? I'm just something on

a magazine cover. Out of circulation in the high Himalayas, and in any case the new number is coming off the presses."

She threw her head back to look at him, and the curve of her throat was taut and clean and beckoning, with not even the finest of lines on the asking flesh.

"What's frightening you?" she challenged him. "Is it only a figure and a face? Or is it that you're scared of someone's honesty?"

"I don't know yet," he said. "But it won't take long to find out. It's a question of understanding. Nothing more."

"And when you understand it, you'll be free of me, won't you?"

"We'll be good friends—which is as much as we should be."

She laughed delightedly. "Oh, Krish, you've such a desperately orderly mind. You really think that by explaining the demon you're going to exorcise it. Hasn't it struck you that just because you want to be such a reasonable person, putting my appeal to you on a rational footing will make it that much more difficult to escape?"

"If I understand something," he insisted stubbornly, "it loses its power to hurt me."

"If you're going to understand anything, my precious, you'd better start by realizing that you aren't getting hurt." She stood up erect and a little arrogant, just the slightest trace of the jungle in her green eyes. It was over in a flash and she was herself again, civilized and normally disconcerting.

"I've played it the way you wanted it, Krish. I'm not here to make you unhappy. Of course, I've got my own feelings too. I'm not to be walked over, but for heaven's sake trust me instead of trying to fight me."

He stood up and gripped her shoulders from behind. He spun her around. He looked levelly and intently at the unflickering eyes and the aristocratic mouth. "Lunch is ready," he said. "Which do you prefer, mutton stewed or mutton curried?"

She smiled at him fondly. "How long do you think you'll be able to keep on doing that?"

She waved happily as she went back for her clothes.

She was out in five minutes, a lesson in how to look cool at a hundred and eleven degrees. Her dress was not the source of the impression. It was a bright lemon shade, and she was sufficiently tanned so that the vigorous color did not wash out her skin. Tanned uniformly too, as he had noticed approvingly at the pool's edge. In contrast to the usual haphazard operation, with layers of brown like geological strata.

They took a table that overlooked the lawn. He ordered lime juice and soda.

"Take something stronger," she suggested. "You'll need it for the truth."

"I'm a truth addict," he replied. "I have to have it neat."

"It's rather difficult to begin," she mused, "but the fact is that my appeal to you isn't because of myself. Or, more correctly, it's many other things besides myself."

"That's right," he said, twitting her, "blame the environment. Sound materialism and progressive doctrine."

"It isn't the environment, either, that's part of the trouble. You could be in half a dozen other places, I could be half a dozen other people, and the result would still be similar, though of course I flatter myself that as I am my pull would be the strongest. That's where you're going wrong, dear. You're firmly entrenched, you're busy building defenses, but what's the use of the fortress if the problem is yourself?"

"Of course it's myself," he said with some exasperation. "What else could it possibly be? That's why I'm trying to unite it to things that are real and rooted, that belong in India even if I don't."

"Pushing files into the OUT tray—that isn't particularly real. You're not honestly tackling your problem at all, Krish, and you know that. You're just shoving it into a situation and hanging on, hoping that the situation will solve it."

"Well, what do you want me to do, go out into the bright blue and build the dam with my bare hands?"

"I don't want anything except possibly you, and I can live without that. We're discussing what *you* want, and that's what you asked for, in case you've forgotten."

It was the first time she had spoken of wanting him, and she said it tautly, as if the admission hurt her pride a little and as if she had come to take the hurt for granted. It wasn't completely unexpected to him; he had even thought of how he might react to it, but now that it was said he was still surprised at the sudden significant tightening, as if the emptiness had always been there and as if, looking at her, he had suddenly found the reason.

He told himself angrily that he was forgetting himself. He tried to push back the stubborn, startled feelings into the shape that duty had ordained for them.

"Very well then," he retorted brusquely. "Go ahead and tell me what I want."

"You want me, of course, and you also want Kamala. Now don't make faces, that's the way things are, and until you accept it you'll just be going around in circles."

He tried to take refuge in facetiousness. "I suppose if I have both of you I'll be able to see straight."

"You want Kamala and myself," she insisted. "Because of what we stand for to you. It's the way you are and the way your life has been. You'll always be torn between conflicting loyalties."

"Don't tear too hard," he warned her, stubbornly flippant. "When I decide, I want to do it in one piece."

"Of course, Krish." Her voice had relaxed, becoming suddenly gentle, as if to urge him back into the seriousness he was sedulously avoiding. "Only, be sure that *you* take the decision."

"It's done already," he told her, hoping that saying it would make him more secure. "You can't live with freedom; it's only a different cage. It's the web the spider spins out of his own body."

She had her own way of looking at the comparison. "If there's an alternative it's only a name for surrender. At least the web is one's own. As long as you make it you can also break it."

"It's done," he repeated. "I've come back to where I had to. I've taken on the responsibilities I had no right to evade."

He had meant it as a reminder of the practical, a declaration of necessity. But when the words came out, they sounded only defeatist. It was how she wanted them to sound, he realized. If they had that echo for him it meant he had moved over to her side.

She saw what was happening in his face and pressed home her advantage in that typical way of hers, deliberate, methodical, yet intense.

"You've got to begin with yourself," she told him decisively. "With the way you are and not the way others have drawn you. And you don't start searching from a place on the map, or on the family swing, or in the cradle. You start from something that happens in your mind, the firmness you feel when you've stopped running away."

Her face was set a little tighter than he had known it, determined yet, under the pride, forlorn, and without wanting it but also not resisting it, he felt the pull in him, the sense of identification, the response of one loneliness reaching out to another.

"Where are you looking for your home, Cynthia?" he asked gently.

"I'm a half and halfer," she replied a little wryly, "and home could be close to you because you're a half and halfer also. Like something in a mirror, the same image but the loyalties reversed."

"It's no man's land," he told her. "You want to live there, between two worlds, under perpetual gunfire."

She tossed her hair back in that characteristic gesture of defiance. "If it's the way you are, then you've no choice but to live there. You're the tension, the conflict, you aren't either side or either way out. The right solution is the one that expresses you best. Don't ever tell yourself that it's the one that hurts you the least."

"If I were to accept that," he said slowly, "I'd have to change my whole approach. I'd have to throw away even the little that I've built."

"I'd like you to be," she replied uncompromisingly, putting the thought up firmly against his wavering. "I'd like you to be and not belong. And as for me," she added with a rueful smile, "there isn't much question of my belonging, is there? I've a home or, if you put it neutrally, a house. I've got security. I could have the future that I ought to want. Why should I be compelled to something far off and different? Because of the statistics I've digested? Because my grandmother was Indian? Because I like you and may come to love you? Or is it because the place doesn't matter; home is the place where my heart tells me it must be, where I can plant the seed and make my reality grow?"

Without realizing it he put her hand in his. The color had jumped to her face, suffusing her features with vitality.

"You're right about one thing," he said. "A man's way to truth is his own. It's in himself, and only he can find it. That's why the disciple chooses his *guru* and the *guru* leaves when the man knows how to discover reality."

"You see," she concluded. "All philosophies are the same. You sit down to think and you get up a nonconformist."

"That's only one side of the coin," he pointed out. "On the other side there's a social order regulated to the minutest detail, every step from the cradle decided in advance, a tremendous, relentless engine of conformity, and that too, oddly, has a religious basis."

"Poor Krish," she teased him. "You're always doing that. Walking around the coin, trying to choose between opposites. Why don't you be yourself, dear? It's easier on you, even in no man's land."

He looked at his watch. It was a quarter past three. "Have to leave in a hurry," he said. "If anyone from upstairs has been ringing I don't know what I can possibly say."

"You were trying to retrieve a file," she suggested, "from the Ministry of Finance. Because that's where all the files eventually go."

All the way back he could see her face in the mirror. There would always be a face there wherever he went, whichever way the road turned. The truth was not going to make him free. It would compel him to choose and decide the limits of freedom.

She was right, it wasn't the shock of the unexpected, it wasn't the easy, asking grace of her body, a curve his sensuality could caress, as the ebbing tide of surf caressed the beaches. She was the pull in his life, the tension that had to be, no matter how he twisted or evaded; the lost face would be there, inflexibly, in the mirror.

Back to the fortress and the yard-thick walls. He sat behind the files, the tight-lipped officer, P.U.C. and Q.E.D., V. S. Krishnan, the accomplished draftsman—for everybody's problem but his own.

7

Krishnan looked at Pratap Singh quaffing his afternoon *lussee*. There was nothing the Sikh could choose. Destiny would choose for him, and Mountbatten was in Simla, giving destiny the informal nudge.

Mukerji stood on the verge of the great mystery. Was the Assistant really alive? In Calcutta, the barricades were up, and the guns trained behind the innocent windows.

He dialed the Joint Secretary's room and made the appointment. He walked up the stairs, since the upper crust lived upstairs. He sat down uninvited, because he was tired of going nowhere.

He said, "I want a transfer."

"You're crazy," the other man said. He'd heard it before, and in May there was too much of it.

"The assistants are coming," Krishnan was going to say. "The faceless men who haven't birth certificates. Something will come soon and it won't be in the index."

He said, "I want a field job."

"You've only just arrived, man. I've heard good reports about you. What sense will it make for you to go scampering off, just when you're beginning to pull your weight?"

He was Eton and Oxford gone gray at the temples. The last of a conscientious line. You could see the end of him written on the calendar. Six months from now he'd be port outside, starboard home. Next year he'd be Colonel Limbo, the forgotten man, fiddling his way down Aldwych—"Never forget your curry, my dear chap. Always remember the wonderful years I spent there."

He said, "I know what you're trying to tell me. You're a square peg in a round hole. It's the commonest disease in this continent of diseases. Every year it ruins more families than malaria, tuber-

culosis and typhoid put together. And there's nothing you or I
can do about it. Just go on with your job and hold your
peace. One happy day like any other day you'll wake up and find,
amazingly, that you aren't square any longer."

"I don't want to seem obstinate," Krishnan persisted. "I'd like
to do something to people instead of to files."

How could he tell him: I want to run away; I prefer the
trenches because it's simpler to live there.

"You're not the district type at all. Scholarly background, a de-
gree in economics, fair in athletics, an indifferent mixer. You see,
I know your record. If you've any place here it's behind that desk.
When you chaps get up here, learn to pick your men too."

"You know what's on the way, sir," Krishnan suggested, as if
what he wanted, as if the fear in his heart, was only flaring up in
the public interest. "I'm from the South. I don't belong to any of
the sides. Wouldn't that help to make me more useful?"

The Joint Secretary looked back at him shrewdly but not un-
kindly. "There's a tremendous job right here. Don't fool yourself
that what you do doesn't matter. Every time you feel your insignificance, that you're out of the current, that you aren't playing
your part, ask yourself what the plan means in administrative terms
and how the details add up in human lives. You can't touch the
people with your hands, of course, but all the time you're touching them with your work. Go home and try to forget it," he
ended. "Take the day off, if it makes you feel any better."

Krishnan went down and took the Hillman home. The wheels
turned and the empty minutes ticked on. What did the radio say,
what could it say? The knives are being sharpened in the land
of the five rivers.

8

"Would it hurt you," he asked her, "if I were to go back to
teaching?"

"I wouldn't be hurt," said Kamala, "but Mother and Father
would. And you know the condition of Mother's heart."

It was the way it had to be, the exits closed and the flames beginning to smolder. No panic, ladies and gentlemen. When your feet begin to burn, it helps you to stop worrying about your ulcers.

What would he teach them anyway? The invisible hand and the frictionless economy? It was coming down from the Himalayan foothills, down the eight hundred turns of the road from Simla to Kalka, the germ of the future in the solemn convoy. A cloud of pain no bigger than a man's hand. When it hit you there would be nothing else to learn but to stay alive and stay human.

What could he tell them? Don't shoot the policeman if he seems to be doing his worst. Subdue the private agony for the public good. Forget about your sister raped, your mother in the ditches and the haunting face that reminds you of the crime, which is everyone's face, wherever the curved knife slashes.

We must rise superior to misplaced emotions. The time calls for the statesmanlike act and the self-denying ordinance.

"I suppose," he said, "that teaching wouldn't solve it."

"No," she replied, "it would be like buying new clothes. For a little while you'd be more self-possessed, and then you would realize that you have the same frustrations underneath."

One day I shall wake up and find myself cylindrical. Gather around me the appointed and the established, come to admire the ideal vivisection. I shall be the curved grace of the perfect scroll enshrining the accumulated wisdom of the archives.

"If I hang on," he said, "I'll eventually get used to it."

"Your frustration isn't that of a misfit, Krishnan. The job won't make you happy or unhappy. It only intensifies what is already there."

What shall I do when I'm in the room with the animal? If it destroys me, that's my funeral, and my decision made it. Let it destroy me, but what if it destroys her—all that sweetness and passionate power of acceptance?

Go out of the cage and into the free air. Go out past Kurukshetra where the sons of Kunti fought, out past Panipat where Babar planted his triumphal tents, out to where the frontier is the claw line and the torn body India.

"How do I fight it?" he asked. "What do I do if I am to make it obey me?"

"It's your problem," she answered, "and only you can tell. Wait for the silence to come and for the right way, like a finger of light in the silence. Then do what you know to be right and do it without fear."

He had the feeling of helplessness that came over him more and more often when he talked to her. It was like walking on water or trying to swim in air. If she would only support him, resist him, give him the solidity he so desperately needed. Loyalty or dissent didn't matter, if there were a claim, an appeal, whether of duty or love. Why did she have to drive him back on himself, down into the whirlpool of his indecision?

"What happens," he asked a little grimly, "if I do it and someone suffers as a consequence?"

Her voice was tense too, as if on the edge of bitterness. This time her principles had leaped upon her and from now on would take their price in pain.

"Don't ask me," she said with quiet determination, and he, sitting beside her, fancied that he felt her shiver, as if the will to be what she should had gone right through her body. "Don't ask me; you can only ask yourself. The problem is to do the right deed, not the just one."

He had not seen her in this mood before and it alarmed him. Was it because she was sure of her own strength or because, under the acceptance and the pliability, there lay some deep and hopeless instinct to nothingness?

"I found where Cynthia's staying," he said, deciding to tell her. "Do you still think we ought to ask her to dinner?"

Let them come face to face, the halves of his existence, and in the collision there might be more than debris. Perhaps they would decide for him, lay down the terms of escape. He would not have to sit there waiting for the silence. The voices of others were always more convincing than the hard, sad voice of one's responsibility.

"Yes, of course," she was saying, "and some of your colleagues in the Secretariat also."

She looked at the calendar and at Lakshmi's blessing. "The month is nearly over," she said, "and Tuesday's the day we were married. Let's make it the first Tuesday of next month."

9

It was in the air, and everyone knew what it was. They knew the principles and the outlines but not the details that would judge the future of thousands. The streets were not filled with hope or jubilation. The comings and goings of the people did not suggest that the great change might be only hours away.

The frontiers would no longer be those of nature, the sand and the sea and the white crests of the mountains. They would be drawn by the minds and beliefs of men, the meat that they ate and the scriptures that they carried.

Five men would draw them and ten million dispute them.

Strange lines, grim lines, in a familiar face. When you burned them in, how deeply would the face change?

It was the beginning of the unprecedented.

Six dynasties had gone down to oblivion in the red sandstone and the Jumna's earth. Always the rivers had been their cradle, the walls of snow and the breaking waves their ramparts. Always, above the warring and the factions, there had been the dream and the obsession of unity.

It would happen now as it had never happened before.

The city went quietly, precisely, to its work. Accustom yourself to the weight of the inevitable. The leaders hesitated, trying to resign themselves to the truncated dream. Then they too bowed to its urgent, angry logic.

It was Tuesday, and Krishnan left his office a quarter of an hour early. He had spent lunchtime exhaustingly at the bank. Six forms had been filled in, and twice he had certified that he was still himself. After an hour of investigation and the cross-checking of several records, he was able to extract what he wanted from the safe-deposit box—a pair of Kamala's earrings and her ruby necklace. He handed them over to her with relief. She had dressed for the occasion in a turquoise georgette, with a restrained but still elaborate pure gold border.

"It's unpatriotic," he said, "to have jewels for your dowry. Government bonds are so much more convenient."

He watched her while she screwed in the earrings. He always felt squeamish when it was done with pierced ears.

"Like them?" she asked him. "Mother bought them and Father said exactly what you did about buying Government bonds. Now they're worth three times as much as his wretched certificates. You can't dress up in the certificates either."

She did the clasp of the necklace, with its beaten-gold setting.

"It's odd how well it suits you," he remarked. "One would have thought it needed a larger person."

He had been seeing it on Cynthia and he crimsoned a little.

But she didn't notice the *faux pas*. Her thoughts were all on the evening. Occasions such as these were rare enough, and she could still derive an innocent happiness from them.

"I designed it," she explained. "So it ought to suit me, really. Besides, it isn't heavy; only a little severe. You don't have to be large, just well proportioned, to wear it."

"You've got the classic proportions," he assured her.

She could still blush when she was paid a compliment, even when it was paid her by her husband.

He shuffled his feet a little. It was an insensitive, maladroit beginning.

The first car arrived, crunching up the gravel.

It was Vijayaraghavan, exuberant as usual, with a Moslem colleague from the Secretariat.

"Shocking news, of course. That Jinnah chap wants a corridor five feet wide and a thousand two hundred miles long, from the Punjab to Bengal. And what's more, he's proposing to line both sides of it with morocco-bound copies of the Koran. What do you say to all this nonsense, Imtiaz?"

"Most of it," said Imtiaz defensively, "is nonsense that you yourself have invented. As for the rest, I'm staying in India, and that should be answer enough."

Imtiaz held his wife's hand protectively as he spoke. Kamala felt sorry for him, a lonely figure driven against the wall of unpopularity. One would certainly accept him and his Moslem brethren, but acceptance was not enough. There had to be something more than toleration; there had to be a positive sense of community to dispel the shadows of frustration and resentment that would cluster angrily around their suspected lives.

"Complicated fellow, this Imtiaz," said Vijayaraghavan. "Like every normal person, he hates his father subconsciously. So instead of decapitating him healthily in the Id, he works out partition as a way of separating himself from the detested presence. I'm a blunt Brahmin, of course, and unable to appreciate such elaborate courtesies."

Imtiaz began to smile. His father was a well-known Congressman, so no one would think the absurd argument true; and not being true, there was humor in its absurdity.

Kamala did not smile. She couldn't help being aware of the element of truth in the carefully frivolous reasoning. Fathers and sons *were* going to be separated. When the line was drawn it would not only be across the wheat fields golden with their harvest but through people's lives, through family relationships, across once-happy rooms where the sense of difference would suddenly harden, and kinship would be subdued to more abstract yet more demanding loyalties.

The Pratap Singhs arrived at the same time as Cynthia. Krishnan looked a little amusedly at his colleague's wife. She was dressed fashionably but unhappily, with the rigorous corsetry forcing her body into unnatural courses. She walked mincingly, as if on egg shells, and since she was obviously unfamiliar with the equilibrium of high heels, each step created a crisis for her ankles.

Cynthia, on the other hand, was dressed with strange sobriety, in a gray costume that did not really become her. Krishnan found a minor satisfaction in revising his judgment of her taste, until he realized that the effect was quite intentional. He had not been at all certain that she would come, and now that she had decided to do so, she was reminding him of his uncertainty by holding part of herself back. Persuading her had not been easy, and at first she had emphatically rejected the idea.

"I never heard anything so ridiculous. What good could it possibly do?"

"It's Kamala's brain wave," he had explained, trying to soothe her and minimize his own connivance in the idea. "We've done nothing that we need to hide. Why make her think that we have by not accepting?"

"How do you suppose I'd feel about the future if I went?"

"How do you suppose I'd feel whether you go or don't go?"

"That's different," she had said with a little toss of the head. "You married her, didn't you, and it's your decision. I'm not taking you from her and I never will."

That was true too, he had thought. If the trap worked, in a way it was the fault of the animal. But how could she brand him with the undivided guilt? Even if she didn't actually reach out for anything, did not the very way in which she waited for it, the almost predatory strength of her expectancy, make her culpable to a certain degree?

"I don't think," he had said, "that I'd be entirely to blame."

"There you go again, Krish. Guilt and shame and the whole morbid, familiar apparatus. If you're trying to suggest that you're not completely responsible for what you do, you're wrong, and the sooner you recognize it the better. You can't share responsibility. You can't and I can't. Happiness yes, but responsibility is one side of loneliness; you have to see it yourself and shoulder it as you see it."

"In that case," he had observed a little testily, "you're just as responsible as I am."

She had been prepared for the parry. "For what I do, yes. But then I haven't done and don't propose to do anything. I'm taking nothing, you understand. You leave her or you don't."

Well, it was her escape, and all of a sudden he had felt tired of arguing. Maybe she was right and you couldn't share it—neither his hesitations nor her confident passivity. Who was he to seek to pass on to her, or to expect her to accept, the germ of his doubts or the tension of his deciding?

"You might as well come then," he had told her. "I'm asking you and it's my responsibility."

"Of course, Krish dear, if it helps you to sort things out."

So here she was, and he shuffled his way through the introductory mumbles.

Pratap Singh bristled when he came to Imtiaz.

Vijayaraghavan sensed the situation. "Pleased to meet you again, Miss Greengage," he said to Cynthia with an exaggerated bow.

"Bainbridge," she corrected him with just the right tone of haughtiness. She kicked his foot playfully, and Kamala, aware that at least one crisis was over, made no attempt to hide her evident relief.

"Look around," said Kamala. "We won't have this house much longer. The tenant's returning, and we're nine hundred and ninety-six in the housing queue."

"Ask Imtiaz," suggested Vijayaraghavan. "He's an enlightened capitalist. He'll give you a place to live in for three times what it's worth."

Pratap Singh stroked his beard. "It would be more prudent," he said threateningly, "to stay clear of Moslem property."

Krishnan's capacities as a host were limited, but he felt it his duty at least to attempt to guide the conversation into more tranquil waters. "Why don't you tell us about your Indian ancestors, Cynthia?"

"There really isn't much to say," she answered, uncertain for once as to how to relieve the tension. "My grandmother was Indian. She died when Mother was a child. Grandfather left a few years afterward, and none of us has been back since. Maybe that's why your country fascinates me. It's in the blood. Only a little, it's true, but far back enough for me to want to return to it."

"That's to your credit," said Pratap Singh grimly. "There are people whose families have lived in India for centuries and who have suddenly discovered that they aren't Indian at all."

Imtiaz flushed, but rose to the innuendo. "You weren't thinking of Indian citizenship, were you, Miss Bainbridge? You'd be so much more advanced than some of my co-citizens."

Vijayaraghavan scoffed. "Let me remind you that citizenship is a privilege. Deeds will be required, not just meritorious grandmothers."

"I don't intend," said Cynthia, "to survive an ordeal by fire."

"I was going to suggest an ordeal by coffee. That is, if you're prepared to drink it in the South Indian way."

"My grandmother wasn't South Indian," she pointed out apologetically.

Shoulders were shrugged and knowing glances exchanged.

Cynthia let them take their time. "On the other hand," she added mischievously, "I know lots of things my grandmother never taught me."

"Bring on the coffee," said Vijayaraghavan.

It was brought in the brass tumblers, and Cynthia watched a little apprehensively, it seemed, as it was poured repeatedly from one vessel to the other. When it had cooled sufficiently, it was handed to her. She stood up, mouth open and head flung back, her bosom heaving, like a middle-aged Brünnhilde aspiring to the High C. Hesitantly she tilted the tumbler, the rim of it eight inches from her mouth. It wasn't a particularly promising pose, and amused looks among the others telegraphed the impending calamity.

The liquid went down without a drop being spilled.

Disbelief melted into laughter and applause.

"Where on earth did you learn the knack of doing it?"

"They laughed when she sat down at the piano," murmured Imtiaz.

"It's Kuppuswami's home-study course," she told them gaily. "All you need is a towel and buckets of the stuff."

"I wish you'd muffed it," said Vijayaraghavan. "Then we could have put you into a sari instead of that horrible dress you're wearing."

Kamala took her by the arm. "Why don't you wear a sari anyway, Cynthia? On a day like this you ought to be one of us."

They went in, and the men looked inquiringly at each other. It was unnecessary to announce a subject which was already an eroding current in their minds.

"Anyone know the details?" Krishnan asked.

Vijayaraghavan poked at the grass with a twig. "Some of them, yes. The bottom's out of the corridor, of course, but the rest of it is what we're all afraid of. But what can one do? What's the practical alternative?"

Pratap Singh clenched and unclenched his right hand. "Who works out the details? Field after field, the houses and the people? Who decides which country is to have them? Who tells us what we're to belong to, or to leave?"

"Two men from this side, two from that, and one above the conflict who'll probably be the only one who matters."

"That's only the beginning of it," said Krishnan. "There's the army and our foreign assets, the railways and the administration. Everything you can think of goes into the slicing machine."

"There'll be procedures to attend to all that. Councils, committees and so forth. Of course, it doesn't follow that they'll do the job adequately, but tidily or not, knowing the consequences, measuring the cost as clearly as is possible, we're all of us resigned to having it done."

They looked past the rapidly lengthening shadows, as the sun set toward the future frontier.

Kamala and Cynthia came back. Cynthia was wearing a shot-silk sari, with flame the predominant color. The border and the *pallu* were in black and gold, heavy and a trifle ornate. It was too dressy for what was really not a highly formal occasion, but Cynthia had the height for bold effects and wore the sari with a lack of self-consciousness that obliged one to take the whole result on its merits. There were murmurs of approval—one or two from the ladies—which Cynthia acknowledged with a graceful *namaskar*.

She sat down on the lawn. It was impossible for her to look fragile, but she managed unexpectedly to look compact.

"Magnificent," said Vijayaraghavan. "Has Kuppuswami taught you to eat on the floor also?"

"I can do it if I have to. I did gymnastics once."

"I've not the slightest doubt that you can, Miss Bainbridge. But what's the use if poor Pratap Singh can't?"

Pratap Singh glared and his wife flurried eagerly to the rescue. "You see, we're a very big country, you know. And in the North we're very much more Westernized." She patted her hair to emphasize the point and smiled sophisticatedly with one side of her mouth.

"Now, now, Raj dear," said Pratap Singh reprovingly. "All it comes to is that they're a little different from us. We mustn't suggest that they aren't just as civilized."

She reared up combatively in the cane chair. "Who said anything about civilization? I admire the South. The only georgette I ever wear is from Mysore. And you know what I look like in it. You've always said that it suits me much better than Benares silk. How could that happen if they weren't civilized? So where's the question of civilization? That's what I'm asking."

"There are differences," said Krishnan, trying to be soothing. "We Tamil Brahmins are a tight-lipped community. Do your job and prepare for the hereafter. There are other values needed to complete a civilization, and maybe we've tended to neglect them."

"That's exactly what I was saying," Pratap Singh's wife interjected. "Up here we're a practical people, that's what we are. We face hard facts and challenging realities." Her alarmingly upthrust bosom quivered aggressively as she stared at the future with the eyes of a lion tamer.

"I can't even remember how all this started," protested Kamala. "What difference do the details make if all of us remember we are Indian?"

They went indoors to dinner. Kamala had obviously given the menu some thought. All the South Indian delicacies were there, including the usual vegetables, deftly spiced and laced lavishly with tender, shredded coconut. Unfortunately the cook combined his talents with an inflexible orthodoxy that refused to tolerate even eggs in the kitchen. Apart from Cynthia, who either knew what to expect or was expert at hiding her feelings, the gathering did not take kindly to the lack of meat in the fare.

"Very interesting food this," observed Imtiaz hungrily. "Of course, I'm not much of a rice eater myself."

Pratap Singh looked suspiciously at the *avial.* He took a large spoonful and then plunged into the *sambhar,* which merely compounded the agony. "Not used to it," he explained dismally between splutters.

"Come, come," said Vijayaraghavan, "you're from a martial race."

Krishnan suggested the *pachadi.* "We don't spice the curds as you do, and it brings out the flavor of the rest."

The consumption of water exceeded that of the food.

Kamala wrung her hands. "I told the cook not to put in too many chilis."

"Too many is a relative term," said Krishnan. "From the culinary point of view he no doubt obeyed you. As far as our guests are concerned, he apparently didn't."

She was glad when it was over and she was able to suggest their going out on the lawn.

Krishnan looked dubiously at his watch. "Better switch on the radio," he suggested. "It's nearly time for it now."

"They'll all be speaking from A.I.R.," Cynthia reminded them. "Isn't that the place to be? In front of the building where history is being made?"

"Yes, yes," said Raj, "there's going to be such a *tamasha.*"

"Please go if you want to, but I'd rather stay," said Kamala. "It will happen differently to every one of us. I don't want to be in a crowd. I couldn't share the joy and the tragedy of it. When it comes, I want to be in the darkness, trying to understand it and to measure it for myself."

"I too," said Pratap Singh unexpectedly. "What have I got to cheer about?"

Something in Kamala's tone convinced them, and they sat quietly in the unlighted room waiting for the event. It was only minutes away now, yet the brief preliminaries seemed interminable.

Vijayaraghavan tried to relieve the tension. "Can't trust this Mountbatten fellow," he remarked. "He'll turn his charm on and sell us down the Hooghly."

"Why be scared?" retorted Cynthia. "Your Prime Minister has charm too."

The silence was even more embarrassing after that sally, but fortunately it was only moments before the historic speeches began. Mountbatten was first, then Nehru for the Congress, Jinnah for the Moslem League and finally Baldev Singh.

Somehow it was all over sooner than they had expected. It was not that the speeches were short ones; but the waiting had been so much longer. And the impact was lessened by anticipation. It had been a dream, and then a call to sacrifice, a hope, and then a future tinged with bitterness. Now it was on them, it was their reality, a new dimension humbling and ennobling, the choice established, the decision made.

They sat there, each one of them drawing the line in his heart, feeling the taste of frustration in achievement.

They were different men, Hindu and Moslem and Sikh, North and South, who had reached across many borders.

They were different men and soon they would be free men.

What would it do to them, what answer would it bring? How would the fact of independence and the challenge of division permeate and order the pattern of their lives?

They had seen it already, the gnarled fist and the curved knife, the burning houses and the screaming flesh, the barriers in the streets and in the eyes.

The shadow had been there a long time, growing and malignant.

The reality was the same except that one could not escape it.

Pratap Singh looked at Imtiaz. "I hope you're satisfied," he said bitterly and quietly. "I suppose you consider this your finest hour."

"Easy," said Krishnan. "Remember, Imtiaz is one of us."

"I can look after myself," retorted Imtiaz. "I've had just about enough of this. My family's worked for independence, we've been in jail, we're decently proud of our record and we don't need lessons in being Indian from bearded numskulls who sit in Government offices."

Pratap Singh leaped menacingly out of his chair. His eyes were bloodshot and he was breathing heavily.

"Try it," said Imtiaz. "You big, fat side of beef. I'll answer to my conscience. What have you got to answer but your pay bill?"

"Stop it, both of you," said Kamala firmly. "What's happened is a tragedy for all of us. But surely it means we should look into ourselves, count our mistakes, and do what we can to understand each other. If the best we can do is to stand here bandying insults, how can we even begin to live as a nation?"

Pratap Singh backed off and shrugged his shoulders awkwardly. "I lost my head a little," he admitted. "If they are loyal they will have nothing to fear."

"That isn't enough," said Kamala. "We have to trust them also."

"If they want our confidence there are ways to earn it."

Krishnan walked over and looked at the calendar. The picture for the month was of two girls in a tea garden. He drew black crosses through the first three days of June. He turned over the pages. August had a picture of the temple at Amritsar. He drew a red circle round the fifteenth. While the others watched him, he counted his way backward.

"Seventy-two days," he said. "Seventy-three days to freedom."

It didn't sound exactly the way it should have.

CHAPTER FOUR

Season of Thunderheads

IT WAS STILL POSSIBLE that it might not be.

The plan was there, but it was only the outline. The people would draw the picture as they wished, but how else could they choose to draw it except as frustration ordered and resentment decreed?

The sky could be any sky, but July was the season of thunderheads, scudding and menacing across the ancient plains. The fields were golden, but you could see the redness where the plow turned up the moist earth underneath.

Tell them that they could choose. Not all of them, but the literate and the propertied, those who might read the writing on the wall or feel the shuddering of the gracious acres, those who could scan the future with intelligence and `chart the course of nationhood with clarity.

Tell them also that they had no other choice but choosing. They would inherit the power, so let them inherit the agony. What was freedom: the recognition of necessity, the sudden understanding of what one could not escape? Or was it the implacable pressure that made man creator and created also, the field where six empires sank to ruin, the eternal harvesting of the dragon's teeth?

The picture was there, the familiar face of the stranger. Nothing had changed, not even the people who drew it. But all of a sudden the shadows had reached into them, dredging the truth, and now it was there, the deep demandings of them, or of whatever molding force of fear or bitterness walked in the scarred skin and incited the blood.

Voice after voice, whatever the people wanted, whatever the heart said or the steel denied, choice upon choice, and the lines on the map would harden and the sentries stand defending the new realities.

Krishnan could feel it in the fortress also, the dog-eared files becoming steadily thicker, the tape grimy and twisted as they shuffled up and down, in the hierarchy soon to be blown off at the top. The fractions were everywhere; in the margins, and around the dockets, and running through the penciled calculations which the hurried assistants had forgotten to erase. Eighty to twenty, four to one, divide by five and take away a fifth. Everything goes into the slicing machine, whirling remorselessly in the plan's enclosure.

He began to take the files home. He would sit under the lamp, peering, drafting and judicially noting, watching the yellow edges crumble with mildew and unexpected use. The borrowed house with the gracious lawns was gone now, and he was relegated to what his position deserved. Since he was a married officer, they were obliged under the regulations to give him two rooms, so they had given one with the veranda walled up. The roof was low. The sun fell directly on one of the windows. There was a table fan with an alarming clatter which beat the air in unsuccessful but frantic attempts to move it. Krishnan scowled and screwed his eyes under the twenty-watt bulb which illuminated nothing but around which the rain insects clustered avidly, cutting off even the poor pretense at light. They lived for only eight hours, so a single minute was like a weekend to them, an unforgettable holiday spent in the garish paradise of the twenty-watter, before they fell back, dying of their happiness, amid the untidy notes and correspondence.

He sat there behind the piled-up papers, grateful for their protection because he didn't have to talk too much to Kamala. It was a genuine and a valid reason, but if it had not been there he would have found something else, and the knowledge made him angry with himself. He wanted the gray limbo of the rain on the tin roof and the naked child splashing in the puddle outside. He did not want to be made to choose, or even be reminded of the necessity of choosing, by what, without her willing it, crept into Kamala's voice, by what she gave up, or didn't ask for because she didn't want to hurt him.

A civil servant's life should be like his files, the pros and cons symmetrically arranged, all the considerations lucidly stated, but the decisions made elsewhere, at some superior level.

The dinner had not produced the alliance against him that might have purged him of responsibility. It also had not resulted in hostilities. That would have been helpful too. An unkind remark, an unfair insinuation, might have put him firmly on Cynthia's side, but the opportunity never came, not because Kamala was trying to be careful but simply because being unkind was not part of her nature. He began to be concerned about her total lack of malice. "She's so collected," she had observed of Cynthia, "so much more effective as a person than I am." He had thought first of saying that she was not being fair to herself; then of admitting the difference, but arguing that it didn't really matter. It took him time to realize that he had to be honest and, having done so, to surmount the problem of how to agree to what she said without discouraging the candor he respected.

"I daresay you're right. She's remarkably attractive."

"She's much more than that. She has an unusual understanding of us. The understanding is Indian, which is what makes it real, but her vitality is foreign, and I think that makes her difficult to resist."

If he were going to concede all that, he would be in trouble, no matter how objective Kamala thought she was. But he could not deny it without revealing a degree of interest which he was unprepared to disclose, and he could not change the subject without confessing his embarrassment to such an extent that she would have no difficulty in detecting his motives.

"How odd that you should put it that way," he replied, as a

happy inspiration seized him. "Vijayaraghavan says almost exactly the same thing."

He was relieved to extricate himself, but he realized that he could not expect to do so always, and that next time the results of being honest might be considerably more serious. So he welcomed the files and the long hours of work that limited conversation to everyday things. He was in a vacuum—not the most comfortable of states but preferable in its quiet neutrality to the stresses and strains that had steadily worn down his sense of discrimination.

Cynthia had left some days earlier. She wanted to spend a week in Simla. "Of course," she had added, "that isn't the only reason. The storm will be brewing in the plains, right underneath, and I ought to have some knowledge of the pressures."

He had taken the news with a sense of loss that must have been more evident than he had thought, to judge from her smile and the pleased manner in which she rumpled his hair. "Cheer up, Krish dear. It isn't forever, and, besides, it'll give you time to think."

Fortunately the train left in the middle of an extremely crowded day. She was gone without his having to stand there, stupidly casual on the bustling platform, isolated and measuring his loneliness, embarrassingly conscious of his dependence on her. She was gone, and opening his mind to the fact of her absence, he was relieved to discover that it did not affect him as he thought it would. Yet it was typical of his state of mind that even this sense of relief began to become a basis of concern to him. What did it mean, he started to ask himself? Did it imply that her effect depended on her immediate presence so that by changing the situation one could get rid of the choice? Or would the alternatives be there, whatever the situation, only in different forms? The question swung him too close to uneasiness, and mechanically he began to swing back, along the much traveled groove of reassurance. Perhaps he had overestimated her live and full awareness, which made her directness, when she chose to use it, so disconcerting and difficult to evade. If the pull were predominantly sensual, it would pass. Time would soothe the raw ache in the expectant nerves, and the friction of events would loosen the rope. If she were not part of him, as he knew Kamala was, he would not have to deny himself to forget her, or change himself, or feel the thrust of absence whichever the eyes he looked at—those green as the jungle depths, or the tranquil brown ones where the *gopuram*'s shadow leaned in.

The days slipped by, and one evening he came back from the office later than usual and more heavily burdened.

"You look so tired, darling," Kamala said.

He waved away the coffee. "I don't want it. It only makes me perspire more."

He patted his neck with a towel where the prickly heat was chafing. "I'm half dead," he said flatly and almost indifferently. "I've just exceeded the average life expectancy. From now on, every day will be taken from someone who deserves it more than I do."

She sat at his feet on the coarse cotton rug. She put her head quietly against his lap. Her hair was damp with the humidity as he combed through it with his fingers. He looked down into the vibrant darkness of her eyes.

"You're like the earth," he told her. "Sometimes the earth is fertile. Sometimes it has nothing to offer. But get away from it and you abandon your strength."

"I'm sorry," she said, unexpectedly changing the subject. "I didn't want to have to say it in this way, but Mother's had a heart attack, and you know what it means to somebody of her age."

Her sorrow hadn't showed at all, and he reproached himself for having let her center her life around him, so that even a disaster to the family such as this was not allowed to be reflected in her face.

"It's a terrible thing to have happen," he said. But he knew when he said it that he was thinking of something else.

"I think the worst is over," she told him. "But she needs nursing and the strength of having her children around her. Oh, Krishnan, please, would you mind very much if I went away for a week or

two? I'd try to make it as short as possible, but you do understand,
don't you, that she needs me?"

Two weeks, and Cynthia would be back in two days. Away
from the earth he would abandon his strength. How could he
tell her, For God's sake, do not go, I need the shade and shelter
of your presence, I'll choose if I have to but don't make me
choose alone.

He said, "Go, darling, of course. For just as long as she
needs you."

"You'll take care of yourself, won't you?" She could have said
it like any formula, when the real source of her anxiety was elsewhere, but she said it with a concern that only conspired to make
his position more difficult.

"There's really nothing to worry about. The bearer will keep
the place tidy. And I can mess with the rest. After all, we ought to
eat some of the meals we pay for."

"The hostel food is poisonous."

"Nobody ever died from it. You really must go, darling. Your
place is at her side."

What would that sound like a month from now, he wondered.
Did he say it because he wanted to be tied to it, because he was
hoping that the ghost of it would haunt him, like some transitory
and misty reminder of the earth?

She kissed him quietly on his forehead and his eyes. She put
the battered leather suitcase with its Yale lock up on the bed
and packed it slowly, with the precise finality of somebody going
on a very long journey. When she had done that she arranged his
own things meticulously in the rickety chest of drawers.

"You don't have to worry," she said. "You wear what is on top
and give it to the *dhobi* and then you wear what comes next."

Yesterday he would have called it interference, but he was grateful for it now because a little bit of her would stay on in the drab
room, helping to pull him back toward reality.

"It isn't for long," he told her, with all possible gentleness. "Two
weeks is not for eternity."

She turned to him and her eyes were suddenly brimming. He

kissed the wet cheeks and tasted the salt in his mouth. He laid
her down and let the cascading richness of her hair out, arranging
it fastidiously over the small, firm breasts. Then he lighted two
incense sticks and turned off the light, sitting in the stillness till
the soundless sobbing ended. His arms went around her and he
bent his head down to the earnest oval face, peaceful once more
against the halo of darkness.

"Dear God," he prayed, "wherever she is, I want her to reach out
to me."

2

The next day was not the difficult one. They were up early for
the Dakota and left for Willingdon nearly an hour before take-
off time. Half a mile out, a tabby cat ran across the road, and
Kamala insisted on going back. The *pooja* she offered to Parvati
was as brief as possible, but it cut into his margin uncomfortably
and he had to hurry in order to make the flight. There wasn't
time to say much; he gave her the usual advice about blowing
her nose and swallowing on the way down. He would have liked
to kiss her, but public demonstrations were foreign to his upbringing. He held her hand instead. The clouds were low, but he reassured her, telling her that this wasn't the monsoon route. Air
travel was new to India, and even after the converted troop transport had taken off and set its course southward, he had to fight off
a slight feeling of uneasiness.

It was just after seven and, disinclined to face the hostel break-
fast, he drove directly to the Secretariat, put the car under a tree
and took up his position in the fortress. He read the United Nations Charter and the *Discovery of India,* from the revolt of 1857
onward. At one minute past ten he inspected the section office and
found it empty. He made a mental note to demand an explanation,
which he knew he would forget or not have the heart to insist
upon.

The work came in steadily, but he had time to keep on top of it,
occasionally turning a phrase to his satisfaction, or applying to his

notations the muted sense of humor which was the civil servant's proof that the job had not overwhelmed him. He did not notice the time too much until it was time to go. He left, played two hard sets of tennis at the club, and came back healthily tired, and hungry enough to make the food acceptable. He cranked the portable gramophone and listened to Subbulakshmi's voice, percolating through the cracked soundbox.

It was a day like any day, a page torn off the calendar, a paper boat for the child in the puddle to play with, an ordinary day, but one day nearer to freedom, one step closer to the agony of choice.

It wasn't the difficult day.

He lay in bed trying to plan it. He would get up late and not arrive at the office till ten. He wouldn't really start until an hour afterward, and by that time the *Most Immediates* would have piled up enough to keep him under pressure for the lunch break, so that he wouldn't be too conscious of the train coming in. If it didn't work, he would call for the superintendent and go painstakingly with him through every pending case in the branch. But it did work, somewhat to his surprise, and on the few occasions when he looked at the clock, it was to check his own schedule, not to remember hers. He worked late, since visiting the club would not be prudent. He drove home slowly, lingered as long as possible over dinner, and listened to Schnabel's version of the "Emperor Concerto" played a tone flat upon the perspiring gramophone.

He couldn't sleep. He told himself that it was the heat and moved the fan to within inches of his head. It made him cooler and that was all. He tried hard not to think. Count the six million Sikhs, he told himself, but at four thousand and eleven he was still wide-awake.

He got out of bed and put the lights on. A cockroach scuttled across the floor. He caught it near the corner with his *chappal* and killed it with unnecessary violence. He put the crushed body into a paper boat, attached a priority label to it and launched it ceremoniously in the puddle. He wished it had been a scorpion. He began to wonder if something else was dying.

He took everything off and pulled the sheet over him. Twelve more nights, five million nine hundred and ninety-five thousand and eighty-nine more Sikhs. Any O.S.D. with determination could do it.

He got out again and put three eighths of his clothes on. A mosquito bit him and he squashed it, not bothering to wipe off the smear of blood. He wrote letters to everyone he could remember. Then he opened the second drawer of the chest and looked at his belongings, neatly stacked as Kamala had left them. With an aimless but still purposeful thoroughness, he jumbled the order systematically. When it was over he wanted to put everything back, but the sequence was gone now, beyond his recollection.

He fell asleep finally and awoke only when the dawn noises came.

He put his head under the tap. The rest of him felt worse but didn't matter as much. His clothes went on as they came out of the drawer. He was a new man; he belonged to nothing.

He remembered to clean one *chappal* with benzine.

Into the office early and alert, up the stairs like the man who takes Sanatogen, with a youthful vigor that belied his years. The Joint Secretary was in, but talking on the phone. He waved to a seat. Krishnan took it gratefully. He drew a guillotine on the note pad with care. He tried to think of something that couldn't be put under it.

"I'd be grateful for five days' casual, sir," he told him. "I've been working nights and Sundays and I feel pretty well done in."

"We all do," Robertson said. It was true, and Krishnan could tell it from the circles under his eyes. He wasn't going to be there when the storm hit, and yet here he was, taut, sleepless, living on his nerves, driving himself to make the ship seaworthy.

"I know, sir," Krishnan replied. "I wouldn't ask for it unless I had to. But when one gets to the point where one makes serious mistakes, it isn't sensible to keep on going."

"I haven't noticed them," Robertson said.

"Not yet, sir. I've been able to correct them so far."

Tired and uncompromising, he stared at Krishnan. He was demanding nothing that he wouldn't do himself. "You've no relatives in danger of dying, I suppose. No lawsuits and no one in the family getting married?"

"No, sir, I haven't. But there are other things in life which are just as serious."

"I'm sure there are, but that's no reason for casual. Hang it, man!" he said with sudden intensity. "What could be more serious than what's going to happen to this country? And it is your business, your darned business, you understand, to have it happen with the minimum of friction. The absolute minimum," he repeated slowly. "Every detail can be paid for with a life."

Krishnan drummed the table with his fingers. He didn't want to argue. It was true and shouldn't have been the kind of truth that a foreigner had to tell him.

"I just can't do it," Robertson continued. "We're understaffed, we've got too many people on summer leaves. You've been here less than four months. You've got to take it, however hard it feels."

"I understand, sir," said Krishnan.

He hadn't really expected anything else. When he went upstairs he wasn't hoping for the exit. He only wanted to confirm that the last door was really shut—as it had to be in the nature of the problem.

"Thanks for hanging on," he heard Robertson saying.

"Same to you, sir," he replied with a familiarity that surprised himself.

He left, watching the ghost of a smile play sympathetically around the elder man's mouth.

He went downstairs. He treated the *Most Immediates* as the blue labels deserved. The clock hands went around and the mechanical work went on. He tried to imagine the life in the margins, between the details, cross every T with blue blood and a man's heart.

At home he didn't have a telephone. He could leave the office and lie down with the cockroaches and the white ants and the strange music of the Indian night. He needn't sleep now since he wouldn't for a long time. He could lie awake and hear the jackals

howling and postpone the decision for another day. For twenty-
four more hours his mother could hold her head high, his father
could point him out in the *Gazette,* and the Mylapore gossip
wouldn't clot on his body like the dead mosquito on his reddening
skin.

He was a Brahmin, a priest by heredity and Manu, the head of
Plato's Republic, he was the knowledge that completed power, the
incarnate force in the social order to which both king and warrior
turned for counsel.

For twenty-four hours he could avert the flesh.

She claimed his intellect too, he told himself. She was the obstinate thirst in him for freedom, the blue sky of loneliness—endless, cruel and futile—against tradition with its consolations, the
ordained path with its solacing confinements.

It was three minutes to the hour, and he could hear the feet going home. Soon the bicycles would be flooding down the ramp,
the small cars honking and the *tongas* clattering. Those who each
day did their daily duties would sit in the corner munching their
chapattis, grimy-eyed and sore-lipped, feeling the rot in their bow-
els, one day nearer the ultimate promotion, nearer to peace and
nearer death.

He picked the receiver up and spun the dial.

3

She wasn't as he had expected her to be. It was her day and
she must have known it. She could have come dressed as if for
celebration, as if to make his temptation justified. If she had conceded anything to the usual ways of triumph, his sense of discrimination might have been able to spring back, and however
little she took anything for granted, she could have found the
unexpected prevailing. But she was impeccable and seemed to
know all about it. She was like yesterday, only more discreet. The
branch of sensuality bloomed in their relationship, so she let it
be, neither counting the leaves nor seeking to cover them over.

He had taken her out beyond the walls of the old city, because the curve of the river and of the flat earth sweeping unobstructed to the horizon gave him some feeling of security and repose. He pointed out the deep, clear distance to her, where the white clouds accentuated the brilliance of the blue sky.

"Out there is Kurukshetra."

"I know," she said. "I've been there myself. It's just a field like any other field."

"How else should it be? It's anybody's problem."

"When I was very young," she told him, "I read it all in that klippety-klop translation. I was asked to read Grimm's and Hans Andersen, but I didn't want to. And when I was older I didn't want *Beowulf* or the *Iliad*. That was when I realized that there must have been a mistake and that when I left Heaven I must have had the wrong label."

"The Greeks never had a word for it," he said. "Homer's was a war of civilizations. It was for Helen's body, but they wanted the body of Troy. The sons of Kunti fought a war of fratricide. It was a war of annihilation to settle finally a gambling debt." He paused, not wanting to go on with the thought.

"I know what's in your mind," she said. "I was in the country to the North and the West. It's coming, Krish. Brother against brother. The battle of inheritance once again."

He tried to speak more firmly because of his lack of conviction. "It doesn't have to be that way. We're on the edge of freedom. Why abandon the dream because it is mutilated? We have an enlightened and a vigorous leadership. We're giving the people what the majority want. Why should the minority take it into the streets?"

"Simply because you're not a pacific people."

"Not pacific. Don't be ridiculous, Cynthia. We owe our independence to nonviolence applied persistently over thirty years. Thirty years, mind you. That calls not only for discipline but for stamina and certain inbred qualities."

"You're a resigned and not a pacific people." She had thought it out and spoke with quiet authority, not criticizing, not regretting, but candidly stating the facts as they appeared to her. "Everything is decided for you by someone else—Manu, tradition, the family, the Government, the rains that don't come or come too often when they do. Every day you live with frustration. Some days you lie down with calamity. There's nothing that you decide or choose. All you do is accept and try to make a room you can live in between the corners of acceptance."

"So we're resigned," he retorted argumentatively. "As if we didn't know it! But how does that prove we're not pacific people?"

She poked him gently in the chest with a twig. "It doesn't suit you to look belligerent, darling. As a matter of fact, I asked myself the same question on the train from Ambala. Resignation and pacifism simply aren't the same thing. Nonviolence takes resignation and transmutes it into resistance. But that's not the same thing as pacifism either."

"You're just juggling with abstractions, Cynthia. It sounds clever, but what does it actually mean?"

"That's what I asked myself when the porter took away my luggage. Then I came outside and saw the man in the *tonga*. He was beating the animal horribly. It didn't kick, but it also wouldn't move. In the end he had to give it something to drink."

"Surely you're not arguing that the beast was not pacific."

"On the outside, yes. And because that was the only way to get the water. Oh, I'm not trying to minimize Congress's achievement. It isn't so long ago, remember, that I stood between the sandwich boards in Trafalgar Square, thinking this was the best thing politics had invented. But nonviolence is easier when it's obvious that nothing else will work and when it fits the natural forces of resignation."

"What else do you suppose will work now?" he asked her.

"Nothing else really! But the people don't think so, and it will take them time and a virtual war to find out."

"You're right about one thing," he told her slowly. "The people aren't resigned any more. They're watching an empire and three centuries of occupation melt away. Why shouldn't they believe that other things will melt also?"

"That's the big change," she said with clear conviction. "Bigger than partition. That's the foundation for either ruin or hope."

He took her back to the car. He had forgotten to fill the radiator and it began to steam a little. He had it attended to at the nearest petrol pump.

She waited till it was done.

"Remember what you said once, Krish? About a relentless engine of conformity? Well, it's an engine without a safety valve."

4

It was good to take her dancing. She was graceful and vital and did what she ought to and usually made it different. She was shocking, like cold water. It was good to know her if you refused to stay still.

She was for the people without roots who weren't frightened of being rootless, who liked the blue, deep sky and the bite of the high passes, for people without the luggage of ideas who took the facts as they grew in the green valleys. He liked her because she never borrowed the answer and wouldn't sit down waiting for the answer to hit her. She was a difficult girl, easy on the eyes and singing in the senses, but the loveliness came out of a core of loneliness, and when he touched her now he could feel the core's profundity.

"Do you think you love me?" she asked him.

"I'll answer that if you tell me what love means."

"It's an old-fashioned word. It's been stared at too often. It's become the mirror of what you want and can't have."

"I don't love you," he told her. "I'm a prudent man. I only love my insurance."

Somebody else might have bristled, but she laughed. "I didn't really expect your love," she said. "A big girl like me has to learn to live without it."

"What is it that you really do need, Cynthia?"

"I need a misfit that some of me can fit into."

He straightened himself out solemnly. "Are you convinced that I really am the right shape?"

She looked at him as critically as she could. She tapped her chin reflectively with her forefinger. "Mmmm," she said, "not bad! Not bad at all! But you must take some of the resignation off those shoulders."

5

They went to the one room and the walled-up veranda.

"It's where I live," he said, "but it isn't where I belong."

"Oh, no complaining, Krish," she teased him. "You belong in a house with seventeen servants and separate cooks for the *iddalis* and the *sambhar.*"

"You'd like to spend the rest of your life this way?" he asked her.

"I wouldn't like it all. But I'd take it if you came with it, and after six months I'd push you into something more sensible."

"No pushing, remember," he warned her. Lightheartedness was a good thing, now that the edge was near. "Do you realize that teachers live even worse?"

"I said something more sensible, not more comfortable, darling. Besides, I think this teacher business is rather a red herring. It's nice to wave around an alternative that won't materialize in quite the way you want it. Then you can dismiss it with a clear conscience and sit ever so much more comfortably in the cage."

He wasn't going to argue about it too much. "You keep your size sevens on the ground," he told her. "You can't live forever on the expanding horizon."

"I don't have to," she assured him. "I'm sure to find it some day. The work that expresses you and in which I can find a place. How long can it stay hidden with two brilliant explorers like us?"

She lay down on the creaking cot and unconcernedly watched a spider on the ceiling. "Relax, my dear boy," she told him, patting his head. "Remember, you aren't the only cook in the place."

He looked at her and then at the four walls. "You're beautiful," he said.

"Thank you, my critical sir."

"But that has nothing to do with it."

"Thank you, but even more so."

He hadn't expected that, and she was amused at his discomfiture. "I want to appeal to your intellect also, darling. What would I think of myself if I were to lose you after the hundredth ice cream?"

He sat down hesitantly beside her. She looked up at him, not with Kamala's deep gentleness but with a searching, almost hard, intentness which he hadn't seen earlier and didn't really like.

"You're sure," she asked him, "that this is the way you want it?"

"It's the way it has to be."

Her body tensed slightly. "That isn't an answer, Krishnan."

When she used his full name it sounded like a rebuke.

He had hoped that she would accept that answer, but she was right, of course, not to. Now that he was up against the commitment, his irresolution began to reassert itself.

"It's the way I've chosen," he said, after pausing a little.

Maybe that wasn't enough. If she asked for more, he had some chance of refusing. He put his hands on her body, and then tried to take them back. She looked at him possessively and not entirely kindly. Her tongue flicked out, moistening the curve of her mouth. Then her own arms reached up to him, surprisingly strong beneath the feminine smoothness, circling his indecision with finality, pulling him firmly, irrevocably down. He felt his resistance buckling, giving way. His mind opened and the wave swept into him, the riptide of her sensuality seeming to wash it clean so that he was conscious only of the thrust of her loveliness, lingering and lissome.

It was the end of a commitment, he could almost feel it weakening, slipping away, as it had to, down his memory. But it wasn't a beginning, there were no stones to stand on, no welcoming soil to wade to with relief. He hadn't the sense of liberation to which the slow growth of expectancy had reached out, only of a strangely frightening freedom, all the more desolate because no longer hemmed in.

His memory reached back to the diagonal of the breakers, the brilliant sky and the unknown horizon, the gulls shrieking and the catamarans on the long, mottled beach going out into the threat and promise of the ocean.

CHAPTER FIVE

The Rebellion

IT WAS EASIER to go on after the choice had been made, no matter how, no matter for how long. A little of you seemed cleaner because of your honesty. There was less to hide from yourself or from the opinions of others that claimed to be yourself.

He was happy with her. He had the security of one door locked behind him. He liked to lie with his head in her lap watching her face in the beginning of gentleness. Today was freedom and tomorrow a different day.

"Which son of Kunti do you suppose I am?" he asked her.

"You're Karna," she replied without hesitation. "The man who couldn't belong."

It was an apt choice and it brought the enigmatic story flickering to life in the corners of his mind.

"Karna was a great warrior," he told her. It was the part of the legend that had always struck him, as if the heroic achievements magnified the refusal, stripping it of all pretext, making the force of rejection even purer. "No one surpassed Karna in valor or skill of arms. He was born from the sun and bred from the strength of the earth. He bent the great bow when everyone else had failed. Even at the end he stayed unconquered. They killed him only by breaking the rules of chivalry."

She began to remind him of the part he had left out. "It's all very splendid," she said. "But what good did it do? What's the use of bending the great bow and all that if Draupadi wouldn't give him the go-ahead signal? His father was a charioteer, that's the trouble. You get nowhere if you aren't in the social register."

"Yes, I know it's puzzling," he admitted, aware how defensive and insufficient the word was. "But there has to be a reason; there always is. Maybe it was presumption of some kind. Or what the Greeks call *hubris*. If you want the moon you must be tamed to accept the earth."

"He didn't want the moon, dear," she protested. "He was the democratic man trying to be judged on his merits. You can't wholly forgive the society which shuts him out."

"It isn't a question of forgiveness. He made his mistake the same way Oedipus did, and the retribution was greater than the flaw. It's the nature of tragedy and you mustn't confuse it with justice."

"Well, anyway," she said, refusing to be discouraged, "he did get close to Draupadi in the end."

"For five minutes, and his back was broken for it."

"Well, what about those Pandavas who finished him?" she retorted. "They weren't such a classy collection, were they? A congenital gambler and a strong-armed thug."

"I'll behave like Karna then," he promised her, smiling. "I'll do it for you even if I have to dig my own ditch."

"If you had half his spunk you'd be three times as handsome."

"Remember, though," he added, "that Karna isn't the whole of the story. He isn't the total picture of our society. If you want to have that you must also think of Nanda."

"I didn't find him in the nursery library," she said. "What happened to him? Did he break through the barrier?"

"He was a pariah. The priests wouldn't allow him even on the steps of the temple. But he prayed and prayed and because of the strength of his devotion to God, the statue of Nandi, the great bull, moved aside, so that he could see the dancing image of Shiva."

Her interest was aroused. "That's much more like it. That's a far better symbol of the India we ought to live in."

"It's the shiny side of the coin," he cautioned her. "It's the face of conscience and enlightenment. But turn the coin over and there is always Karna."

"How depressingly like you, Krish dear," she protested. "You and your famous coin. For every plus there has to be a minus. But you know very well that even the most stuck-up of them had to recognize Karna's valor in the end."

"They never accepted him," he pointed out. "He offered them his sword and shield. They took it. They didn't want him; they only wanted his courage."

He continued with his thoughts, contriving his explanation because the lack of one disturbed him, because, despite his own warning, he could not dissociate tragedy from justice.

"Perhaps the trouble with Karna," he suggested, "is not that he didn't belong but that he insisted on belonging somewhere else."

"You're beginning to sound like the rest of them," she reproved him. "Wake up, Rip darling, this is the middle of the twentieth century. Or shall I remind you with some of that gorgeous South Indian coffee?"

It was good to be with her, to feel her obstinate freedom, to watch her fine body and the defiant fling of her hair. Her skin was white, but under the skin she was Indian, and not simply because of good intentions. There were plenty of facts in her head; but what surprised him was the number of facts in her bloodstream and the live, just awareness which she brought to her comprehension of those facts. Yet, in her heart she wasn't Indian at all; she'd never learn the meaning of acceptance. "I am I," her interior strength seemed to say, "and the rest of the world might just as well get used to it." That was what fascinated him: the vivid and quite deep Indianness, and underneath it, yet in harmony with it, the exotic core of stubborn individualism, which he wanted to see take root in his reality.

"Half and halfer," he called to her. "Which half of you do I want?"

"I don't know," she answered happily. "I hope you never know either. Because then you'll have to want all of me, all of me, the whole mixed-up debacle."

2

He was with her always; there was no other place where he wanted to be. He let himself be seen with her. When the door shut, the room became different and there was no reason not to make that clear, even to those who looked in from the windows. He began to pass on responsibilities in the office, and the files disappeared with exhilarating rapidity. He canceled his appointments and, when he could not, cut them shorter than courtesy allowed.

He met Vijayaraghavan at a dinner he could not avoid. "I don't think you should play with her," he told Krishnan. "She's a decent girl. She's really one in a thousand."

"I'm not playing," said Krishnan.

Vijayaraghavan's eyes widened. "What's come over you? You must have a screw loose somewhere."

"What's wrong with Cynthia anyway?"

"Nothing's wrong with her, but she isn't Indian."

"She's Indian enough for me," he retorted with heat. "She's a darn sight more Indian than some of the specimens at this party."

"By the way," inquired Vijayaraghavan blandly, "I nearly forgot. Was I wrong in having the impression you were married?"

Krishnan flushed unhappily. "Sometimes a man can do the wrong things."

"Then he stays with them till they become right."

It was true enough to hurt him, and he retorted with some of the anger that had been building up slowly under the pressure of his embarrassment. "From the way you talk one might very well conclude that you're attracted to Cynthia yourself."

"If she were Indian I might conceivably have married her."

"But you won't because she isn't."

"I'm not interested in having half-caste progeny."

"A fine answer indeed." Krishnan's tone was bitter and scornful. "Particularly from a so-called progressive. I'm surprised that you haven't learned to be more tolerant."

He was aware as he spoke the words of something deficient in his reaction. His primary feeling was, naturally enough, one of personal insult, but what surprised him was that he did not feel, or at any rate not to any great degree, that Vijayaraghavan was mistaken in his attitude.

"I can be just as tolerant as you want," his colleague replied. "But the children at school won't be. The other families and the relatives won't be. They won't grow up in the storeroom, you know. They'll grow up in India, whatever its defects."

Krishnan tried to sound as if he were practical also. "It'll be a long time, surely, before there is any question of their growing up. And all the time things are changing. In twenty years it won't be the same India."

"It isn't going to change to that extent. And anyway," his friend added inexorably, "the future is not yet your problem. The present is. Specifically, Kamala is."

"I intend to make every provision for Kamala."

"How do you propose to give her back her status?"

"I can't have my life run just to keep her status intact."

"Your life," said Vijayaraghavan with biting indignation. "Is that all that you can see, you blind fool? Don't you realize how many other lives are woven into yours and could be torn up by it? Kamala's life and both your parents, and hers, and all the other members of your families. You want all their names to be mud? You want them to become the butts of Marina gossip?"

"I know," said Krishnan tiredly. "Don't think I haven't thought about it over and over. But someone has to get hurt, whatever one does. I wish, I desperately wish, it weren't so. But it has to be. It's the cruelty of choice."

"Then why don't you try being cruel to yourself? You're only one person, and I can assure you, you'll survive it. What right have you to injure fifty others and to fly in the face of tradition and normal decency?"

"It isn't just me, it also has to be Cynthia."

"Cynthia's expendable!"

It was said in the heat of the moment, but in other circumstances the injustice might have been discounted. This time, Krishnan was in no mood for understanding. He had been on the edge, this was the reprieve he wanted, and all the emotions and the defeated arguments grouped themselves aggressively around the insult to Cynthia.

"If that's what you think of her, so much the worse for your logic!"

He gritted his teeth, strode from the room and slammed the Hillman viciously through its gears.

Two against fifty. A mathematician ought to know better. There were other variables to be considered also—the depth of the injury, the value of the people on whom it was inflicted.

His mind went back to the incident on the beach and to the logic of the charge against him. Merely in order to avenge a friend, to defend himself from a sadistic policeman, what right had he to ruin a demonstration?

It was the same typical, unvarying reaction, the treatment of him as if he didn't exist, as if all that existed was the reflection in the mirror, the shadow in other minds of what he should be. It was blackmail, nothing more, he told himself, stiffening his anger with the slap of the word, to say that he should not protest simply because his protesting might hurt others. Iron out the man for the convenience of the machine. If the system resulted in unreasonable consequences, blame the individual for getting in its way.

Cynthia was on the steps in front of him, waving, the look on her face melting his rancor away. She got in and he put his arm around her. Her happiness went through him and the reservations tensing his mind relaxed.

"You're wonderful," he told her. "You're worth ten aunts, twenty uncles and forty-seven grandmothers."

"Thank you," she said, smiling back, flattered but bewildered. "Thank you, darling, because I know you mean the compliment. But why put it in that extraordinary way?"

3

How was he to tell Kamala? How do you tell someone your life has ended, consider yourself as born again tomorrow, lovely and twenty-one, without a past? Put it away among the spiders and the scorpions, under the secret stone behind the storeroom vessels, in the black tin box that no one has ever unpacked.

You will not need love, even as a cloak for kindness. Put it away with the unnecessary jewelry, the *vodyanam,* the belt of beaten gold with the bells hanging from the scalloped edges, the heavy headdress with the sun and the moon at its borders, the circlet with the swan upon the lotus leaf, around which the bridal roses cluster.

Tomorrow you will have no need even of the memory. Hold your head high as you stand among the unwanted, growing old, the small body sucked in and shrunken, wearing the saffron robes without respect, the quiet life flickering in the wayward margins, as the feet slip down to the peace of the last river.

You will not even be as the widows with shaven heads, scolding and railing on the black Cuddapah stone, while the children gather around, curious and awestruck, accepting the magic that must flow from renunciation. You have no status, not that of age, not even that of honorable exile. Bury the past and look into nonentity, the days driving by shadowless and endless, lay your unasked-for hands over the harvest in the child's eyes, bury the tin box and treasure the vacant years.

He could tell her by letter, the end coming normally in the dirty brown envelope that the post office sold for the cost of the stamp. He would be away from the blow. He would not see the hands trembling and the blood ebbing from the sorrow-stricken face. Part of him would have to die, but it would be in another country and at a forgotten distance.

"You mustn't just write to her," Cynthia told him. "She deserves something more than that. Besides, you can't get out of it. She'll come here and you'll have to face her in the end, and all her relatives and yours into the bargain. It may not be pleasant, but if you're thinking of another way, you're deceiving yourself."

"It's a terrible thing to do to her," he said. "I can't even trust myself to do it. I can go there with all the phrases arranged, all the emotions organized as they should be, and then her suffering will hit me and tear the order up and I won't even have the resolution to go on."

She didn't bristle at that. She didn't say, This is the acid test. If you really love me you wouldn't hesitate. Do as a man should, or never again darken my portals. She said that she herself was fond of Kamala, she would feel awkward and a little shabby doing it, and he must feel worse since she was that much closer to him. She didn't suggest that he should think it over. It was his choice (he had said so himself), and she paid him the compliment of presuming he would adhere to it, while not pretending that she wasn't aware of how many it would hurt, or how much, or of the retreats urged on him by his indecisions when he was compelled to look through to the end of his acts. She had counted his hesitations but she did not chide them, and, proposing nothing, she still succeeded in giving him the confidence that honesty would prevail and not prevail too cruelly.

Her understanding relieved him. Before now he had had the sense of being maneuvered so that sometimes only the action was his and not the state of mind that made the action logical. She no longer gave him that feeling, at least not to the same extent. Perhaps he was changing, perhaps he couldn't have changed until he had made the commitment and let his mind grow from it. Perhaps it didn't matter how the road was marked out if a man could be sure that he traveled it himself.

But he was still worried about the details of it, the way the denouement would sting, how he could numb the others to its impact, what kind of kindness would serve as an anesthetic.

"There will have to be a provision for Kamala," he said, trying to push his uneasiness down to normality. "It won't be easy managing on what's left. It'll be a twenty-four-hour, nose-to-the-grindstone life."

She too reacted with relief, glad to get his problems into a ne-
gotiable area, away from the region of private responsibility.

"I can work too, you know. I'm good at earning a living."

"I'm sure you are. You can go on at the Palladium."

Her eyes glinted mischievously. "You want to dare me, Krish?"

"I know better than to dare you by now. You'd probably be so
good at it that I'd be miserable ever afterward. I suppose," he continued, making the suggestion to demonstrate his hardheadedness
but not really expecting her to take it seriously. "I suppose that in
due course I'll get rid of my prejudice against working wives, and
then you should have no difficulty getting an Embassy job at twice
my pay, if I'm fool enough to stay on."

"Even if I don't work," she suggested, "we can live on the family
fortune."

His response was immediate and gave away his pretense. "Oh,
no, I couldn't possibly do that."

She was amused at his conventional attitude. "That's right,
Krish, be virtuous. It's tainted money anyway. I'm sure Father
squeezed it out of the proletariat or, what's even worse, made them
work harder by giving them a share of the profits."

"What makes you think," he asked, "that your family will let us
touch it? They haven't been told about us, have they? How do you
suppose they'll feel when they find out?"

She was completely unperturbed. It seemed that no matter how
minor his misgivings she was determined to combat them with
confidence, as if to force him forward, as if to melt away any
reservation on which he might later fall back.

"There aren't any elders. You know that, Krish," she said. "Except for an uncle in Brighton who's too busy writing his memoirs
and swearing at the Socialists to spare me more than a patronizing
snort. Of course, if he thought about it long enough he'd probably want to lock up all the money. But he doesn't have the legal
right to do that."

"So the financial problem is solved," he conceded reluctantly,
wishing that once in a while she could bring herself to admit the

existence of an obstacle. "I wish we could do the same with Kamala's status."

"That's much more difficult. It needs a social revolution, and neither of us can achieve that."

Now that she had done what he wanted, he would have preferred her to have persevered with her confidence-building program.

She saw the misgivings in his face and cut in before they could develop. "I know it's a painful problem, darling. But, remember, you'll suffer a loss of status also, not as much as she will, of course, but mean things will be said or, worse still, left unsaid and used to mop up the floor of people's high and mighty moralities. And don't forget that I too have to pay a price."

He *had* almost forgotten it, and the reminder brought back his receding sense of proportion, making him realize that he owed her certain amends too.

"Honestly, Cynthia, I'll never understand why you did it. You're a wonderful girl, alive and lovely and intelligent. You could have had someone so much more worth while than I am, and there would never have been any question of going through all this unpleasantness."

She kissed him on the forehead, the reassuring, nonsensual kind of kiss, the measured appeal to his better instincts, falling short so nicely of the bribe of passion.

"I want your love, darling, not your gratitude. And as for Kamala, no one would be more concerned than I if you didn't do it in the way that hurt her least."

Of course there was an element of calculation in it. But perhaps all it meant was that she had thought out her conclusions a little more clearly than he had. Perhaps the most humane course was that of the made-up mind moving to its objective, shunting aside the hesitations which were the beginning of havoc.

"I know," he made himself say. "You wouldn't hurt her any more than I would."

Typically, she took the admission not as a compliment to herself but as a step onward for him. She went on with the process of re-assurance. "There are others who'll be hurt too, not only the rela-tives, but even you and I to some extent. The mud has to come off everybody's clothes. I'm not saying that there isn't a terrible price to be paid. But do remember that the real pain is usually less than the thought of it. It isn't pleasant and it's even worse when you have to inflict unhappiness on someone else, but you mustn't let the uneasiness of doing it become an absolute barrier to the life you want."

He looked at her with deep fondness. He let her argument, dis-creetly and reassuringly organized, drop into his mind, where he could feel its ripples widening. She was sane and sensible and sym-pathetic, and her feeling for him had gradually exposed a gentle-ness which he had not known, and which strengthened his sense of security. All his reservations had been soothed away. She knew about his lack of resolution, his fumbling diffidence when he ap-proached the barrier. Yet she had confidence in his ability to sur-mount it. It was the best that it could be, yet within himself he still felt the obstinate core of his misgivings.

4

The next day he got Kamala's letter. Her mother was much bet-ter, and she would be returning by the next flight. She sent him her love. She had made an offering at Tirupathi for their happi-ness. To his surprise the news did not unsettle him. He did not find himself rehearsing the argument, putting the words in their places like the shirts in his drawer, trying the civilized and reassur-ing approach, trying to fight down the suspicion of his caddishness. In an odd way, the knowledge of her coming relaxed him, even though it made the inevitable conflict more imminent. Perhaps he had known this was the only way to say it. Perhaps not worrying about how and where and when made him more certain of the act itself and what its content should be. What the blow did was not his problem, at least not to the same frustrating extent, since the context had been decided, and half the responsibility taken from his hands, leaving him, as he reassured himself, a little cleaner in the lightening of his burden.

The plane came down out of the afternoon sky, and he was happy when her feet touched the earth, his earth. He did not know why, but as he saw her approaching, the gentle surge of identity went over him and he had the conviction of something shared between them. She was looking better. She had added freshness to her delicacy and her eyes were as they used to be, deep and persuasive pools of understanding. A porter put the luggage into the car—one suitcase of thirty-nine pounds, but of course it was infra dig to carry it. She sat in the bucket seat beside him, fragile and strong, something beyond the nightmare.

"It's so reassuring to be down here," she said. "You aren't aware of the storm. The only tension is the expectancy of freedom."

He asked her the mechanical questions. Her mother was better but would benefit more from a less taxing climate and would probably leave for Bangalore within the week. Father sent his regards. He hoped Krishnan would stick to his occupation even though he didn't feel it to be entirely congenial. Government service was no longer more important than business, but it was still solid and dignified and when you went on leave you still got your name in the small type. Kruger was in the midst of an exultant Jeremiad. Prejudice had triumphed over reason, which only proved that it should have been allowed for in the first place.

She had bought a Yakshi, a perfectly realized image, an anonymous dream transmuted into poetry. She couldn't wait to put it up. There was no room for it unless she transferred the vanishing cream to Krishnan's drawer. When she opened the drawer she saw the clothes rumpled, and her face changed, but her reaction didn't show in her voice.

"Kruger gave us a Nataraja," she said. "He'd been wanting to for some time, but you know how finicky he is. He found this in a little shop outside Chidambaram. He was so happy at being able to satisfy his taste without having to empty his pocket completely."

She took the image lovingly out of the straw and tissue paper.

She put it in the only place it could be, and two bottles of coconut oil and a tin of Amrutanjan were demoted.

Krishnan didn't know how to begin, and then he reminded himself that it didn't matter how and that no matter how bland the words or adequate the reasons, they couldn't blunt the cutting edge of the fact. He might just as well blurt it out, it was ugly however unavoidable it was, and why should he try to disguise or civilize it?

He said, "I've been seeing Cynthia all the time you've been away."

He heard the words dropping like stones into a deep well. He expected the pain to splash into her face, but if he hadn't seen her hands closing and the nails driving into her palms, he might have told himself that she had shown no emotion.

"I know," she said very quietly. "I have been told about it."

It wasn't surprising; there were a dozen people who could have told her, but he could not avoid the feeling that he should have been the first. He tried to reassure himself that it made no difference, that he hadn't concealed anything and that her knowledge was the proof of it and of his intention to be straightforward with her.

"I can't go on staying with you, Kamala."

"I don't expect you to."

There was nothing in her voice, no bitterness, no resentment, not even curiosity about the manner of her defeat. She wasn't trying to reconvert the facts, to suggest that he might have misunderstood himself, to leave him a margin for his indecision, to hold out forgiveness as a bribe for change.

This wasn't what he was ready for. He had expected the claim on his pity, the reproach, however muted, to his disloyalty, and he had braced himself instinctively for the scorn and the appeal. But it wasn't going to be that way at all. He realized with horror that she wasn't going to resist him. He had made the decision by himself, so he and he alone would be responsible, and she wouldn't have the responsibility diluted by explanations, justifications and the minor withdrawals which were the resting places of conscience.

Actually, knowing her as he did, he should have realized that this would be her reaction, and, indeed, her strength of acceptance, which he had once prided himself on perceiving beneath her apparent pliability, made such a reaction entirely in character. But logic was not what one looked for in a crisis. Tragedy was supposed to strip one to one's essential dignity, but more often than not, and so it seemed in his case, it merely reduced one to the roots of conventionality—lust, fear, hate and accidental or unavoidable courage. It wasn't so with Kamala, and the recognition confused him, as the collection of accidents that is a normal person stands bewildered in the presence of integrity.

He didn't know what to say next and tried to persuade himself that it didn't matter, that with his mind and her reaction made up, the tone of his voice and the choice of his words could not materially alter the injury.

"Of course, I shall make every possible provision for you. There is never going to be any question of hardship. The first claim on anything I earn will be that of your comfort."

It sounded so mean, the much-rehearsed phrase that was to establish his fairness, and hearing the shallow tinkling of it, he wanted the lash of her anger back in his face.

"As you wish," she replied. "We have no children, and I can earn my living."

She might have said it as if it were something she was being forced to say. Or she might have said it as if it were something she would have thought of doing anyway, if marriage hadn't persuaded her to a different solution. She simply said it clearly and calmly, yet with no particular effort at being collected, almost as if she were describing someone else. She must have thought of it all the way home in the airplane. But now it was in her and she wasn't acting at all. She was being herself, and that was the focusing lens, the pitiless mirror. She would surround him with the facts, the facts created by his own decision, brilliant and blazing and stripped of all emotion and a fire of truth that would compel him to understanding. He was shocked by her, shocked most of all by a poise that, he was beginning to see, could not have been cultivated, now that the hard rock of her personality was evident.

He said, "Is there anything I can possibly do?"

Her answer was simple. "I can look after myself."

No claim on his conscience whatever. No appeal to his better nature, to his capacity to give, which was developing into a yearning. And yet he knew that she was not indifferent. She was letting him be what his decisions had made him, so that he could see and accept the consequences.

"I feel awfully mean," he told her. "I can never really forgive myself for what I've had to do to you."

She didn't say, "I'll forgive you, but come back," or even, "There's nothing to forgive," the phrase which even at this late moment might have turned him around and opened the door behind him. She said, "Only you know whether what you're doing is right," and that was her way of telling him that forgiveness wasn't in it and what he needed to have was the strength of his convictions. If he had, then the injury he was compelled to inflict would disturb but not deflect him, and while the consolation of some remote forgiveness might diminish the human cost of his act, he would know that the price was not the justification. It's asking too much of me, he told himself, but he had to recognize that she had not upbraided him, or solicited his pity, or held up her own pain, or the pain of others close to her. Even under the shock of what he was inflicting, she still remained on his side, giving him the only kindness that remained to her, that of complete candor and an understanding of his freedom to choose. Go back to her, the voice began to tell him, but what could he do now, how often could he change, how many loyalties could he demand and then repudiate?

"Do you want to go back to your family?" he asked her.

He had a sense of relief, a bolt on the door, a part of him thrust into the liberation of the past, today's dull pain becoming tomorrow's memory. The future would not be happier but it would be simpler, and in simplicity too there was some relief.

"I'm not going back," she said with quiet finality.

"I'll try to find an opening somewhere for you," he assured her. "By all means stay as long as you wish."

It was quite meaningless, the first part of it at any rate, since both of them were aware of his complete lack of influence. But he was a little surprised at her acquiescing in staying on, not by any word or gesture but by the fact of her silence. Perhaps she still hoped to change him by the reproach of her presence, the inevitable conclusion in her face when he returned home, the silent entry in the books of his conscience, made each time he put on his better clothes or looked longer than usual into the cracked wall mirror. There was nothing to hide. He had often said so himself. It was over and done with, so why treat it as a perpetual exhibition? He was beginning to anticipate the bland inquiries over the morning coffee or, worse still, the oppressive silence and the belligerent, uncomfortable stare of his self-vindication. A week of that was more than he wanted to think of. But he could hardly throw her out; there were proceedings to be gone through, and till then she was entitled to use her pressures, unless he could persuade her that it would make no difference and would hurt her as much as it embarrassed him.

"I'm going out to dinner," he told her. "Do you mind?"

Cruelty was no more difficult than any other habit. He straightened his tie and went out awkwardly, with his hands in his pockets, about to whistle until he realized that it would only sound as if he hadn't convinced himself.

It had not been his intention to go anywhere. He walked the mile and a half to where the memorial arch led on to Kingsway, watching the bicyclists come and go like fireflies and the stars shine on the man-made openness. Hawkers were treading the once immaculate lawns, and some of the pools were beginning to look unkempt. In the bustling lights and the babel of voices, the mingling and flowing of many tongues and manners, he seemed to feel something of the turbulence of change and the essential ruthlessness of change to its inheritance. The old order was passing, and, for a period, order too might pass. He held the thought in his mind without regret. He was glad in his heart that something else was dying.

5

He passed the morning behind the protection of the newspaper. They exchanged political platitudes. It was odd that the breaking of a bond, an arranged bond, should leave between them this ashen, aching emptiness where emotion could not move lest it stir the embers. There were no tears in her face, yet she had not made a mask of it. It was simply that her inner strength seemed to have controlled her so that she sat there unflinching and erect, neither proud nor tragic nor pathetic but with an unassailable dignity, as if she were entirely at peace with her acceptance. What he did to her would flow over her. It would be like water in the rock pools after the storm had subsided, leaving behind the image of its life in concentrated clarity, as his own self seemed focused in her loneliness and in her soft eyes with their pitiless candor. There was nothing he could say to her. All he could do was to leave a place where his own lack of integrity had no foothold.

He left for the Secretariat, driving slowly, so preoccupied that he forgot to change gears, and his car stalled on the ramp. He scratched at his work, but his thoughts were on the calendar, which was down now to single numbers. The unprecedented advance was nearly upon them, the birth of a nation, of two nations, the cataclysm without a historic parallel. Millions of men would know that the earth was their earth and look down at it, watching the withered paddy and the wheat stalks, and then look up into the hostile sky, where the kites forever wheeled in their sinister circles.

What was freedom—the same proprietor for the mud hut, the same boat for the fisherman upon the angry sea? It was the red line upon the trembling map, established by deadlock, defended by the law's guns, ripped at and eroded by the violence of fear. Freedom for him was the bolted door, the room behind him where he could not hear the sobbing, the erect, taut figure forced out beyond emotion, the tears he would never find on Kamala's pillow.

Pratap Singh saw him looking at the map. "Just wait," he said. "It won't be long now. Just wait till the transer of power and till the eminent Radcliffe presents his notorious award."

"Is that what you really want?" Krishnan asked quietly. He knew what the answer would be, but that didn't mean it had lost its power to shock him.

Pratap Singh spread his hands in a deprecating gesture. "My dear man, I'm an anonymous, minor civil servant, and what I want doesn't concern the national interest. My mother and father have both been killed, of course, but that was a reprehensible accident which the League leadership solemnly deplores. It hasn't affected my impartiality, has it? It has made no difference to any Moslem in my section." He put a loose pin back into the sagging pincushion. "But, my friend, when it happens the way it is going to, without my having done anything about it, do you want me to say this is intolerable, this will solve nothing, I implore my colleagues to be gentlemen, please, particularly after the others have been barbarians?" The paper knife in his hand stabbed down at the blotter. "Don't tell me it isn't some kind of justice."

It was like chain-smoking, Krishnan thought—each little death of frustration lighted another, and then all of a sudden the pain burst out and the barriers exploded. He had killed something too and had done so without provocation. What right had he to cavil if the end of one life called for the taking of another and if, without discrimination but with a blinded sense of purpose, the hand struck down from the burning house of memory.

He didn't answer Pratap Singh. He scribbled away behind the protection of the files, trying to put humanity in the margins, emptily waiting for the hour of exodus. He went home in the great daily outpouring of conscientious men and ideal husbands, to whom the promised land of freedom beckoned, the bicycles weaving erratically toward it, and the feet of those too poor to have bicycles, their shoes thin soled, the leather cracked from the heat, moving forward eagerly, hopelessly, in the resigned, eternal torrent of their yearning. How long would the great walls and the crumbling ramparts hold? How long would it be before the strength of

their need thundered down, like a ferocious river, into the ancient
streets, over the altars and the great bull's body, leaving even the
apex of the *gopuram*'s thrust a buried appeal beneath the ravaging
waters?

He detoured on the way home, seized by an impulse, and bought
a Kashmiri powder box for Kamala. He wanted to buy a box for
her *kunkumam* also in the same delicately worked papier-mâché,
but there was none in a corresponding design. It seemed mockery
at first that he who had taken away so much, and all of it irre-
placeable, should want to offer her this trivial gift; but anything
more elaborate would have been a claim on her sentiment and a
pretense that he could restore some infinitesimal part of the depri-
vation he had inflicted on her. Perhaps she would accept it as a
token that good will had not entirely died between them. Yet he
knew while he was thinking that it was not a question of good
will—she would always bear him that, only with no tinge of personal emotion. What he wanted the gift to say to her (and words
would not assist him, since, too directly, they struck at another
loyalty) was that he had seen some of the defects of the reflection
in her true mirror and could not turn that mirror to the wall.

He went in, calling her name. He thought she had left for the
hostel and was going to follow her when he saw that her box was
missing. There was no note on the chest of drawers, or by the fan,
or on the small stand in the walled-up veranda. The fan had been
left on and might have blown it on the floor. He searched carefully
and found nothing. He questioned the bearer and was told what
he expected to hear. She had left three hours before in a taxi, saying nothing and leaving no address.

He went back to the bedroom. His eyes fell on the Yakshi, and
he opened his chest of drawers. He found his clothes in their customary disorder. There was nothing there that she wanted to say
to him.

In the bathroom he stared at the broken mirror with its finger-
marks and its dried smears of toothpaste, seeing the truth in trivial
smudges only, wondering how he could understand the rest.

There was nothing he could do. He turned the lights off and

opened the window wide so that the darkness would flow in. He pulled the fan over and lay down on her side of the bed.

The pillow was wet, and not with perspiration. He put his tongue out and tasted the salt of her tears.

6

He was glad that Cynthia didn't kiss him when he told her. If she had, he probably would have left her on the spot, but she was gifted with an almost unfailing sense of when not to behave like a character in pulp fiction. In fact, she felt that he hadn't been concerned enough.

"You Indians are all alike," she reproved him. "It's the result of being too sensitive. First you care too much and then you don't care."

She rang the police station. He would have known better than to have done that, of course, but she stayed on the line, arguing and expounding, and reminding him by her persistence that there was a practical side to kindness. It took her twenty minutes to scold her way out of the lower echelons and to persuade the skeptical officer to whom she had been referred that her inquiry deserved some marginal consideration, even in the face of the imminent riots that menaced the city's security.

She was told she would be contacted later. Her perseverance made her pretend to believe otherwise, but she was seasoned enough to understand what that meant.

Then she rang Vijayaraghavan. He expostulated, since by now he was feeling a little guilty, that it was a waste of time, the man couldn't be in a position to know anything.

"You just stay out of this," she told him bluntly. "You're like all men. You don't care enough and you give up too easily."

Krishnan let the criticism of the male sex pass, and after five minutes she put the receiver down, puzzled.

"I don't understand," she said, knitting her brows. "He knows something, but he doesn't seem to want to tell me."

His first reaction was a rush of anger that put him firmly on her side. Cold-shouldering him was one thing, but she had injured no one, and there was no justification for snubbing her concern as if the mud had washed off on her.

Then the second wave hit him and he saw it. It astounded him that he hadn't seen it before. What else could it mean, the admiration she couldn't conceal in the hospital, his not being married when everyone else in his community was, the way she went to him at the very first crisis, and finally even his lavish compliments to Cynthia, thrown into the wind to turn Krishnan's nose the wrong way. So that was why Kamala never made a claim. That was why she let his conscience twist him, hoping all the time his loyalty would break, so that she could walk out, wearing martyrdom like a September sari and he take the smear for what she really wanted. It was treachery, he told himself. Betrayal, nothing less, the innuendos and the mockery flaming up, as he stood there glowering, with his jaw set, hardly aware of Cynthia's nonplused look.

He pulled his coat on and fished for the car keys. "It's my problem now," he told her, tightening his belt. "He's going to tell me; he has to. If he doesn't, I'll take it out of him all the way back to the first lie."

He rushed out of the hotel and into the Hillman, driving it recklessly through the sullen, sodden night. The downpour was persistent and solid, and the fog reminded him mockingly of himself. He drove dead-center through the almost axle-deep puddles, splashing the less agile citizenry with his anger.

The little house, with the unkempt grass in front of it, loomed up, and he crashed forward to the entrance, through the solitary flower bed, storming right in without bothering to knock.

The man was sitting in the cane easy chair drinking lime juice and looking as if he thought this encounter was going to be a pleasure.

"Where the devil is she?" Krishnan exploded.

"In the bedroom, naturally," said Vijayaraghavan, waving him on.

Krishnan was through the curtain, across the open doorway,

before he realized what an ass he was making of himself. The room was empty, as he would have known if he had waited to catch his breath. He came out three degrees cooler and two shades more scarlet.

"Sit down, my foolish friend," said Vijayaraghavan blandly. "Don't behave like a tomcat that's been seen in the wrong neighborhood."

"I've a right to know," demanded Krishnan sourly.

"You'll go back, won't you, if I tell you where she is?"

"Damned if I ever will," retorted Krishnan. He was striding meaninglessly up and down, uncomfortably conscious that he wasn't looking menacing.

"In that case," said Vijayaraghavan, "your future course is obvious. Go back to Cynthia and the body beautiful. Drown yourself in her; it's a fine death for a Brahmin."

Krishnan glared at him as intimidatingly as he could. "I can wring your neck if I want to," he observed.

"Go ahead, my dear fellow. You've done worse things in your time."

"You love her, don't you, damn you? All the time I've been tormenting my conscience you two have been going on behind my back."

"Love," reflected Vijayaraghavan, sipping his lime juice. "What is love but an Occidental inanity? A scarlet thread with which to tie up confusion."

"So you've done it, you scoundrel, without even being in love."

Vijayaraghavan got up, nearly knocking over the glass. "This is really quite alarming, my dear friend. You must have left your brains in Cynthia's baggage."

"I take it that you'll at least be ready to marry Kamala. After your pious words about her loss of status."

"Yes," said Vijayaraghavan, his voice suddenly crackling with anger. "There isn't anything that I'd rather do. If I could have her, that is. I'm not in her social class. I couldn't presume to get near her. All I could ever do was stand and look and wish I had been born a little different. And you," he added, his voice rasping, sur-

prisingly close to savagery, "all *you* had to do was pick her out of
a line-up. You only had to stand there and decide that she was
better than the other ones offered to you in marriage. And now that
you've got what you can't deserve, you dumbbell, you don't even
know how to stick to your good fortune."

"So you love her," Krishnan declared triumphantly.

"I could make her life something of what it ought to be. If she
and I could come to share one life. But she won't, curse you. Can't
you understand that she won't? She only wants you, you pea-
brained, bumbling baboon."

Krishnan listened to him, feeling the barometer dropping, the
slump of tension going all the way down.

"I'm sorry," he said limply. "I didn't know how you felt. I hope
it works out—works out for you, that is."

It sounded trite and it didn't seem to register.

"Take your time," said Vijayaraghavan, his voice toneless. "Take
your time going, but go. Every time I see you it reminds me of
what you did. I'll make it my business that you never hurt her
again."

Krishnan went out with most of the passion drained from him.
He almost had to push himself into the driver's seat. His anger
was gone, and something else had gone with it. He was tired, so
tired that even the reproaches didn't stand up to browbeat him.

He told Cynthia what had happened. Her first response was of
relief that Kamala was safe, and the reaction glowed in her face so
that even he felt easier and more real in the warmth of it.

Then she looked at him, her sympathy reaching out, the touch
of understanding coming so long before the bodies touched, making it clear that there could have been no mistake.

"You won't be hurt either, any more," she said.

He put himself against her, letting the drowsiness float in. His
arms went around her, firming the arch of her confidence. She let
herself go down, the eyes half closed, the receiving loveliness upthrust, the yielding line of her expectancy tense, as if inciting the
onrush of darkness. Then she opened it all, as if there had always
been innocence, as if there could never be any other sky.

Was it pity for him or a deeper kind of gentleness?

"Drown in her," the voice said as he gave up his mind to the wave.

7

The news hadn't got around, but he could see them imagining it. He took Cynthia to the club, where he was now a full member. It didn't matter now, he told himself. This was his rebellion, it was his own act, and the act had made him real for the first time because of a real devotion. He was ready for the whispers, the sidling voices, the averted faces, because he knew that out of the corners of their eyes they would be looking at her, watching her grace, admiring her vitality, and that, in their condemnation of him, envy would be the principal substance.

Even Pratap Singh's reaction didn't upset him as it would have once.

"What's this I hear?" the Sikh said. "You've sold yourself that fancy piece of goods. I saw you on the floor the other evening pushing her around like a senior-scale promotion."

"I'm in love with her," Krishnan proclaimed.

He had begun to mistrust the word, but he couldn't find anything less resounding or more accurate.

Pratap Singh responded as Krishnan had feared he would. He leaned back delightedly in his chair, slapped his oversized thighs and roared with laughter.

"Of course, it's plain you love her, my dear fellow. Your eyes when you look at her are like two Diwali lanterns. But that's the trouble with you priests and pundits. The very first time a woman tickles you, you're done for."

"You think that's all there is to it?" Krishnan demanded, his pride beginning to simmer.

"Oh, no. I'm told there's ever so much more. But this comes first; why bother about the rest?"

He saw Krishnan's face and abruptly dropped the jibing out of his voice. "I'm not running down your motives, my dear fellow. You're an intellectual chap, one of those South Indian examination miracles. I suppose what really sent you for six was the shock of discovering she didn't have a third-class brain. But let me give you some purely friendly advice. Don't jump in so far that you can't climb out. Take what you can but be sure you give nothing away."

"I love her," repeated Krishnan with sonorous persistence. "It's what we think of each other, not what other people think of us."

"Whatever you think, in six months you'll think differently. It's the result of your foreign education, my dear fellow. Too obstinate a taste for the exotic."

"I should have seen that coming," Krishnan replied as crushingly as he could. "You could have told me it was the desire for rebellion, that I fell in because I wanted to break out. It wouldn't have been true but it would have been less inaccurate. But that wouldn't strike you, of course. The only reasons that you know are carnal reasons. And even in your carnality you can't avoid being snobbish. It's her foreign extraction, the color of her skin."

Pratap Singh shook his head. "Not any more, my friend. As an independent country we must revise our standards. White women, pah! They're not the scalps they used to be. No prestige, my dear fellow. They no longer add anything to the length of one's beard."

He pulled a magazine out of the top drawer and thumbed it open at the most vivid of its pages. "See her," he said admiringly. "A real Swaraj product. She can do everything your foreigners can and sing too."

It had irked Krishnan more than a little while it lasted, but five minutes after it ended his anger was over. It wasn't in the bucket seat beside him, a nudge of derision all the time he drove home. He could walk up to Cynthia, open his mind to her welcome, and the little sneers were no more than what they should have been beside the fact of her love, the sense of fulfillment which bloomed from its reality.

He was happy with her because she wanted only him. There was no frame that he had to walk through for the fondness to come glowing into her face. They lived on an island, and the days could glide by, time slipping easily into the pellucid waters, the past never clouding the clarity and the affectionate candor of the present.

On Independence Day they were part of the crowd, like everyone else in Delhi or in India, waving and stretching and straining eternally forward, craning their necks for a fleeting glimpse of the great, happy and united in the common surge of history. She held his hand, she stood on tiptoe with him, her eyes were shining so there must have been triumph in his, but in that sudden lucidity of loneliness that only strikes one in the heart of multitudes, he was aware that something should have been in him and was not.

He was on an island, self-sustained and ringed by his contentment, but in front of him the continent lay—bleak desert, barren snow, jungle and village and the volcanic rocks of poverty—calling to him, inciting him, but no longer to be touched, the challenge there only to be looked upon across the blue happiness of his separation.

It would always be so, he began to remind himself, as long as the bond existed and the roots of his being had to be shared with her. However quick and vital she might be in her sympathies, however perceptive in her appreciation, an alienness remained in her, maintaining that infinitesimal yet decisive distance that made it impossible to share the sense of community with her when the pride of being Indian mounted in one's blood. He had not previously thought of her in this way, for, while always aware of a certain separation, he had, up to this point, regarded her slightly off-beat perceptiveness as focusing rather than blurring his understanding. It would still be so, he tried to reassure himself, throughout the area of their personal relationships, in every normal aspect of self-fulfillment and happiness. The intense sense of nationality which had disturbed him because he could not impart it occurred only rarely, and to see it involving anything more than a transient separation was, he protested, unfair and even perverse.

He stubbed the thought down as firmly as he could; but it had smoldered once, and he had the fear that it might light again, a murderous flicker of honesty in his eyes when his body went down into the depths of her love.

It would be the end, and an angry end, when that happened. Cynthia's tolerance might subdue her other emotions enough for her to forgive the conventional infidelities, though, having appreciated the tension of her possessiveness, he himself was inclined to doubt such an outcome. But she was a proud girl, perhaps even more proud than possessive, since pride was what made her happy in her rootlessness and gave her the distinctive *joie de vivre* that stayed so felicitously on this side of abandon. Did not that pride mean also that in the deeper exchanges of personality it would not be possible 'for her to blind herself to another's reservations?

She had never known how to compromise. She had always wanted it all. Could she reconcile herself to the anger of discovering that there was a core of difference she could never enter?

Could she learn to lie down and to live with the basic deceits?

8

The consequences of his decision were not quite what he had anticipated, and woebegone relatives did not beat a path to his door. Part of the explanation came in his father's irate letter.

"It will cost me a thousand rupees to get to Delhi and back, and since I probably will not be able to persuade your scanty intelligence to undo the consequences of your emotional imbecility, I have decided not to risk throwing good money after obstinate flesh. Do as you please, but don't come to us to patch up your mistakes. I cannot bring myself to disinherit you completely, but dead or alive, don't expect me to contribute, morally or financially, to any part of this folly."

Mother's letter was more conciliatory, the good will surviving, notwithstanding the deep and completely unexpected injury.

"I shall never be able to understand what has become of you. Let us hope you realize before it is too late what a terrible mistake you have made and how many people will have to suffer for it."

There was a tear smudging the ink, and the handwriting had wavered.

"I suppose Kamala must bear a little of the blame too. If she had not been deficient in some aspect of her wifely duties it is inconceivable that you would have deserted her for this foreign girl who cannot bring you happiness. It is just as Desikan the astrologer said. She should not have married anyone west of the Cauvery. If only you had listened to us and chosen Menaka, we would not have to undo the damage of this tragedy."

Kruger's letter arrived the day afterward. It was hectoring, like his father's, the barb directed this time at his morality rather than his intelligence.

"An affair with a white woman shows a lack of taste, comprehensible in a young man even if it is not excusable. But to desert Kamala is not merely cruelty, it is not merely infantile self-indulgence, it is also defiance of the laws of one's nature. Any man can chafe at his *Karma*. No man can expect to overthrow it and not pay fully for the consequences."

Now that the torrent of objections was waning, now that the gossips had glared and the relatives spoken, he felt his position a little more secure. The scorn and the rebukes had failed to shake him. The criticisms made—maltreatment of tradition, disrespect for his caste, indifference to the ignominy suffered by his family, an uncontrolled and immature surrender to emotion—were remarks which stung him but which he could disregard, since they were not related to his inner struggle and to the terms in which he had experienced his conflict.

The letter he had feared was the one from Kamala's father, but that, when it came, was characteristically tight-lipped, written in suave prose that discounted its emotions, and merely expressing the hope that he would realize his error while it was still possible to undo it. He wondered what force had controlled the elegant language—the old man's pride or Kamala's deep knowledge that acceptance was sometimes the surest form of protest.

He was emotionally tired now, grateful for a respite, anxious to keep the temperature down, and Cynthia, aware of his state of mind, responded, putting the uncomfortable thoughts discreetly away and expertly shaping the situations that he walked through.

She had the charm and depth to give the island variety; she could taunt him repeatedly with the pride of her body, engage him creatively with her firm, courageous mind. Her beauty came to him with a casual unexpectedness, like a mountain rivulet in a deep glade of beckoning. If there was contrivance, as there must have been in her, it had sunk far inward, so that she followed no pattern. Her love was sometimes stormy, sometimes peaceful, but the storm destroyed nothing that the peace could not restore, so that, lying becalmed with the atoll of their contentment around them, he could feel the rhythm of change without its cruelty.

But the breakers came through. The Award was the match that lighted the long train of dynamite, snaking and ravaging across the chosen frontier. The violence broke out of honorable men, a lust in their eyes, a smear of satisfaction on the thirsting knives, the burning homes its beacon and memorial. The words, the inflamed reports, the provocative rumors, were like bacteria in the air that one breathed, and before reason could summon its reserves against the menace, the contagion had seized you, and you were its screaming puppet. And after the flaming sky and the broken bodies, after the wailing and the useless appeals, the stripped flesh and the soliciting knees, raped, mutilated and torn into the silence, the exodus came, column upon column, blindly marching upon the vacant future, million upon million of the dispossessed, in what seemed to be history's greatest tide of suffering. They had nothing to look for, only something to flee from. When the sun rose again in the grimy and blistered eyes they would be a little further from the memory. They passed each other, the endless processions moving westward and eastward, all that remained of yesterday carried on the humped backs, like two rivers moving irrevocably forward, unseeing, as the immense pressure of their pain dictated, in a despair too deep for even revenge to agitate. But on the banks of the disaster the anger festered and smoldered, destroying and pillaging with a compulsive, purposeless violence, as if an eternity of frustrated acceptance was there, inching forward in the implacable orgy, flooding the brain with its unappeasable fever, reaching down, forcing the demented hands to yet another and another convulsion of hate.

The pride of being Indian, of having helped to bring to its unprecedented climax a generation of struggle in which the sword had not been lifted, was submerged in an emotion in which shame was a component less compelling than helpless bewilderment at the fever and its virulence. It could not be escaped. It was in every line that one read and every face one looked at. And now even in the capital, where the call to order issued, it was no longer safe to walk in the streets, and the Moslem houses with their constricted entrances huddled together in the clenched city's heart, shuttered their windows and waited for the assault, while the home-made, petrol-soaked incendiaries were flung in, primitive but deadly in that murderous congestion. Old Delhi was a city made for burning. And the Moslems, so it was said and echoed in every narrow street, had stores of arms hidden for an uprising. So it was preventive war and anticipatory looking. It was vengeance for the hundreds of thousands who had poured out from the North and who now sat shuddering behind the walls of the old forts, sleeping together in holes in the crumbling masonry, under culverts or in the shelter of ditches, expecting nothing, since, numbed by catastrophe, they were nothing themselves but a collection of needs which a body tied together. In two short weeks the human tide had doubled the population, and even in the new city with its immaculate lawns, and the roundabouts where the leisurely traffic circled, the misery drifted, carrying its foreboding.

Vengeance and agony in the ferocious, endless cycle. How long would it last, how deeply would it wound the newly born reality? How many must die, how many be dispossessed, how many scars be inflicted on the uninjured, before the pestilence devoured itself, leaving behind it the unwashed blood on the stairway and the flickering fear walled up behind the great stones?

"It's terrible," said Cynthia. "I knew it was coming. I've even tried to prepare myself emotionally. But until it happened there was always the hope that it wouldn't, and now that it has happened, nothing I imagined is remotely like the shock of it."

"It's your fault," Krishnan retorted hotly, shame spurring him to language in excess of the facts. "You made this awful thing grow. For a whole generation you British have stirred up the trouble. It's you that made the religious divisions take priority over our common political interests. Communal electorates, communal representation in the civil service. Communal this and communal that. Even the cricket matches were communally organized."

Cynthia listened, first in sheer astonishment, and then with the surprise on her face hardening into an anger that she still kept under control. She hadn't reproached his country. What she had said had really been offered in sympathy. But now her own people had been attacked, and however deep her feeling for him, it didn't go so far that she could ignore the rebuke.

"In all our three hundred years of occupation," she said levelly, "we haven't done what you've done in three weeks of your freedom."

She spoke with a careful neutrality so that even her tone of voice did not put quotation marks around the word *occupation*. She was anticolonial and was reminding him of that. But she was English too and didn't want him to forget it.

He wondered what had come over him. He had to recognize that ninety-nine out of a hundred of her compatriots would not have said *occupation* even in quotation marks. Though he still believed in part of his accusation, he realized now that it hadn't been called for by her remarks. If an Indian had spoken the same words, there would have been a bond of feeling, not a reaction of guilt.

He tried to be more reasonable. "I don't want to question your right to judge. I'm not even saying that there isn't some truth in your judgment—"

"I know," she interrupted. She too was a little contrite. "It isn't fair to ask you to judge your people. If it happened in England I can imagine how I'd feel."

But it hadn't happened and never could happen in England, not in that green, cool, soft-toned, decorous civilization. This was a different continent. The sun and rain lashed it to an angry brilliance, and every furrow of the plow in the soil turned up the frustration that might darken into violence. Could she imagine that? With her sympathies, yes, with the force of her fondness for him, perhaps even with her heart, but the heart was not the blood, and this was the time of the blood, molding and stating and establishing the difference.

"It's like a fever," he said. "You cannot judge a fever. You just sit down and do your best to cure it."

"It will be cured, of course," she said, and her tone was not one that questioned the assertion.

He was grateful for her confidence but aware of it as largely an effort of good will. They modified their positions mutually after that, anxious to be reasonable in a climate of prejudice. In the end they were close together but both were ill at ease knowing that it was a negotiated, not an instinctive, agreement.

He was more keenly aware now of the roots of difference and began to wonder whether only a crisis exposed them. England might not be her home, as she had once said, it might not be the place where she could grow her happiness, but it was her background, just as India was his, and the mingling of backgrounds, creative though it might be, involved an inevitable friction of dissent.

She understood what was passing through his mind. He had found her directness disconcerting once, but that was when she was trying to throw him off balance, and now that it was important to give him a sense of security, he was amazed at how much she knew how to leave unsaid. She did not refer to his job. She knew that the routine was a sort of insulation, and it was as if she wished his unsettled nerves might harden before exposing them to a different experience.

"You ought to write," she told him more than once. "It's the solution for people who don't belong. All writers are children who gaze at their dreams through brilliant plate-glass windows and go home sadly, not daring to throw the stone."

But she didn't speak of it as something to be thought of this day or the next; only as a solution that he could enter if he chose to, being sure always that he would find her beside him. "The in-betweens see both sides of the question." He agreed, but argued that precisely for that reason the in-betweens saw nothing as it really was. She didn't accept that. "A writer doesn't stand wholly with any character, any philosophy or image. He's neutral. He establishes the tensions but doesn't make the choice." How much like himself, he thought, and then realized that that was precisely why she was saying it. She wanted to make his irresolution creative by giving it a standing and a purpose. He appreciated that, knowing that someone less perceptive could have made cutting remarks about the Hamlet mentality.

What was it, he wondered, that made her so reassuringly self-sufficient, so that she was able to tend the private garden of her happiness, not in obliviousness to the world outside but with a renewed and deeply personal understanding of its problems. Was it because she was rootless, as she had said so often? Or was it because of the character of her background, because she came from a tradition which included nonconformity and dissent among its attributes? She could do as her heart dictated, create her own life style in sturdy independence and yet not feel the deep interior sense of alienation, of being cut off from the strength of one's soil. In an island civilization, how radical was it to choose a smaller island?

His background, on the contrary, was one of complete conformity, where the map of one's life was drawn even before one's first cry. All the emotions and responsibilities were systematically charted—to the village, to the government, to the complex yet precise hierarchy of the joint family, the relation of man to society, man to man, even the relation of a man to his wife, so that all that remained for private definition was the deep, personal mystery of a man's relation to God. And even that mystery was set in a ceremony and process rigidly prescribed to the minutest detail, so that, while the discovery was one's own, the only possible way was that of all men.

His was not the neat, washed country of semidetached realities where a man could sit comfortably in his slippers, warming his hands in front of his isolation, hearing only the louder quarrels on the other side of the common wall, or the unexpected outbursts on the radio. It was the public square, the streets in front of the temple, the milling multitudes seeking the *darshan* of saint or political leader; it was the constant struggle to maintain the shape of a personal life against the torrent. He was not in sympathy with such a background, he would spend much of his life trying to protest against it but he began to realize the extent to which it controlled him, however comprehensive the character of his rebellion. For him the maintenance of his individuality required an unceasing pressure of self-assertion, whereas for her it was merely the application of forces which society had long recognized and to some degree respected. She could never understand the force of the pull and the weariness of resisting it, the pitiless vigilance needed to preserve the island, intact and serene amidst the collective sea.

9

Kruger arrived a day or two later to see him in his office. He would not go to Krishnan's home; home was contamination. He looked at Krishnan in sorrow as well as in anger, the living embodiment of a Brahmin disgraced.

He had not come for any specific purpose. There were manuscripts in Benares that he had long wanted to consult, and when one came that far north one might as well go on to Delhi.

Krishnan went back with him to the cheap room in the hotel. He stood in the corner on one foot, scratching it with the other one, while Kruger eyed him from the creaking cot.

"Why don't you see her?" Krishnan asked. "See her before you decide against her."

"Whatever she is like it wouldn't make any difference."

"That's just like you and the rest of you. She's Indian in any way that matters. She wears our clothes, she eats our food, she speaks our language—well, not the words maybe, but most of what goes into them. What else can you expect of her?"

"I expect nothing from a foreigner," said Kruger. "What counts is what I expect from you. Fidelity to your thread and to your calling."

"Then tell me why you object to her."

"I object to her firstly because she is not your wife and can't be. I object to her secondly because she was reared by a flesh-eating mother who bathed only once a fortnight and cannot possibly have given her a sensible upbringing. It will take several incarnations to overcome such a handicap."

"You're objecting to her background, not to her."

"Objection is not a relevant term," said Kruger. "You introduced the word and I reject it. One does not object to a goat. But, equally, one does not enter into a wedding with it. She is English, and Manu makes no provisions for Englishwomen, whereas he has at least laid down regulations for goats. The truth is," concluded Kruger with deliberate emphasis, "that you are defying your *Karma*. No man can do that without severing his relation with reality. You are cutting off the branch on which you stand."

"*Karma, Karma.* We're always being told that. It's the infallible reason for never changing anything."

"It's the law of life," said Kruger quietly. "You cannot change it unless you have endured it."

"I suppose if I behave myself I can have Cynthia in my next birth."

Kruger was shocked. "She cannot possibly become a Brahmin by then."

"I'm sick of it," said Krishnan. "Philosophy, my foot. It's a cosmic swindle for perpetuating the status quo. At least if you're a Moslem you get your Paradise without any of this red tape. If you're a Christian you get it after judgment day. But what happens to us Hindus? Do as you're told and when you're reborn you might be given an increment. No wonder we're a race of civil servants."

He got out of his corner and got ready to leave. Kruger looked at him dejectedly.

"I can't understand it. It must be because you went to Cambridge too early. It's never happened to anyone who knew Sanskrit."

Krishnan left, banging the door behind him.

10

On his birthday he took her to Mutthra. He was not a temple-goer, he had long since abandoned and very largely forgotten the elaborate sequence of a Brahmin's daily prayers, but from time to time the sense of immensity seized him as it did all those who had listened to the thunder and looked up to see the sky, flaming and pitiless above the appealing earth. Mutthra was Lord Krishna's birthplace, and its unremarkable temple at least harmonized more aptly with its landscape than the multicolored edifice at Delhi. They made the short but uncomfortable journey by train, and then, feeling that the ancient Buick cab with its unshaven driver and its crocodile-shaped hand horn was unsuited to his mood, he and Cynthia took a *tonga* instead. He had an awareness of history's irony in visiting places like Kurukshetra and Mutthra, so hallowed by legend and philosophy and now only plain fields and unimportant junctions. Yet there was something right about their drabness: the place did not matter; but the truth that was born in them did.

He made the preliminary purchases necessary for the *pooja:* the betel leaves and nuts, the flowers, the saffron and the incense. They were the ordinary possessions of all families rich or poor, remind-ing him that the divine was in every household and that to feel its presence a man did not change himself but only became himself more truly.

He had not expected the feeling of elation that welled up in him when he saw the temple, with its squat silhouette, and the familiar *gopuram,* like the upthrust strength of the earth. There it was, brown as the soil, securely belonging to it, with every detail of its architecture confessing the strength of infinity in the smallness of everyday things.

They took their shoes off and proceeded quietly toward the place of prayer. He walked as slowly as he could. He wanted to feel each step as a further addition to the depth of his experience.

Coming up to the entrance, he was almost joyously conscious of the leap of feeling in him, a feeling not simply of remembrance but of something approaching restoration. How different the square doorway was from the Gothic arch, with its erect, pointed curve directing one's awareness to a superior order, and the scalloped Moslem arches endlessly superimposed, so that the perfection of the style was realized when the many blended into the illusion of one. The Hindu arch was a trestle—a beam placed horizontally upon two vertical beams—the simplest of architectural forms, yet, in its sophistication, the strongest and most fertile. And the strength carried through into the temple's rectangle and the tall tower of the *gopuram* itself, the blunted thrust giving aspiration solidity and earthiness. It was there too, in the patient carving, vaguely similar yet never exactly the same, brown stone proudly declaring the earth's promise, so that in the apparent riot of diversity one felt the presence, not of a pattern but of a unifying force, straining upward into the spiritual, penetrating down into the sensual, until the borders of division melted away and the two worlds were extensions of each other.

Perhaps, he told himself, a little of that force would kindle in him, restoring him to some constructive community with the parched land and the frustrated roots, clutching defiantly at the unyielding soil. He would invoke the benediction in the thousand and one names rather than in the shorter ceremony, and the cadences of blessing would flow across his mind, soothing it into creativeness, like running water over the hard, smooth stones which its constant erosion had polished into shape.

He was deep in his thoughts and unaware of Cynthia. He came to the priest with the gifts in his hands, and something of his mind now dropped into tranquillity, reaching forward into the offering fingers. He was going to ask for the blessing when he saw the question in the grave eyes and the benevolent yet impassive face. He knew what the question was. He should have known it before they took their shoes off to walk up the steps, before he had visited the bazaar to make the purchases, but he had wanted the blessing for them both and wanted it too keenly to remember.

There was nothing to do now. His hands fell stiffly to his sides, holding the useless bundles. He turned and went back down the unending steps, each step an addition to the distance of exile. They put on their slippers. She was wearing a sari, and as he looked at her, she could have been Indian except for the hair and eyes, but that didn't make their separation less. He did not know what to do with the garland, so in an awkward gesture he put it on her shoulders. When he saw it on her it reminded him that he had meant it for a deeper devotion, and he took it off clumsily and a little roughly in his haste, so that the string bit into the nape of her neck.

She rubbed the sore spot gently with her fingers. She wasn't angry, and that made it even worse.

"I didn't want it," she said. "I was going to return it anyway."

He had done it all wrong, and the knowledge drove him to harshness. "Let's go," he told her. "We can just make the five-ten."

She said nothing most of the way to the station. The disappointment was not in his face but in his hands, nervously twisting and unclenching. She waited, watching them until they relaxed.

"It's because of me, isn't it? He couldn't bless us both."

"It doesn't matter," he said without conviction. "Wherever a Brahmin is, there is a temple."

Perhaps it was because she was not on the inside of the words, feeling their hollowness as he did. Or perhaps she simply wanted to believe him and to persuade him to believe himself. But she smiled at him with an expression approaching gratitude, which he hadn't seen on those familiar lips and the face he knew best, with its confident sensuality. She sat by the window in the train looking out at the alien land, watching the rise and fall of the wires strung between the telegraph poles, in the monotonous installments of their journey. When the pride rubbed off, there was a different kind of beauty underneath, and looking at it, Krishnan felt some of the old feeling, but not all of it, come back.

He moved closer to her. Neither of them wanted to speak any further of what had failed to happen, so he told her impersonally of Lord Krishna, the child carried to safety across the unpassable torrent of the Jumna, which subsided into a quiet stream at the

touch of the infant feet. There was another flood now, and innocence would not be enough to tame it. Then he told her the more
familiar stories of Krishna's childhood and youth. He did so with
a slightly stiff formality which would have amused her at another
time and made her tease him for being too schoolmasterish. He half
hoped that she would do so now. He wanted to see the crinkle at
the edge of her eyes when she laughed at him, and to feel the affectionate shock of her debunking, pushing him back into their
chosen reality. But she was too tense and too uncertain to try it.
She waited till he had finished and then said what she did only
because she felt she had to say something.

"He was consistent, wasn't he?" she observed. "He graduated
from butter and milk to milkmaids. He should be the patron of the
dairy industry."

That was a long way below par for Cynthia, but now when he
too could have broken the ice by teasing her he couldn't summon
the necessary fondness. He let the hour's journey slip into the silence, putting up the invisible but tangible barrier between them.
They dined, went back to their rented home and sat there trying
to form again the old images between which much more than affection had lingered. He put his arms around her. Her body still
had its beauty and the surge of its passion and, looking into her
eyes, he could still see the gentleness which his love had planted between the determined lights. Was she aware of the difference, of
the small kernel of hollowness? Did it show in his fingers, or in
his muscles, or in the caress of the words spoken between them
that joined their two minds in the communion of peace? The gestures could all be there. The rite could be celebrated with the same
absorption, the same desire with affection as its margin. There
would always be the same deep pull and ebb of his emotion, the
overturning of himself in the shaping power of darkness, whenever
the white breakers of oblivion rode in and the yield of her body
rose to combat his pride. It would always be so, and what was the
power if not the power of love? Yet something had died, and they
could lie there, both of them knowing it but unable to point a finger at the evidence. And after the storm had passed, the silence

would change its quality, becoming not the blanket of peace but the tormenting whisper of their emptiness.

Perhaps he was too sensitive. Perhaps the change had to come, and the crisis was only its acceleration. The dying down of intensity was inevitable, and one would not even be aware of it if it came gradually over the numbing years. This way was more dramatic; but it was different only in its tempo, not its nature, and merely required a more dramatic adjustment.

Her eyes were closed and she was breathing steadily, not moving when he touched the thin, red string mark on the nape of her neck. The scar of the experience would pass off with the night's sleep. Perhaps she would forget that the scar had ever been there. Perhaps it didn't matter, since she had done what she could.

He could stay with her, and it didn't need even loyalty, only the sacrifice of that ultimate honesty to which no man is entitled when the truth tears the happiness of another. A man had nothing but mistakes to live with. But love did not miscalculate; it turned again and was rekindled with the error.

He put his head against her, and her arm went around him in her sleep, drawing him back into the protection of the island. All night he felt the thunder of the sea's surf and the strange emptiness of a death without pain.

Next morning he made his attempt to be contrite. "I'm sorry I went off the handle like that," he told her. She replied that he ought to be ashamed of himself, but her tone was friendly and encouraged him to explain the reason for his reaction.

"Rejection by the family, by other people, by society, is one thing. One expects it automatically and is prepared to meet it. But this was so much deeper. It was so deep that I had forgotten my defenses."

"I never thought of you as religious, Krish." She tried to keep the surprise out of her voice, but the effect only made her concern more dominant.

"It isn't religion. It's just something deeper than society or the family. You take it for granted until you realize that it isn't available. That's what happened to me. It never struck me that I'd have to do without it. Never, until I looked into the priest's eyes. And then I knew what it was. After I'd lost it, of course."

She tried to reassure him. "You're overestimating it, darling. You'd set your heart on something, and it was simply the force of disappointment. When you get your distance from it, it isn't going to be any more serious than all the other rejections that you've been through."

He shook his head. "Why did Nanda pray on the steps of the temple? Was it only to secure the priest's acceptance? He wanted something more. And that's what I've lost. It would be easy if it were just the blessing."

Her voice took on a slight edge of exasperation. "Krish, I'm trying hard not to be prosaic. But what else have you lost besides a blessing? If you've made your choice, if you're prepared to stand by it, the deeper acceptance, whatever it is, has got to come from the knowledge of having done right. It can't come from something done with flowers and saffron. You said it yourself, remember, coming back to the station. Wherever a Brahmin is there is a temple."

She was more right than she knew, he thought. It wasn't the exterior rejection that mattered but the change in him which the rejection had made evident. If he hadn't changed, he would have lost only the blessing. But he had changed, and something else had gone too. How was he to tell her that? Or conceal it from her without her coming to know it? He tried to reassure himself that it would not be a lie, only a restraint in telling the whole truth, which would give the unsaid, undesired part of it an opportunity to evolve into something better.

"You're right," he said slowly, hoping that the words wouldn't seem like a mask for his real emotions. "It isn't what people think or customs allow. It's the inner conviction that one has done right to the best of one's ability."

She didn't ask whether he had the inner conviction. At least for the moment, she was willing to share his readiness for deceit, to participate in his reluctance to press honesty to its brutal, ultimate limits.

It was the only way, he told himself. There had to be a tactical lie, a bridge thrown temporarily across the chasm, which one could cross over and later on destroy. But, going to the office, he remembered that he hadn't felt the same solicitude for Kamala. She had compelled him into uncompromising honesty. He tried to assure himself that he had become a little wiser, that what one achieved was never worth the suffering, that people changed and that there was no point in stating exhaustively and destructively what might be only a transient phase in their relationships. But, sitting engrossed behind his desk, behind the smudged tape and the tottering piles of paper, he began to wonder whether what prompted him was practical wisdom or the fear of his emptiness.

II

He went back to the house as late as he could. It was the first time he hadn't wanted to return, and he didn't need to tell himself that he felt that way because it mightn't be home much longer.

Two pegs, downed fast, straightened out his ego, and he saw himself the way a realist should, five-seven, slim-shouldered and ready to face the future.

"Don't do it," she told him, "unless you're afraid of the truth."

"Who's afraid of honesty?" he replied, scowling. "The big, bad wolf. All it can do is to frighten away one's happiness."

She took the third one away from him. "I'm a truth addict as you were. I like to have it neat."

He pushed the drink closer to her. "Try it without the soda," he suggested. "It burns going down just as the truth does, but it doesn't give you as much of a hang-over."

She looked at him discouragingly. "I think we should get out of here."

He took her out. She looked good with the moonlight poured upon her. Her beauty, though familiar, was still new. However often he saw her, she still looked as if she'd just come off the calendar.

"You're much more lovely than you ought to be," he told her. He would stop being refined and concentrate upon that.

"Better watch the speedometer," she warned him.

"You tell me where I'm going and I'll watch it."

"A road is to take you where you want to go." She removed his arm firmly and put it back on the wheel.

He shook his head. "Not this one. Somebody else has planned it for us. Every furlong post is an additional mistake. And you see that car behind us with the blazing headlights? That's honesty and its home-made machine gun. Two minutes from now our tires will be blown off."

"Better stop here," she said. "It's more open, and maybe it would help if you let some fresh air into those fancy metaphors."

He got out. The road was empty, but at the end of it there was a dull red glow, ominous against the night sky. His head was aching, but it was clear enough for him to look at her and to know what was coming. He could see the blaze starting in her eyes and knew she was beginning to demand the truth.

"Cut it out, Cynthia." He tried to keep the appeal out of his voice and to accentuate the firmness. "It won't make us any happier or freer. Let's stay with the facts, and we can get used to them."

She faced him squarely. "I'd like to but I can't, Krish. I've got to know now. I've got to know whether you're beginning to feel different."

"You've always fascinated me. You still do."

"That isn't an answer," she retorted angrily. "That isn't an answer, damn you, and you know it."

"I don't love anyone else. Is that an answer?"

Her face seemed to lose a little of its tenseness. "It is, but it isn't enough. We've got the weight of custom against us, we've got everyone's hostility and nobody's approval, and we've hurt so many by what we've had to do. All we have is each other and we must have all of each other."

He had turned a little sideways to her, and she spun him back with surprising strength, gripping his shoulders and looking at him with an intent possessiveness that was almost animosity.

"Don't you see," she said flatly. "I've got to have it all."

He extricated himself and tried to subdue her. She was breathing harder and arched away from his touch.

"Don't be unreasonable," he said. "Nobody can have that. Only death can make that kind of a claim. If you want to stay alive, if you want to remain yourself, you've got to agree to something being kept out of it."

"And how much have you kept out? How much of you walked away when she left?"

"About half of me," he said a little tiredly. "I stayed because I thought that the essential part remained."

"So you don't love me," she declared accusingly.

He hadn't expected that of her but he had to see its justice. The crisis had hit her, and she had broken down into the conventional inconsistencies, frightened that she might lose him, angry because she had never completely had him, wanting what she could never be given and disdaining the loyalty which he was eager to give, unprepared to lie down with the illusion, yet injured by and indignant with the truth, which she had forced from him against his better judgment. It was all quite illogical and completely predictable. It could happen to anyone when the coherence of their natures broke up under the impact of events. Only Kamala was unpredictable, with that strange consistency that seemed to intensify in the presence of crisis.

He had to think of something to say. This was the big question, bidding for the jackpot, and the machine was supposed to come to life, delivering the proper answer in pink ribbons. But he couldn't hear the bells ring and the wheels whirr. He was ready for the lie, but not that kind of lie, only for the avoidance of the whole truth, the best possible statement of what he was able to give. She had made it mean too much to her. If he said yes now it would be a blank check drawn on his insincerity, an infinite deception to which the future would bind him.

"No, I don't love you," he found himself saying, and he was surprised at how easily the words came. Perhaps it was something he had wanted to say for some time. He wondered, though, whether the explanatory footnote had got through in his voice. Short of the impossible commitment she demanded, there was still so much he was prepared to give her.

She hadn't expected it. She was demanding the truth and yet she would have taken the big lie if it were sufficiently plausible for her possessiveness to cluster around it. She'd bid high, like anyone who bids high, because the small consolations were no longer quite enough.

She came back fighting. The forest fire in her eyes had had its answer.

"You've got a nerve," she told him. "Nobody asked you to come to me. But you come blundering into my life, ruining someone else's in the process, and now that it's time for a change, or so you think, you want to walk out as if nothing had happened. It's a wonderful way to work out your problems, isn't it? Experimenting with what you want, provided someone else pays for the mistakes? How irresponsible do you suppose you can get?"

"I never said anything about leaving," he reminded her. "I want to stay. If you'll just consent to keep the temperature down, there's still a great deal that we can give each other."

"Loyalty," she retorted angrily. "Even a dog can give that."

"There's much more than loyalty in it."

"Go on," she challenged him. "Go on, and tell me the difference."

There was a difference, and in a calmer climate he might have been able to define it, but here in the crisis and under the fire of her belligerent questioning, he was in no mood for exercises in semantics.

"If you don't know the difference there's no point in my telling you."

"Just as I thought," she said with bitter triumph. "You walked in because it meant a good time. A few things didn't happen the way you expected they would, and of course it isn't quite the same thing after you've got used to it. So you want to quit. But you've been brought up with certain principles, or maybe you can't stand seeing what you actually are. And there's your mile-wide streak of resignation, anyway. So you must stay put. It's your precious cage, and this time I'm the bars of it."

The tone of her voice was hardening and rising. He could feel the words stinging across his face.

"If you love her, go back to her."

"I'm not sure that I love her," he replied. "Something of me will always be with her, yes. But I never even tried to conceal that."

"Then go back to her anyway," she said, and he could see the tears starting to her eyes, though her voice still held itself firm, high and a little contemptuous. "Go back to her. She's a Hindu wife and she'll accept your loyalty. In an arranged marriage you've no right to expect more. She doesn't have to be like me, wanting something deeper that you've probably never known about."

"Yes, I have," he protested. "Believe me I have. But you've no right, either, to ask for a total commitment. When I lost her I abandoned some of myself. It was much more than I thought. It wasn't simply what I left with her, but so many other loyalties and attachments—to her world, her society and mine too, which just can't be re-created on our island."

"So you've miscalculated. The world is full of grownups who can't add. I suppose," she added wryly, "that I can't complain at having bumped into one of them."

"No, you can't," he told her. "Anyone can make mistakes. Living with them is the test of one's character."

"I don't want your sermons," she said impatiently. "I gave you something. I've a right to ask for the same."

"We each give what we're capable of giving."

"You've no right to give less than you receive. If you couldn't give everything, then you ought not to have started it."

"You said once," he reminded her, "that you could live without love. All you wanted was the right kind of misfit."

"That's just it," she retorted. "All I ever wanted was you. But you've always wanted much more than myself and made that a condition for committing yourself. I can't give you the blessing of the priests. I can't give you the family's forgiveness. You've known that, you've always known that, Krish, and if those things were that important, what right had you to come to me?"

"This," he said curtly, "is about where I came in. It's my fault, yes, and up to a point you're entitled to cudgel me with it, but now we'll either sit down and work it out or I'll find some other place to be."

"Go back to her," she said, her eyes flaming, her voice hardening almost into a scream. "Go back to your belonging and your bondage."

She brought her hand up and hit him square and hard across the mouth.

He didn't back off. He took out his handkerchief and dabbed the edge where the blood was beginning to trickle.

"I'll take you home now," he said gently.

He drove her back. She sat erect, staring in front of her, her hands trembling.

"You needn't come in," she said when they arrived. "I'll send your stuff on later."

"I hope we can still be friends."

She didn't seem to hear the platitude. "I hate you," she said, and for the first time the emotion was out of her voice, making the statement even more emphatic. "I hate you and I never want to see you again."

She walked up to the entrance, opened the door and switched on the light. Then something struck her and she turned, facing him in the doorway.

"I made it easy for you, didn't I? She never did. There's something mean about nonviolent people."

He was still near enough and she had pushed her tears back far enough for him to see her half-smile and to understand what it meant. Then she shut the door with emphatic gentleness. The night was his own now as the headlamps of the small car cut out from the darkness the endless and quivering ribbon of his life.

CHAPTER SIX

Day Train to Disaster

THE NIGHT was a sticky, compounded stupor, the double result of humidity and depression. He lay in it, squirming and turning, the fragments of dreams shuffling his past mistakes. He had forgotten to let the chicks down, and at six in the morning the sun slapped his drowsiness open.

He pushed his eyelids apart, tried to pry out the granules. He groped his way out of the embryonic naggings of the advancing light and into the bathroom and the wash of normalities. He oscillated his head across a toothbrush, dunked it under a tap, put it lethargically on chiseling terms with a razor. After the second gouge he concluded that he still retained a vested interest in it.

The blaze of reproach was coming in through the window, tapping the base of his brain, forming and re-forming the kaleidoscope of error.

He went back, counting the milestones. But who could tell when the beginning ruptured, if the first flaw fell from action or from thought, or if there were no cause at all, but only an endless condition, the circle of flames in which the dancer vaulted, the destruction glittering from the eye of his light. Perhaps to fail was his *Karma,* his necessity. Perhaps there was only disappointment for him, since the will was born in the body, striking from it, and, whatever distance of serenity it strove to, had to be held and maimed by that dark flesh.

Could he even say that the failures made a pattern, that they
trapped a meaning, however distorted and dimmed, that he could
take himself back, explaining and judging the milestones, feeling
the perspective, the direction, emerge? Could he say that or would
he have to admit that the distance was a journey, not a progress,
that he could never find a road to lead him anywhere, except
through the rending of other people's lives?

He could go down the street and watch the Jain devotee stepping warily so that he would not kill the cockroach, the mask on
his face, the very breathing subdued, lest by drawing breath he
might destroy a microbe, since life was sacred, except that by being
alive one threatened continually the lives of others. The cows were
sacred and their multitudes roamed the market place, their holiness
aggregating, giving merit, as the barbed bones thrust through the
perishing flesh. The serpent was sacred, the ancient legend said so,
the cobra's hood was the umbrella of Vishnu, the fang in the leg
God's way of getting you somewhere, the divine transfer for the
eternal civil servant. The monkey was sacred, and so the descend-
ants of Hanuman leaped into railway compartments, giving frantic
women their glimpses of divinity, gobbling up all the *bania*'s fat
bananas.

Life was sacred, and five feet from where the Jain had spared
the cockroach, the maggoted body would lie in the scarred streets,
still open with the pain of yesterday's battle. The nonkillers of
cows and the nonslayers of pigs would join their darknesses in
compulsive carnage. Life was as sacred as it was four thousand
years ago, when the last Kuru went to his death in the field of
a million, and the triumphant Pandavas, the five that were left
of them, rose in the divine holocaust that the song of Krishna
justified.

The leap of the dancer rang through every temple. Was it evil
alone—the demon—that the foot trampled, or was the macabre
energy indifferent, choosing nothing but the pure circle of form?
Did the soothing of the image mean only that cruelty lived and one
had always to live with it? Was that the condition of a man's life,
his *Karma,* the cost of the truth, the toll of being human? Was that

the prison no one could escape from, the body of the mind so
much more treacherous than the other temptation with its simpler
singing?

He couldn't escape it, but he could discover its contours, feel
out its obstinacy, its perversions; he had to live in it, but he could
also tame it, tame it so that the energy turned inward, the harsh
frustrations hurting only him. It was time to stop thinking of himself. He would walk like the Jain, afraid of injuring others.

The last mistake was the nearest, the easiest to reach, the kindest
to undo. He could go back to her if she wished. He could
swallow pride, the mildest of known poisons.

He let the remembrance of her smooth out the untidy morning;
his mind slipped back over the curving, yielding length, lissome
and answering as she always had been and, in the sight of recollection, lovelier. He formed the picture as exactly, as passionately,
as he could. Then he threw it down and made himself walk over it.

There was still enough to go back to, enough for much more
than loyalty to cherish. He had chosen her against all pressures, in
his obstinate, lonely act of self-assertion, and out of the exactions
of sorrow and of chagrin there had to come something of the
truth in himself. She was the receiver of the only pure commitment, the act had been free, it was himself uncompromised, and
in the reality which it planted, the meanings that he sought could
stand and grow.

But had he really chosen or been chosen? It was his body, his
desire, in a sense he had even made the very frustrations from
which it germinated. Was it his logic that swept into the act? Or
had he merely signed the paper, initialed the consequences?

He remembered the whole picture now, the penumbra of doubt
which the lamp had also illumined, and which he had overwhelmed then with the body's dedication. He had entered the
act as if decreed to do so. What had drawn him in was not the
strength of freedom but the hope that liberation would lean from
the far side.

It was her arms, the encircling eagerness of her yielding, that
had held him down, making his conquered vagueness the horizon

of her proud, definite and compelling body. She had chosen him,
not abandoning herself, but letting his possession of her shape him,
revealing the certitude and clarity of her own strength. The weight
of his need had fallen across her, and she had taken it to her,
giving it a more confident universe.

At no time had she even thought of compromise. She had made
him reach and she had let herself be given, the green of her country when he was ready for it, its loneliness, the cascade of its
vigor. But the price of her dedication could not fall short of his
complete acceptance, his readiness to live in her world entirely,
and in her happiness, to its island limits. If a little of him went
back to another frontier the rest would follow in reluctant sequence, and she had held his mind too closely not to know that.

It wasn't only Easterners who saved face. There was a kindness
in pride, if one knew how to control it, and she had done it that
way, clear-eyed and deliberate, driving the quarrel on until it even
possessed her, pushing it fiercely to that stinging climax which
perhaps only her determination wanted. She had hurt herself but
she had made the break clean.

She had made it easy for him, so she had said. He could flatter
himself that her womanhood wanted him back. But she was a
little more than that, a little prouder. In her obstinate strength she
wanted him to go onward, because any other way, any other kindness, would destroy even the remembrance of the island and the
affections it still held in their hearts.

She wasn't nonviolent, she wasn't like the Jains, but, beating out
her solutions, she had spared more than a cockroach. She had
pulled him in and now she had pushed him away. In the end she
had made him go back to himself. Perhaps it was her final reassurance, the last gift of her tight-lipped English haughtiness.

He took himself down, on the road and up the ramp, parking
his mind in the garage of the office. It wouldn't purr, and the files
didn't tune the engine. But he came out ready for a different
journey.

He nosed along the road, among the wavering bicyclists, in that sudden darkening, like the end of life, the night seeming not to come but to drop, almost at the turning of the day's back.

The white house was still there, only a little less white, blistered and peeling from the rain and the sun. He could still see the swathe where he had cut through the flower bed, it was not yet quite healed by the rainbow of new growth.

The lime juice was there, a couple of inches farther down in the glass, and the man, a little more acid, was in the chair.

"So you want to go back to her," Vijayaraghavan said.

He hadn't come with that specific intention, but now that it was put to him, it pulled his vaguenesses together. He pushed away the answer that sprang to his lips, reminding himself that he had turned to a different chapter, that it was time to think of others also.

"I want to hurt no one," he answered.

Vijayaraghavan eyed him quizzically.

"It's no good, my dear fellow, you're only a bull in a china shop. Don't try to be a saint. If you do, you'll spoil something more precious than the crockery."

Krishnan went through the motions of being gallant. "You've much more reason than I have to be with her."

"It's a world of law and not a world of reason." He said it with a controlled and level resentment, as if he were demolishing his own feelings with the sentence.

"I wouldn't even know how to begin," Krishnan confessed. "I wouldn't dare to ask her if she wanted me back."

"You don't have to ask her," Vijayaraghavan said. "The law is made for man and she obeys it. Just walk into the house where you have no moral right and take the woman like a cast-off bangle."

It was not simply the scorn in the words that unsettled Krishnan but the knowledge, flung at him, that he had to humiliate Kamala, even in the process of apology.

"I can't do it in that way," he protested. "If it has to be so I'd rather not do it at all."

"Then go back to your consort with the white skin. Go back to where you've neither law nor reason."

"She threw me out," said Krishnan. It was an exaggeration, but thinking of what he might do, he felt it necessary to bring on the rebuke.

Vijayaraghavan jumped in as Krishnan expected he would. "So much the better for her," he said gleefully. "I've underestimated Cynthia's intelligence."

"I deserve it," said Krishnan. It was true this time. "I can never forgive myself for what I've had to do."

"Forgiveness?" asked Vijayaraghavan, obviously puzzled. "Surely it's reserved for a higher order of sin."

"Then you don't think I've done wrong?" Krishnan responded unthinkingly.

He was aware too late of what he had let himself in for, but he was still surprised at the way Vijayaraghavan took his opportunity, jumping out of the chair, intense eyes flashing, striding up and down, eager to scathe and to wound.

"Of course you've done wrong, you poor fool," he declaimed. "You've done wrong in the ordinary, idiotic way that anyone does in any third-rate movie. The only difference is that your blundering has injured two people who are vastly superior to you."

"Perhaps," Krishnan cut in, "I can heal the injury to one of them."

Vijayaraghavan continued, ignoring the interruption.

"I suppose she'll forgive you," he observed. "It would serve you right if she didn't, but she will. Yudhisthra and Nala threw away their kingdoms at dice games, but Draupadi and Damayanti took them back. You've only thrown away your self-respect, which to a Brahmin should matter more than worldly possessions. But she'll forgive you. Forgiveness is her only weapon. I hope to Heaven that she hurts you with it."

"If she does take me back," said Krishnan soothingly, "I'll try my very best to be worthy of her."

It only set off another scornful tirade.

"You'll have a hard time doing that, I assure you. If your sin had profundity your repentance might have value. But what have you done? Lost your head over a woman. Any imbecile can do that. And don't tell me you have reasons. Any imbecile can delude himself with reasons. Trade follows the flag and philosophy the flesh."

He paused to catch his breath, as well as to plan the next thrust, and Krishnan, feeling the sting, was sorry for him also. He realized that the man had no other whip.

"Let me remind you," Vijayaraghavan resumed, "that adultery and desertion are the most trivial of sins. They just don't have the quality of grandeur. Nala and Yudhisthra committed their kingdoms to the caprice of the unknown. You only did what was predictable and, at least as far as your precious welfare is concerned, you never did anything you couldn't undo. Nala and Yudhisthra spent ten years in the wilderness. You're planning to get away and you probably will, with twenty minutes on my front veranda. You call that sin, my dear fellow? A Brahmin should know better and do worse. It isn't sin but an inferior and sottish stupidity."

Krishnan forced the smile on. It didn't require the effort he expected. There was a sense of frustration in his friend's words that drained away the scorn and its effects.

"I deserve it all," he admitted disarmingly. "All that you want to say and more. If you'd like the next round with the punching bag you're welcome. Or if you've had enough we can get down to brass tacks."

He didn't say it defensively, but with a matter-of-fact consideration that surprised him a little. Vijayaraghavan saw the point of it, the anger slumping suddenly to fatigue.

"What is it you want to know?" he asked.

"I want to know where she is."

He flared up again. "Damn you, why can't you find out for yourself? Why the devil must you come here expecting me to tell you?"

"It's easy enough to find out," Krishnan said gently. "Her father, my mother, any one of our relatives. But I want to learn it from you. If you say it, you'll be saying something else. You'll be telling me that you want me to go back to her. I wouldn't do it if you didn't tell me."

Vijayaraghavan swallowed, his face going tense, his fists unconsciously knotting. "She's at Shantihpur," he said thickly, pushing the words out.

"My God," said Krishnan, aghast. "It's the center of the hurricane." The apprehensions thronged in, and his voice hardened. "What the devil came over you? You said you'd look after her, you said you'd make it your business. Don't you know what she's in for? How long do you suppose she'll stay alive?"

"Don't try to tell me," said Vijayaraghavan angrily. "Don't think I didn't try every way to stop her. She insisted on going there. She almost welcomed the danger. She was hurt, viciously hurt, although she wouldn't let you see it, and she must have thought she could diminish the pain if she could lose it in something larger." He put his face in his hands, and his voice trembled. "You forced her to go there, you infatuated fool. The violence is breaking out everywhere around Shantihpur. It'll be a miracle if the place escapes. You've driven her there, you blundering numskull, and if anything happens you know where to point the finger."

"I'll take the first train tomorrow," Krishnan said lamely.

Some of the old sarcasm flickered in his friend. "Borrow a beefsteak done rare," he suggested. "Wave it around aggressively. If you do it long enough some patriotic Punjabi will reduce you to mincemeat and relieve Kamala of the problem of your existence."

But at the doorway he paused and put his arm around Krishnan in a shamefaced, hesitant gesture. "I'm sorry," he said awkwardly. "I never touched her and I never will. I can't even touch her with kindness. If you didn't hurt her it would matter less."

"I know how you feel," said Krishnan reassuringly, wishing he could say something a little less inadequate.

Vijayaraghavan shrugged his shoulders. "It's a world of responsibility, not of feeling."

The aphorism seemed to comfort him, a symmetrical peg, a shaping for his life. He went back to his position in the cane chair, took up the lime juice, the route march, the routine. It was a tight-fitting glove; there was no room in it for emotion. He would live in his pose, and the pose would slowly become him, until a different night came on him with its quietness, and the skin slipped off in the invading dark.

2

The station was always bedlam, but this time it was compounded with misery. The chaos lay everywhere, stuffed into brass vessels, gathered together in the frayed and shabby shawls, huddled in the tense faces and hunched shoulders, over which fear would take no backward glance. This was the beginning, and whatever one brought to it was in the trunk with the tin plate showing through the enamel, and the roll of bedding with its blankets striped blue and green, the family jewels hidden in the stuffing of the hard mattress. No matter what it led to, all that mattered was that it led away, and so the people stood patiently and milled and squatted, straining dangerously toward the platform edges, the hubbub rising and falling, and every now and then broken by the high, shrill scream of a hysterical memory.

The train came in—the mode of deliverance, of escape, of putting your back to the nightmare, and the telegraph poles with their soothing installments of distance between the vacant future and the crumbling house and the body with torn clothes flung out of the flaming window. It came in wheezing, whistling and inadequate, while the tide of exodus surged into it and above it, through every official or conceivable entrance, over the roof and in between the bogies, pajamas and *dhotis* and bronzes and bedding and brass, a cascade of humanity flowing like lava over it, till it stood there overwhelmed, stuffed and overflowing, plastered and encrusted with the white figures, and the toes and hands clutching at every protuberance. Krishnan was swept in with the mélange of elbows and the flailing voices, the tin trunks used as battering rams or held solicitously above the conflict, descending on unfamiliar and protesting shoulders, with the original owner sucked away by the vortex. The lower berths had been filled long before; the upper ones were stacked with huddled figures neatly arranged like ninepins, their legs dangling in an erratic curtain, through which the lower occupants peered out irritatedly amidst the calves and *chappals*. The floor was littered with squatters sitting astride their luggage, trying to assert their modest territorial claims with legs and pots and elbows, while the flood surged steadily in, reducing them inexorably to their minimum dimensions. A man with a moneylender's physique was stuffed into one of the windows, filling it with a hipline that must have seen numerous *jilabis*. Krishnan found himself with only one foot on the ground. The other, as the result of a chain of events which he could not clearly remember, was on top of a tin trunk surmounted by two rolls of bedding. Under it, an old lady in saffron with a shaven skull had located herself, two children and a caged myna. It was no position in which to pass a three-hour journey. Realizing this and striving to extricate himself, he rotated slowly on the grounded foot to the accompaniment of uncomplimentary epithets, and with the awkwardness of a man unaccustomed to even emergency acrobatics. He decided against putting his foot down on the blue and gray striped shirt with its temptingly plump shoulder which beckoned to him halfway through his gyration. When he had worked himself through a sixty-degree arc a happy inspiration seized him as he saw his toes pointing at the sign on the lavatory. He plunged forward through the torrent of imprecations and put his shoulder hard against the door.

It gave in. He came through on his hands and knees, dragging his suitcase across somebody's belly. The man kicked savagely, was unable to connect with the receding rear end, and had to console himself with a vivid dissertation on Krishnan's family origins. He slammed the door shut and bolted it. He looked around. A man sat on the toilet seat, his *dhoti* crumpled, a part of the *tilaka* mark on his forehead rubbed off and the triple thread of his Brahminhood showing beneath the soiled shirt with its upper buttons undone.

"Have you a first-class ticket?" Krishnan asked him, having recovered his breath.

The man shook his head. "There's no need for them any longer. A train is for anyone who can't stand it."

"Then please be good enough to move over. I've got a ticket, and a first-class passenger is entitled to a seat."

He hadn't expected the man to move but he did. He dumped the bedding roll opposite the toilet and sat down on top of it. He fingered his thread nervously. Krishnan wondered what meaning it possessed for him, how deep a sense of community it stood for, so that even in these incongruous surroundings he still wished to be reminded of its presence.

"I see you're a Brahmin," he observed. The man's gesture seemed so insistent that he felt he should react to it. "I happen to be one myself."

There was a flicker that might have been interest in the man's eyes.

"You're not a Southerner, are you?" asked Krishnan.

The man responded with unexpected hostility. "What difference does it make to you where I come from? Nobody told you what I am or am not."

"It doesn't matter," Krishnan answered soothingly. He was taken aback by the other person's reaction but he reminded himself that there were doors he shouldn't attempt to open. "It's nothing at all— just simple curiosity. You see, I'm from the South myself."

"I'm from the North," the man said.

It was time to try a different kind of friendliness. Perhaps an attempt at hospitality would help to relax his taciturn companion. Krishnan pulled over his suitcase and fished out a tin of cigarettes. There was nothing else he could share. He lighted one and offered the man another, pushing the suitcase back against the door and leaving the tin on top of it.

The man waved the tin away. "I never smoke." His refusal was brusque, even a little contemptuous. "I'm a Brahmin. Possibly Brahmins are different in the South."

Krishnan decided not to respond to the barb. Three hours was a long time for them to spend in a lavatory glaring at each other. It was worth some price in self-restraint to break down the animosities in the man's mind.

"South or North, we're the same. Don't make the mistake of judging Southerners by me. I'm not at all typical. I'm really rather a renegade."

The man showed no interest, so Krishnan tried a different approach.

"By the way, are you a Vaishnavite or Shaivite? I'm a Shaivite myself," he added quickly, giving him the alternative in case he wanted the way out. "Not that it means anything in particular; it's only a question of different ways of worship."

"There is only one God," the man reminded him curtly, an edge of irritation forming in his voice.

"That's exactly what I was driving at," Krishnan persisted. "Different ways but they both lead to the same truth."

It was a vague agreement, if indeed it was one at all, but he accepted it almost eagerly, hoping it would develop into something more solid.

"If that's what you think," the man demanded suspiciously, "what business is it of yours whether I'm Shaivite or Vaishnavite?"

"Oh, it isn't my business," Krishnan reassured him. He was hurt by the systematic manner in which his friendliness was being snubbed, yet that very fact provoked him to continue his explorations, as if to find a reason for his mistreatment. "I wasn't asking the question in that sense, but simply to find how much we have in common. We're both Brahmins. We ought to be able to talk. It was meant as a social question, nothing more."

"Society," the man growled. "I've had just about enough of it."

Krishnan was beginning to concede defeat now, but he was still reluctant to accept three hours of antipathy, the staring at each other in the confined and swaying space, all the more disconcerting because there was nothing else to stare at.

"I can quite understand," he said a little helplessly, hoping that the conventional train of thought would succeed in striking a chord of sympathy somewhere. "I know what it means; I've felt some of it myself. The pull of something different, something higher. Maybe it's the only truth, the only solution."

The train had gathered speed, and the wheels clicked across the rail joints in their familiar, strumming monotony. The man took a book out of the bedding roll and began to read it. Krishnan was able to make out the Sanskrit characters. It brought back recollections of the only Sanskrit he knew, and impulsively, with the awkward intonation of one to whom not just the words were unfamiliar, he began chanting the *Gayithri:*

> *Invoking you, earth, heaven*
> *And every world of darkness*
> *Let us meditate, communing*
> *On that bright steadfastness*
> *God of the shaping light,*
> *Dazzling that shines into*
> *Up-striving intellect*
> *Raising the climbing mind*
> *Into truth's calm*
> *And unattached tranquillity*
> *Peace be with wisdom, Peace.*

"It's a wonderful invocation, isn't it?" he enthused. He had a feeling for the heart of Hindu philosophy even when the subtleties escaped him. "It's so typical, the reaching up to a knowledge that is above emotion, perhaps above reason itself. In these times we need that kind of tranquillity."

"I wouldn't know," the man replied, with his familiar, guarded aloofness. "I'm not familiar with South Indian languages."

"But it isn't South Indian," Krishnan said, astonished. "It's the *Gayithri.* It's what we all learn when the thread is laid upon us. Just fancy that. And I went so far as to tell you I was a renegade."

He was, if anything, happy to find a Brahmin less one than himself. He suspected nothing. But as he spoke, he saw the flash in the man's eyes and heard the click. When he looked down the blade was there, gleaming and pointing straight at his heart.

"Don't move," said the man, "and keep your mouth shut if you want to stay alive."

He should have seen it coming, Krishnan thought. He should have known enough to leave the unsaid alone. He'd no roots himself, but that was no reason for keeping on with his questions, all the way down to the center of the man's pain. He'd gone in too deep now and he'd have to pay for the answers.

"I never argue with a knife," he responded wryly.

The phrase came out without his having designed it. He knew it was wrong as soon as it was too late. Facetiousness was a flimsy way to hide fear.

The man shook his head warningly. "Sorry, no sense of humor. It got cut with my wife's throat. Maybe," he added, stroking the threat with his voice, "maybe it would save trouble if I were to cut yours also."

"It wouldn't work," Krishnan said. His presence of mind was beginning to edge back and he spoke with the tightly controlled calmness of a man who knew that his life depended on his staying cool. "It wouldn't work. I'm heavier than you are and there would have to be a struggle. I'd yell the place wide open. People would break the door down, and then what? Even if I go, you'd be going also."

"I suppose so," the man admitted. "But don't try anything fancy."

"Mind if I smoke?" asked Krishnan.

The man spat on the floor. "Go ahead if you want to. It isn't the same thing as courage."

The cigarette tin was on top of the suitcase, and Krishnan pulled it to him. The tip of the man's knife nicked his forearm. The cut wasn't too deep, but deep enough to warn.

"You don't need a suitcase to smoke with," the man said.

"Sorry," apologized Krishnan. He wanted to stanch the blood, but he dared not take the risk.

The man grinned mirthlessly, bringing the knife closer. "Next time you won't be able to be sorry."

He watched Krishnan's fingers tremble as he lighted the cigarette. "You've no guts," he jeered at him contemptuously. "You Hindus don't have them, and numbers aren't a substitute. The British ruled you for two hundred years. Now somebody else will have to do the job. You don't have it and it isn't in your blood to stay free."

Krishnan let the jibe go in. He tried to focus his mind on what to do next. He had paid enough to get the suitcase where it was needed. The next time he would have to make certain, he would have to finish the job, he couldn't afford the second installment of warning.

Perhaps the man wasn't aware of the stratagem yet. He sat there, judge and executioner also, enjoying the situation, the preliminary trickle of blood, the slash that was pain now and would gradually become fear. He would wait for the breakdown, slowly nurse the fissure, killing only when he had an image for his contempt.

Should he play the game his way, pleading with him, imploring him? It would buy time, yes, but not the one moment of distraction that he wanted. It would put the man on the road he had mapped out already, with the end clear and beckoning to his appetite. He would toy with Krishnan, but with a catlike vigilance. It would only focus his instincts on the climax, brace him for the elation of the ending.

He had to do it another way, to lull him. The risk would be murderous but he had to take it. The man had to be made to remember, had to be asked the questions that would push him back into the nightmare of the past. Krishnan couldn't tell what the reaction would be, whether recollection would blur the cutting edge of action in the present or move the man more swiftly, more relentlessly, into the obsession and the climax of vengeance. But he had to take the chance, accept the gamble. It could buy distraction or buy a short cut to death.

"How did it happen?" he asked him, taking the plunge.

"How did you expect it to happen?" The man spoke tautly, mechanically, not even seeing Krishnan at first. It was almost as if the shadow in his mind had asked the question itself and dictated the answer. "There were six of you against myself and my wife. You did the only thing you know how to do with a woman, and when you'd done enough of it you killed her."

"It's fiendish, absolutely fiendish," Krishnan said hotly, the horror of it leaping into his face. He was so shocked that it didn't strike him that the man might be lying or that if it was done it was also done on both sides. "You were there, you saw it happen, didn't you? It's something no memory can forget. I only hope you made them pay for it."

"I was there," the Moslem said, his face flushing as the remembrance flooded back. "I ran away. I wasn't able to stand it."

"There's no need to be ashamed of it," Krishnan said gently. "There were six of them to fight with. If I couldn't have done anything, I'd have run away myself."

"You're a Hindu." The man dismissed him scornfully. "The courage you don't have won't teach you any better. I'm a Moslem. A Moslem doesn't run away from death."

His eyes were flashing, back at the brink of action, and, hastily, Krishnan had to change his approach.

"You were married a long time, weren't you?" he asked.

The man's face softened into a different memory. "One doesn't count the years," he said. "Happiness—it isn't something torn off the calendar or added in an account book. One counts it by the children and the harvests and the extra room I was able to add to the house. It's a good house too, far better than its neighbors. They started the same as I, so they can't grumble either."

Krishnan let him talk. It was working as he had hoped it would. This time perhaps curiosity might save him. The memory was coming back to the man, blurring the present with its swaying floor and the clicking chant of the train over the sleepers.

"I wanted to send my son to Lahore. I'd saved enough to start a small shop for him and he was a good, practical boy who never ran away from hard work. None of this college-education nonsense for me. Give them money, I say, and they can develop their own brains. But he never made it; he went ill of typhoid. He should have got through it, really. Heaven knows we'd raised him strong enough, and his mother was at his bedside night and day, but he was like the younger generation—they think too much and give up a little too easily, even though it's my son I'm saying it about."

Without realizing it, the man had eased back a little on his roll of bedding. He continued talking, ostensibly to Krishnan, but more so to his present desperation. He moved through his reminiscences with a sense of gratitude for what they put away.

"His mother was brokenhearted, she couldn't sleep for weeks, but the next year our daughter was married, above our social position. The father-in-law still hasn't got over it, but you should have seen my wife's face at the wedding. But it left us alone, of course. It's a funny feeling, the house suddenly seems so big, and the fields empty except for the wheat growing. You have to look at each other. There's no alternative. And it had been a long time since there'd been the time to do that. She wasn't much to look at but she was enough to come back to, enough to remember, enough to lean against, at the end of a long day, one day nearer the next year. . . ."

Krishnan waited, listening to the voice going back, to the past becoming alive, waited until he was certain of the moment, and the knife had softened, died away in the man's eyes. Then he kicked the suitcase forward with all his strength. It caught the man coming up, and Krishnan was on top of him. He drove his right fist in savagely, hardly feeling the spurt of pain as the blade meant for his heart slashed fiercely into his left arm. The man was off balance or the damage would have been worse. He went back, the suitcase clattering on top of him, his head hitting the wall as he fell. Krishnan stepped across, banging his foot in viciously where it hurt most. The man's mouth stretched back and he doubled up with the pain. The knife fell out of his hand.

Krishnan picked it up, panting, feeling dizzy himself. He shoved away the suitcase where it couldn't be used against him. The breath was whistling out of the man, and Krishnan stood over him while he fought to get his wind back.

"I'm sorry," he said. "Maybe I should have told you. A Cambridge education equips a student for anything."

The man straightened slowly and began to nurse his abdomen.

"I'm a Moslem," he said sullenly. "A Moslem knows how to die."

"You're going to stay alive," said Krishnan. "You're going to learn a lot of things you don't know."

The man scowled at him. "I suppose I have to thank you."

"Not if you don't feel like it. Sit down and take it easy. This could be the beginning of a beautiful friendship."

The man edged over to the roll of bedding.

"The other corner, if you don't mind," suggested Krishnan suavely. "And keep your legs crossed. That ought to assist you in your Brahmin pretense."

The man looked at the knife and then did what he had to. Hastily, Krishnan lighted a cigarette. He needed it badly—enough to take the chance. The man didn't jump him. His legs stayed as they were.

"You've got no guts," the Moslem insisted stubbornly. "You haven't even got the guts to kill me."

"Give any man time and he's sure to kill himself."

"Smart guy," the man said scornfully. "I knew a shopkeeper who went to Oxford once. He had more sense than you've got. But that didn't save him. He's pushing up tomatoes in a field outside Lahore. You Hindus have no guts," he proclaimed a little more cheerfully, "but I must admit you make excellent fertilizer."

"Don't stay alive too long," suggested Krishnan. "You might find out that Hindus have other uses."

The man sneered at him and subsided into silence. Krishnan took another pull at the cigarette. The blood was oozing steadily from his left arm. At first it made him feel mildly heroic, but then it began to look the way blood looks when one doesn't have too much of it. He was feeling a little faint. He told himself that it was only the aftermath of the recent violence, that it would go away as soon as his nerves were more settled. But it didn't. It neither got better nor got dramatically worse. It merely continued on its insidious course, a monotonous, regular, pulsating ebbing away that would have been almost soothing if he hadn't had to fight it. And he knew there was nothing with which he could fight. It would go on as it had to. The faintness would grow, the dizzi-

ness expand into a singing softness, and he would have to struggle
to keep the images, the swaying compartment and the landscape
separated, till they merged also and he could no longer keep awake.

He passed his right hand slowly across his forehead, feeling the
perspiration becoming clammily colder. He knew what was going
to happen now and he knew that the man with the legs crossed
knew it also. It was only a matter of time. A little more time,
another two hours or an hour gone by, and the telegraph poles
would blur in the clicking distance and the man would be on him
and the knife in his heart. There was nothing he could do, and
time would do it. He could throw the knife out, but the man
would take him anyway, and when the strength drained out there
were a dozen ways to kill. He could throw the door open and call
in the marines, but it was a mixed crowd, half Hindu and Sikh
and half Moslem, and the blood on his sleeve would be the signal
for slaughter. He had to kill the man; there was no alternative.
Now, while he still had the strength. He was fast on his feet, and
if he did it quickly, his wounded arm stifling the nascent scream
in the man's throat, maybe the crowd on the outside wouldn't
know. He had to take the chance. If the door opened they would
kill the Moslem anyway. He would only be doing what was going
to be done. It was self-defense, a man had to save himself, and if
he did it this way he might avoid the slaughter.

He looked at the Moslem. It was going on in his mind the same
way and to the same conclusion. He saw the man's lips twist downward, and that made it clear that both of them knew the same
thing.

It was as the man had said: he didn't have the guts. The truth
was he would rather die than do it.

The man's eyes were narrowing, concentrating, looking avidly
at the blood on Krishnan's sleeve. The knife was back in his eyes
now. In a little while it would be back in his hand.

The whistle shrieked. The train backlashed and ground itself
to a convulsive stop. In the compartment outside, the hubbub suddenly died down and then flared up again, but this time with a
different quality, the tense and sibilant quality of terror.

Out of the upper half of the window Krishnan could see the top of the cutting leveling off, the spokes of bicycles and the tires of a jeep and the armed men, hard faced, exultant, sliding down the sides, their curved knives gleaming, and here and there a revolver showing among them.

They had chosen the place well, a tree trunk across the cutting was enough, and if there was any trouble such as armed guards (though that could seldom be afforded) the line of fire was restricted by the slopes, and the road was probably close by for a speedy getaway.

"It's a hold-up," said Krishnan, seeing the query on the Moslem's anxious face. A surge of relief swept through him. He knew what was coming, but the law was out of his hands.

Panic showed in the Moslem's eyes as he lunged for the door.

"Stay away from it, you fool," said Krishnan warningly. His voice was down to a whisper. "If you go through it they'll kill you. Stay down and keep your mouth shut and there's just a chance that they mightn't think of looking here."

The Moslem went back to his corner. Krishnan sat down on the toilet. Outside, there was a brief subsidence and then the sounds of struggle, mounting in intensity. The butchery was in progress now, and the door that protected them could only veil the screaming.

The blood came oozing underneath the door, deepening in color, licking its way toward them.

The tumult began to die down. It thinned enough for them to hear the thud of the bodies being flung out of the windows. Then it was quieter still, quiet enough to hear the individual voices. The men were talking jubilantly, stamping their feet on the floor.

The doors slammed on the left and on the right.

The Moslem's face was beginning to live again.

Then they heard the body moving outside, the sound of the lock being rattled, the deep voice rising angrily, the tattoo on the door growing into a fusillade.

Krishnan looked at the Moslem's ashen face. He threw the knife back to him. "Take it," he said, "and sell it for what you can."

Something close to gratitude leaped into the man's eyes. He held his hand out awkwardly. "May Allah be merciful," he said.

The door burst open, and the Sikh came in. He was a big man, big enough to fill most of the entrance. He looked like his job, too. But he wasn't a professional. He'd learned it from his hands the way it happened, and some other time it need not have happened at all.

"What the devil do you suppose you're doing here?"

"I'm a Government servant," said Krishnan lightheartedly. "I need privacy for my priority files."

"Government servant be damned. That's what they all say and it doesn't save them."

Krishnan produced his passport, his Secretariat pass, his fuel ration card and his wedding photograph. The Sikh examined them carefully. He took a good look at Krishnan.

"South Indian, eh? No wonder you're a crackpot. Better be careful," he warned. "It's always better to be safe than funny."

Then he moved further in and saw the red on Krishnan's sleeve. "How the blazes did you get that?"

Out of the corner of his eye Krishnan saw the appeal flash furtively in the Moslem's face.

"I was on the town," he explained. "The girl was Moslem and she had different ideas."

"Good boy," the Sikh said. "It's the only way to live now." He didn't actually believe that, but it was the right fib, and both of them had to strut through its pretenses.

The Sikh turned to the Moslem. "Who's this string bean supposed to be?"

"He's a holy man," said Krishnan. "He's taken a vow of silence."

"Vow of silence eh! Well, he can break it long enough to say his prayers. Go on and say your prayers," he shouted.

The Moslem said nothing.

"I thought as much," said Krishnan. "He's scared of you, of course, but he's much more afraid of Shiva."

"I've had enough of this tomfoolery," the Sikh grumbled. He turned to the Moslem. "Take your *dhoti* off and we'll see how holy you are."

The Moslem's face went white and his eyes tensed.

"Take your *dhoti* off, you circumcised son of a pig."

The knife flashed upward in the Moslem's hand.

The Sikh was much bigger and he was fast for his size. The *kirpan* slashed at the other man's wrist, almost cutting the hand off. The knife clattered down, and the Sikh kicked it away. He crashed the Moslem against the wall and forced him back as he slid down, arching him helplessly against the roll of bedding. The *kirpan* plunged downward. The Moslem's uninjured arm was still free and at the last moment he was able to fight the thrust off; but the Sikh had the leverage, and after a brief struggle, he broke through. The blood spurted up. At least, thought Krishnan, it was where he would die quickly. The Sikh struck again and, unnecessarily, again, like someone carrying out a textbook plan, a movie script without regard to the facts.

He came off, and the Moslem's eyes were already glazed with death. He managed to slew his body around enough to be able to hold out his hand to Krishnan. The gratitude could still be seen in his face, even with the pain spreading over it, blotting out its humanity. Under the dulling and the crimsoning mist there was something he was struggling to recollect and make clear.

He found it, as well as the unsuspected margin of strength that made it possible for him to force the words out, against the death rattle choking in his throat. "Shiva be with you," he said. The first word came clearly, a conciliation held out; the rest, as the defeated body slumped back, was spoken more with the lips than the voice.

It would have been too much to say that he had died forgiving, but perhaps there was an end of hostility, a beginning of peace, in the mask of his relinquishment of life and the conflicting calm of acceptance it had frozen.

The knife was still there, plunged into his body. The Sikh looked at it uncomprehendingly, almost as if he didn't know who owned it. He pulled it out impersonally, tidying up the place, wiping the knife scrupulously on the nearest piece of cloth, which happened to be the fringe of the Moslem's *dhoti*. When it was bright once more he clapped the flat of the blade tentatively against his thigh. There was no exultation in the gesture. It wasn't the chest-beating of the triumphant animal. He had no reaction yet—neither exhilaration nor its converse, guilt—and Krishnan couldn't help feeling that he was puzzled by the lack of one and was trying to act his way into a response.

When he looked at Krishnan he must have seen something that loosened his emotions, because he straightened up, his chest heaving, his eyes beginning to smolder. "What the devil are you staring for?" he demanded thickly. "Don't tell me you've never seen a dead man."

"I've never seen a murder," Krishnan said. He was sickened more than a little by what had happened, and if he faced the Sikh squarely it was not out of courage or even righteousness but simply to avert his eyes from the alternative.

"Murder!" the Sikh roared. Some of the reflexes were beginning to come back. "Whose side are you on, anyway, you South Indian weasel?"

"I'm an Indian," retorted Krishnan, deliberately unemotional, so that the sense of repulsion wouldn't accidentally leak into his voice. "It may sound stupid, but I'm on the side of India."

"You think I'm not Indian!" The Sikh blazed at him furiously. "You think we haven't paid for being Indian? The thousands that are dead and the millions that are homeless. The rich land abandoned and the lives we've left behind. That's been our sacrifice for making India. What have *you* done that gives you the right to talk?"

"Of course, I've no business to lecture you—" Krishnan began.

"Then go on and spill your infernal lecture anyway. I can see it all over your sanctimonious face. If you weren't a Hindu, if you weren't hurt, I'd cut you into shreds with this *kirpan*. People like you deserve to end up dead."

"Take it easy," urged Krishnan, reasonable but helpless. He had to continue with his side of the argument, but he was beginning to feel that he wasn't reaching anything, that no matter how insistent his appeal for moderation, it would merely bounce off an armor plating of anger. "I know how you feel, but it isn't a solution. You pay and they pay, and each time the bitterness is bigger and the end of it a little farther off. The scores may be level in the end. But does it make sense if all of us are bankrupt?"

"It's easy enough for you," the Sikh retorted, his hands clenching, the anger flaming in his face. "You people sit in air-conditioned offices, decide our fate, agree to our death warrants. It's noble to preach sermons. But it's we who pay for all those fancy principles. What would *you* feel like if it started to happen to you? What would you do if you came home one night and found the house stripped clean of everything you possessed, and your wife dead on the floor with only blood for her clothing? What d'you suppose you'd do then? Would you sit on the floor and preach your sermon to her? Would you put your hands in your pockets and tell yourself that somebody somewhere has to die for freedom? Or would you run into the street bellowing about brotherly love and turn the other cheek till they bashed your head in?"

"I'm sorry," said Krishnan gently. Now that the Sikh's torment had worked its way to the surface, his own aversions had begun to relax. The ground between them was clearer, less unpromising. There was space upon it for understanding to begin.

"I'm honestly sorry," he repeated. "It never entered my head to lecture to you. But it must have sounded that way. Maybe when the flood has diminished and the fever got back to normal, and the light shines differently, it won't look like preaching."

"I left her there," the Sikh said, not hearing the apology, speaking as if he were re-enacting a dream. "I ran away from it, wanting to forget, like the other thousands who'd lost their homes and families. But it was impossible. I could never leave her. Night after night I'd struggle not to remember, but no matter how thick the walls, the blood would come through, and in my dreams I'd hear her screaming and pleading, and my mind would be trampled by the images of their filthiness. Then I'd wake up, my hand on my *kirpan,* and until the dream stopped the house would be burning with anger. I'd never killed a man till five minutes ago. I'm a mechanic; my job is to put things together. But this man, this vengeance, I've killed more times than I can ever forget."

He paused and looked narrowly at Krishnan, stating his justification, not expecting to be understood. "When my hand went down it wasn't simply my hand. And when it was over something else was over also. I was different, a chain had suddenly broken. I wasn't owned by the remembrance any more."

"And then I had to barge in," Krishnan said. "With the look on my face and the self-righteous talk about murder."

"You weren't wrong," the Sikh said. The conflict in him had subsided enough for him to be able to make and afford the admission. "I'm not saying that I didn't want to do it. I'm my own master, I'm free to do what I want. But this was something which I *had* to do also."

"It's in all of us," said Krishnan. "Someday the ember flares up. But most of the time we put it out before it gets to the dynamite."

The Sikh pulled the chain of the toilet. His face relaxed as he imagined the water running. The blood lust had never been there. He had a different look, a look of deeper relief, the relief of a man who had done an obsessive duty and whom the furies had at last forgiven.

"You wanted to save him, didn't you?" he suddenly asked Krishnan. "He wounded you and still you wanted to save him."

"I wanted to kill him once," Krishnan confessed. "I simply couldn't do it. Trying to save him was all I had the nerve for."

"I don't understand," the Sikh said, furrowing his brow. "He wanted to make mincemeat out of you. You managed to prevent that but you were too squeamish to make mincemeat out of him. Then I turned up, roaring and ready to do it, only instead of dropping me one small hint, you did everything possible to put me off the scent. If I weren't so tolerant you'd be mincemeat anyway."

"It's because I'm a Brahmin," Krishnan explained. "My reasoning processes are extremely complex."

"Maybe you're right," the Sikh said. "Or maybe you're like me, neither right nor wrong. A man does what he has to, and that's all. There's a worm eating you and you've got to obey it. Maybe there's only a different worm inside you."

He patted Krishnan on the uninjured shoulder. "You're a good sort," he told him. "But next time be more careful. A man can get killed trying to be broad-minded."

"I hope there isn't a next time," Krishnan reminded him.

"I hope so too," the Sikh said. "But this is something that we didn't start. We're living inside it, trying to keep ourselves straight. But it's more than we can reach through. Something else besides us is needed to switch off the nightmare."

He looked at Krishnan's arm. "Time we did something about that."

He went out into the compartment and rummaged in the debris. Unexpectedly, he fished out a half-empty bottle of gin.

"Put some of this in your gullet."

Krishnan did. He hadn't realized how close to unconsciousness he was, until the shock of the liquid pulled him together.

"Ready?" the Sikh asked. "Because this is going to hurt you."

He poured some water into the bottle, ripped Krishnan's sleeve off and slopped the solution into the open wound. It was worse than Krishnan had expected. He sweated and clenched with the pain of it, but he hung on and managed to keep his mouth shut.

"You've got guts," the Sikh told him admiringly.

It was too much for Krishnan, and he burst into a peal of laughter.

"I don't understand," said the bewildered Sikh. "There's no one braver than a Sikh is, but even to a Sikh this is no joke."

"Sorry," said Krishnan when his laughter had subsided. "It isn't funny at all. But it reminded me of something else that wasn't funny either."

The Sikh looked at him as if he thought Krishnan's brains were softening. "It's time I took you out of here."

He pulled a pashmina shawl off one of the dead women, ripped away the embroidered border, and made a bandage with it for Krishnan's arm.

"Let's go," he said, grimacing. "It makes me as sick as I suppose it makes you."

They went out, across the track and up the slope of the cutting to the road beside it. The Sikh had a jeep about a furlong away. "Where do you want this to take you?"

Krishnan told him. The Sikh shrugged his shoulders. He looked at Krishnan pityingly. "Nice place for a vacation, ain't it?"

"My wife works there."

"Why the devil is she mixed up in all this?"

"I was mixed up with someone else. But it isn't that simple; this is not the rebound."

"I can see from the photograph that she's a good-looking girl," the Sikh said. "If she is careful she can live to fifty. But this is no way to bring down her insurance."

"She's a South Indian," said Krishnan. "She's crazy, like the rest of us."

"Nobody has to tell me," said the Sikh.

The miles ticked off. Krishnan was grateful to have the sun pouring down upon him and for the makeshift bandage that kept the flies away from his wound. The jeep jumped up and down, jolting the pain into his arm. It wasn't much farther now: the turn into the town and the mushrooming fringe of tents where hopelessness huddled.

Kamala hadn't even an address. But the Sikh asked at the post office, and they knew her. Everyone did, they said. Sixth row and seventh tent on the way in. Jolting along among the kerosene tins and garbage, a man on a stretcher and a child in a bucket eyed the jeep with wide-eyed curiosity. Number seven, like any other place, an anonymous white igloo, with nothing to identify it but the counting fingers.

"Want to be helped in?" the Sikh asked.

"I'm feeling fine. I can make it on my own steam."

The jeep drove off, accelerating furiously into the cart track's dusty envelope. Krishnan lifted up the flap and lurched into the tent. He tried to open his eyes against the darkness.

Kamala didn't see him. There was a baby in the corner making faces at a picture of Krishnan and drinking milk out of an Allenbury bottle. When he saw Krishnan he kicked the picture sideways. Kamala put it back. Then she saw the original.

Her lips were moving but he couldn't hear what she said. Through the thickening haze her hands were reaching out to him. Then the floor hit him and the welcoming darkness swept over, deep and forbidding, like a curtain of peace.

CHAPTER SEVEN

Shantihpur

WHEN THE WORLD came back to him it was first of all her face, confirmed in the gentleness in which it always lived, not as an expression it wore but as a constancy it held to, beneath the slowly deepening lines of care and the muted play of emotion around the fine mouth. She did not smile at him. Her hands upon his face were almost impersonal. Yet he could lie there looking at her seriousness, feeling it only as a different kind of welcome.

He let it continue, reassembling itself, all that fragile, indestructible security, the lap only big enough to hold his aching head, the curve of the body exactly modeled but held back, as if a strength deeper than femininity restrained it. Her face was timeless. Tomorrow could make it haggard, pushing its sorrows under the lustrous eyes, draining the hair of its deep, glossy vitality as if each tress had brushed the body of darkness. Tomorrow could make her flesh and blood alone, instead of that radiance of earnestness which was a lamp only and would go out when the rain fell. Take anything from the face, and it would be a mask of nothingness, not even symmetrical. Take anything from her body, and even the minimal curves would start back, shriveling closer to their beginning of dust.

Tomorrow could take it all—there was so little—but tomorrow passed caressing the cheek of her gentleness, and one could look up at her and see the light still shining. She was too easy to destroy so the flood went by her unaware of the real strength. Her fragility was beyond change. But one's recognition of her changed by approaching her constancy, by seeing more clearly the strength of her receptiveness, by leaving behind one the mistakes the cruelty of which she had accepted and forgiven.

He let his silence speak to her first, since she was a child of darkness, her quietness spun out of it, her eyes with that softened serenity of the moon emerging into a rain-washed sky. He needed no words to tell her he had come back, and she gave in to his returning, accepting all of him, the hot face, the torn clothes, the blood-crusted bandage, the body he had become, without asking for its history. She did not chide him with any explicit reproof, did not mention, however matter-of-factly, the stark conditions he had forced her into, did not even indulge herself in that sudden accession of happiness which might have made clear how much he had denied her.

"We threw each other out," he told her, when he felt himself ready for the admission. "Or maybe it was something else which came to its own conclusions and then threw out the two of us."

"Silly," she assured him. "It doesn't interest me. I just want to know what happened to your arm."

He had got around the other, the more serious, pain, and the relief of it made him mildly facetious. "It's the only way for an officer to obtain leave."

The smile pulled at her, but she managed to subdue it. "You mustn't pretend to be tough," she admonished him. She could let herself reprove him for the less essential things. "The pain comes through no matter what one does, and in the end those who survive are those who bleed most easily."

He told her the whole story of the train ride, watching it happen all over again in her face. His hand caressed her, pushing against the firm flesh. Her skin was taut, responsive and translucent. Anyone's pain could reach her body through it.

"You were brave," she concluded unexpectedly, and to his surprise he saw the flash of it in her, the same admiration as when she spoke of another man, sardonic and unflinching, giving a

crowd back its dignity and courage. He remembered Vijayaraghavan's body, unconscious on the white sand, and the look on
her face when she spoke of him in the hospital. He had felt
ashamed then when the same look was denied him. Yet now that
it was given him, he found no pride in accepting it.

"Brave!" he protested, embarrassed. "Because I didn't have the
nerve to kill him?"

"Because he was your enemy and you put your life in his hands.
And when the other man came you kept on trying to save him."

"He died," Krishnan reminded her. "I didn't save him, did I?
I should have killed him or the Sikh instead."

He was starting up from her lap, and she pushed him down
soothingly.

"Bravery isn't always the feeling of courage," she said. "If you're
not used to it you may even be ashamed of it."

He fidgeted a little in her lap. "I'm an ordinary person, nothing
more. I do what I'm told to by my hands and my heart. If it goes
wrong I want to be spared the blame. When it's right I don't
deserve any testimonials."

Something incongruous struck her, and this time she couldn't
suppress the laughter. "Kruger won't give you a testimonial," she
pointed out. "Imagine how he'd feel. Gin in a Brahmin's bloodstream."

He caught the mood from her and was anxious to prolong it.
"It's our country, isn't it, Kamala, and our happiness? There's room
in it for every alcoholic. We're in the land of the five rivers, each
of them big enough to wash it all away."

"When it's all over," she said, "we'll do the penance in style.
We'll go to Amarnath in the spring's earliest pilgrimage, only
slowly, as slowly as we can, exploring everything, folding it into
remembrance, so that we can reach back always to that purifica-
tion, flower by flower in Pahalgam's beautiful valley."

"When it's all over," he echoed her, thinking of the truth outside the tent, putting the dream up against the nightmare's angry
solidity.

She wasn't disturbed by being reminded of it. "When you've

been here, when you've let it all go over you, the hope survives, just because nothing else can. Nothing—not even despair. It's like a child; it just wants to be bigger and different, it doesn't need a promise or a reason."

A yell from the corner interrupted the train of her thoughts.

"It's the child," said Krishnan. "The arbitrary dreamer has awakened. Attend to him. He has longer to live and his needs are much more serious."

She put the curved bottle in and tickled the child's navel. It gurgled and kicked responsively, then subsided, sucking contentedly at the white world. Krishnan liked the way Kamala tended the baby—not with a nurse's detachment, not with a mother's avid tenderness, but with an unaffected fondness that was simply and supremely reassuring, establishing neither a claim nor a dependence.

"How did he come to you?" he inquired.

"I don't know exactly," she said. "I really never asked. Not that it doesn't matter tremendously, but when there is so much sorrow one doesn't want to explore it, only look after the promise that it gives. Maybe his parents were killed before everyone left, and somebody found him lost and brought him away. Or maybe they died in the attack along the route. All I know is that I found him, the youngest, with only a gold *mohur* chain on his naked body and a copy of the *Gita,* which he kept on chewing. I suppose, really, it was because of the book that I took him."

"Don't tell me," he said, touched, "that his name is Krishnan also."

"How could you have known?" she asked with beguiling innocence.

He went over to look at his adopted image. The child stared at him with truculent curiosity, jelly-necked and tire-thighed, proud because he owned a body and two legs. He looked at the picture and at the original masterpiece, both manifestations of the same enormous fuzz. Then he raised his foot like an umbrella, shutting infinity out, focusing himself on the supreme fascination of belonging to his big toe.

"He's like me," concluded Krishnan. "Unable to face reality."
She put the child across her hip.

"It's time to leave now," she said. "You haven't shaved, you look positively villainous. Nobody will believe you've really reformed."

She went out into the street, or whatever it was that the two lines of tents had marked out and the coming and going of the unshod feet had flattened. The weight on her hips was vociferous and vivacious, and gave her stride a rhythm it hadn't previously possessed. But she had an additional confidence; it was not poise, or self-assurance, or anything ostentatious, but the quiet glow, the satisfied sense of purpose, of one who had accepted the law in its cruelty and survived it.

The hospital was some distance away and was, naturally, the town's noblest building, which meant that it had a tiled roof in addition to four walls. There were planks supported by upended drums of DDT on which the less stoic of the patients sat. But there was matting on the floor, which wasn't necessary. There were flowers, and insecurely hung pictures from calendars, which showed that the grace and affection of a woman had walked through. In the corner Shiva danced, the out-thrust arms pulling the flames back to the verge of life, and the *Gita* lay open at his feet at the page where Lord Krishna said that nothing died.

Krishnan had to take his place in the line in front of the medical officer's room; Kamala was not one to give him any special position, even though he was her husband and was injured. He waited with the others who had a life to wait for, a gift unknown, perhaps to them unwanted. The future was the white tents, the brown, deep distance going east and south, a mirror that one could look into and see any face, except those over which the past was healing. There were sick men there, with cataracts in their eyes, or the twitch of fever, or knife wounds of battle under the makeshift bandages. It was right to go on as if there were no other sicknesses. One healed what one could, and death or understanding would have to heal the rest.

It was two hours, perhaps a trifle more, before his turn came.

There was no wall, only an improvised screen, to mark off the medical officer's room. He pushed aside the discarded sari covering the orifice which was supposed to be the doorway.

The M.O. had the only desk in the place—two packing cases with a purloined swing across them to give the furniture that luxury look. He was an inch or so shorter than Krishnan, a precise, small-boned, economically built man. He could have been dapper in another country with a higher grade of tailoring. At this moment he had the slightly unreal expression of someone trying to cure himself of insomnia in a hurricane.

"You're Krishnan, aren't you? Kamala's wandering husband? Won't you sit down and tell me about the milkmaids?"

Asking him to sit was an abstract courtesy since there was no chair. Krishnan helped himself to a cleared corner of the desk.

"The original Krishna had ten thousand wives," he said. "You're much more like him, with five thousand patients."

He took his shirt off, and the M.O. looked at the bandage.

"Nasty, isn't it? Did the Englishwoman bite you? I'm told they do that when they're emotionally aroused."

"It was done with a knife," Krishnan answered lamely. He had wanted to tell the whole story, but having gauged the M.O.'s reaction, he concluded that any explanation might sound boastful.

The doctor's retort was in the mood he had set, in character, but obviously so, a little too proclaimed, too aggressive, to be real. "How temperamental. The Italian style. I go to the movies, you see," he added unnecessarily. "The poor man's substitute for foreign travel."

He made the innuendo plain enough. Cambridge education be damned was at the bottom of all that he said, of the alert eyes with their put-on, penetrating look, worn so continually that it was part of the man: a hospital is where you take off your pretenses; you've come to the right place to be seen through.

Krishnan couldn't help wincing as the doctor dressed the wound. "This ought to have happened in a movie."

"Kamala told me about it," said the M.O. "Wonderful girl. What business has she got here?" Even his gestures were, like his sentences, clipped, precise, unnaturally labor-saving, as if he were conforming to a picture of himself.

"She made her own decision," Krishnan said. "So there has to be a reason, there always is one with her. Not superficially, of course. But deep down in her there must be a question, and being here is the beginning of an answer."

The M.O. looked incredulous. "It's a pretty way of thinking," he observed. "But you wouldn't believe it if you watched her at work. She was sick the first time she saw blood. She still shivers whenever she puts in the needle. She isn't paid for what happens to her, is she? Or is she?"

"She isn't so different from you," Krishnan argued. "Naturally you've no choice but to remain here if this is the station to which you've been assigned. But there's no reason to kill yourself trying to look after others. Unless, of course, the reason is humanity."

"Humanity be blowed," the M.O. exploded. It was plain that he mistrusted the word, that it opened dangerously for him into a nonclinical and therefore sterile vagueness. "Just put humanity on a twenty-four-hour stint, and you can throw it away like any cast-off bandage. You don't need humanity to deal with an avalanche. All you need is a strong arm and a good shovel."

"And the desire to use them," Krishnan added.

"You don't have to call that humanity," said the M.O. "It's a sense of duty, that's all, if one wants to sound pompous about it. Or professional pride, if one prefers to be honest." An afterthought struck him—which it seldom did. "Maybe it's different with Kamala," he conceded. "She's so gentle she makes pride seem indecent. But if the ordinary man stands up, it's only because he's built around a backbone. What he needs is a function, a job and not a philosophy."

"Only," objected Krishnan, "the job has to fulfill him."

The M.O. looked at him almost pityingly as he wound the bandage. "Fulfillment, self-expression!" He spoke of the ideas with a resigned exasperation, as if they were hypochondriac patients. "They're very nice zinnias, but in a different garden. They can't be cultivated in our soil. Out here a man's fate is frustration; he's born for defeat. You'll learn what it means when you've had it happen to you. When you've had to face them coming out of the North in thousands and put them together—the little one can—from the pieces. It can't be done on the basis of self-fulfillment. It isn't enough to live with a cash register, adding up satisfaction with every piece of carpentry."

"I never said," protested Krishnan, "that self-fulfillment was enough by itself. But you know perfectly well that pride isn't the answer either. There has to be something else—faith, I suppose, if one wants to be grandiose, but at least the feeling that one's honesty is part of a larger will, and that little by little the will can alter the facts."

"Pride," said the M.O. emphatically, putting the lid down on the troublesome thoughts. "It's the poor man's Scotch, the all-purpose tropical medicine. If you try to face it with reason or your so-called faith you'll go crazy. If you face it with sympathy you'll bleed to death in five minutes."

He had finished the bandage and made a sling for the arm.

"The gin saved you from gangrene," he told Krishnan. "If you're sentimental, worse things can happen, of course. Come back on Tuesday; you'll be two days wiser. Kamala's brew won't save you from the scorpions."

Krishnan went back through the anteroom into the street. Kamala's workday was still far from over, so he drifted back to the tent. He warmed a chapatti on the makeshift fireplace, ate it and shaved himself, trying to confirm his reformation. Then he lay down on the rainbow-striped mat, leaving her the worn, soiled mattress. The pain in his arm seemed to leak into him; it numbed him and added a not unpleasant weight of exhaustion to his drowsiness.

It was night before she came. He awakened, sensing her presence as she entered, her frail shoulders slumping, the child asleep at her hip. She called to him, asking him if he wanted supper. It was the day's last duty, and he pretended not to hear, letting her slide down beside him, too weary to undress. She was asleep as soon as her head touched the pillow. He waited a little to be sure he would not disturb her and then lighted his cigarette, watching the small glow pick up her frailty from the dark. Curled up in repose, she was even smaller, and as he looked down her length it was over so quickly, so disturbingly quickly, that he had to do it again to make sure he hadn't left anything out.

An hour or so later the child cried, and she stumbled across the floor to give it its milk. When she came back her eyes were open and, looking at him, she saw his open too. Her wan smile showed her exhaustion, but the darkness sweetened it. He drew her to him, treasuring her fragility, trying very gently to coax the tiredness out.

"Kamala," he said. "Why must you do it, Kamala? Is it because of the difference it makes to others?"

She pulled herself closer, nuzzling her head against his chest. "No," she replied. "It wouldn't be right to pretend I'm that unselfish. It's simpler here. In all the sorrow and maybe even because of it, one feels a certain sense of explanation. When everything ordinary is broken you come closer to understanding the little that won't break."

"You don't feel defeated," he asked her, wanting the conviction he could not quite reach, "by the size of it and by everything you can't do?"

She was too tired to carry on a discussion, but the answer came from her like a response of her body, something that was unshakably herself, that must have grown through many such misgivings.

"Sometimes," she told him, the slumber floating in, "everyone feels defeated. But then the very size of it becomes a means of hope. It should be irresistible, yet there is always something it cannot sweep away. It brings you close to the heart of everyone's dignity."

He held it and the relaxing body with it, and then let them go down into that quiet fulfillment where a profounder peace than sleep possessed her. It was her law, he realized, and her life. But what could it mean to ordinary people who sought fulfillment in less frightening places and who, when they were driven against disaster, arose to fight it with a more animal dignity? Were the

consolations the same whatever the person? Or was the M.O. right
—did it have to be something else, the religion of habit, custom,
prejudice, pride, any stupefaction but the clear cleansing light from
which there could never be any hope of concealment?

2

When he next saw the M.O. things had got worse, not for his
arm but for the standards it was supposed to hold up. The last
influx had been the largest, so large in fact that Kamala had
not come back. He had waited in the tent till his own futility
seemed to stretch further than the shadows that he could almost
imagine in the brilliant moonlight. Then he had left to see what
the uninjured half of him could do with the whole problem. He
had wandered in, well meaning but aimless, the better side of
him toward the camera, passing bottles and bandages into bedlam.
He had helped to lever a screaming person onto the makeshift platform they had to use for surgery and had watched with sickened
fascination the futile attempt to pull together the grim lips of the
deep gash, so that the ebbing of the lost life could be uselessly
protracted.

There were more atrocities among the refugees than before. The
little settlement had seen blood and sickness often, but the sensation was different this time, like the painful twitch of feeling in
numbed flesh. There had to be an end to it somewhere, people
were saying. There was only one way to talk back. Nobody wanted
it but one had to answer for the sake of self-respect, and in the
end that meant self-preservation also. If the sword wasn't used people would think one was afraid to use it. Those on the other side
respected only strength. They were fanatical men, they had lived
with ancient demons, they had ruled India and wanted to turn the
clock back.

The people came together, emotion gathered in knots, the common surge of anger holding hands, joining, rejoining, till the

solid wall was built. The air was heavy, threatening, eager for the flame and the explosion.

In the hospital the mood was less intense. The patients were too tired to call for vengeance, and Kamala was everywhere, putting her gentleness between them and the memory. But even in the rooms the tension mounted. Those who were helping began to wear different faces; they had suddenly had enough, the meekness ended, it was easier to maim than to redeem. The toll might be larger, but the books would be balanced.

The M.O. saw Krishnan and waved mockingly to a crate. "Mount it and deliver your lecture on humanity. See if you can stop this one with your preaching. Tell them the saintly and the shocking moral. Anyone's life is worth more than your own."

"You've no business in this room," retorted Krishnan. "The place for the war dances is outside."

"I'm a civilized man," the M.O. said. "All my life I've lived two inches from the end of it. I know how much it means, how little it is worth. I stand around in a white suit and save lives, it's my job, my function, it's simply what I'm paid for. I could be the same man in a uniform and be paid to take life also."

Krishnan passed him the swab for which he was reaching. "You're just pretending," he answered. "You're scared that there won't be a meaning, scared of the questions that you'll have to ask. But pride needs an explanation also. Why should you stand up when it's easier to fold up?"

"When I was very young," the M.O. said, "I saw the movie that changed my whole approach. The man was six-two, with photo-genic biceps, an ox of a swine, with 'white man's burden' written all over his shoulders. The woman toyed with the handsomest local nigger because in a humid climate there was nothing better to do. The husband couldn't forget that he'd been to Oxford, and since he was sensible the termites ate him. When calamity came the brown men like me collapsed. He had a terrible time, the white man, even with that physique, carrying the whole of Assam by himself. But he fulfilled his destiny and the woman also."

He pulled the thermometer out of a mouth and scanned it.

"Nothing worse than a common chill, thank heaven. He can lie down in a corner and shiver it off."

"If that's all you remember," Krishnan told him, "you must have had a peculiar adolescence. There must be something else wrong with you besides your having gone to the wrong movie."

"It's all I need to remember," said the M.O. "I hate the white man because I hate his legend. I hate the exclusive clubs and the snooty memsahibs, and the pimply brats who won't play with our own. They've gone out, rubbing their hands, pretending to be noble. They think if we're left alone we're going to fall to bits, that we haven't the stamina or the pride to live through. I hate them because they think we're vermin."

"But they've left anyway," Krishnan protested. "What happens to us depends entirely on us. It's what we do that counts, not what they think."

The M.O. walked over to a basin and slopped some water into his face. He was swaying a little with the weariness. He rolled his sleeves back and his hands were trembling. "I know what England means to you. You stayed there through its greatness. To you it's the beaches of Dunkirk and the Spitfires climbing in the sky of Kent. To me it's my superior officer, dead drunk, telling me that brown men have no guts. It's the torrents of people coming down with the rivers, all the sick bodies and the blood and the misery. It's what they left me and what they think I can't handle."

"They've gone," insisted Krishnan. "Surely that's all that really matters. Nobody leaves a house clean. Isn't it enough that they had a sense of history, that they weren't entirely blinded by the past, that they saw what was coming and left before it was too late?"

"It's a great virtue," the M.O. said sardonically. "Particularly when you're going downhill."

"Well, it isn't a virtue that every country has. And it's rather more than being conscious of the writing on the wall. In a sense they taught us how to do the writing. I don't think of them as a nation of philosophers, but it does take honesty to swallow one's own lessons."

"You're quite like Kamala," the M.O. said. "You think that forgiveness is the same thing as cleanliness. Being angry is a better disinfectant."

"I'm no more forgiving than you are," Krishnan assured him. "Maybe I've learned a little of how to face it. You want it to be fate, the inherited agony. It's every Indian's instinct for a *Karma,* the rock of circumstance, one cannot hope to alter. It's the hidden consolation which you don't dare admit. But it isn't true. Of course it isn't true. You can change it as well as simply fight it."

"I'll take my medicine," the M.O. retorted harshly, "the way my ancestors and the foreign devils brewed it. I look at my life, and England is every insult I have suffered. I look at the map, and it's a not too shapely island, with an oversized rump, turning its back on Europe."

"It won't work," warned Krishnan. "You've got to spit in order to stay alive. It won't work because there isn't enough saliva."

Kamala came in, putting the pot down and rubbing her eyes with her free hand. She had concocted something with rice and ingenuity.

"You must eat," she exhorted them. "I don't know what it tastes like but it's warm."

"Magnificent," enthused the M.O. after the first spoon. "It's what your husband should have said, of course. Now that I've done so, he can tell you the truth. He's training himself to be a specialist in that."

"It's nothing to rave about, naturally," Krishnan confessed. "But the wonder is, Kamala, that you did it at all."

"You see," she proclaimed happily to all and sundry, "how unflinchingly honest he is. He can even face the fury in its kitchen. And you haven't looked after him," she told the M.O. reproachfully. "Just look at his filthy bandage. You're jealous of him because he has only one arm."

"He doesn't deserve to be normal," scoffed the M.O. "He came

all the way up here in a lavatory and then has the nerve to tell
me I can't spit."

"He's absolutely right," said Kamala firmly. "You're supposed
to be an example."

"You're all against me," the M.O. complained, but more matter-
of-factly, without his earlier tenseness, "because I won't see beyond
the blood and the dirt and the suffering. I've got a job to do, I
need the will to do it. I can't take the risk that there isn't a meaning. So I don't waste time and confidence looking for it. Let it
happen whatever way it has to. There isn't much of me but I'm
ready for the worst. I can't change it but it also can't change me."

He got up, thrusting his hands in his pockets, propelling himself unsteadily to the sickroom. Kamala seized him gently by the
sleeve.

"You must rest a little. You're too tired to go on."

"I'll take a vacation when the enemy does."

"You want to do the job, don't you?" she cajoled him. "You'll
do it better if you come to it refreshed. Go in and lie down.
There isn't anything that won't wait for two hours."

He grumbled a little but he was half out on his feet and was
asleep almost before he lay down.

"Oughtn't he to have a pillow?" Krishnan asked.

"He'd throw it away even if I could find one."

She moved closer to Krishnan across the colored mat and rested
her head on his uninjured arm. "You must be ever so tired, dear,"
she said. "You really ought to sleep too."

"After you, dearest," he responded gallantly.

Looking up into his, her eyes shone gratefully, and then, despite herself, her head drifted down. He stayed there, supporting
her until he felt her relax. Then he edged around gingerly, lower-
ing her to the floor, cradled in his free arm. When she was fast
asleep he maneuvered the arm out. He knew that the child's cry
would awaken her so he went across and sat down beside it.
When its eyes snapped open he popped in the bottle. It sucked
and gurgled approval of his timing. It lay there waiting, cogitating,
kicking. It didn't care what the enormous future contained, it was

innocent energy which was the same thing as hope, the world was a gigantic, fascinating fuzz, and little by little it would push its way in.

He tickled the child and it looked back at him with a faintly scandalized, peremptory brilliance, its head wagging unsteadily in pleasure and reproof. It fell asleep when it seemed most wide awake. The toy that fed it would return when its eyes opened.

It must have been all that Krishnan had been waiting for. A man called for water and he poured it out of a *cooja*. Then he lay down beside her, snuggling his head against the small breasts, scarcely moving in the plain, uncared-for bodice.

Everything dimmed and even the sensation of her presence hazed away slowly into a distant perfume.

3

He awoke with the nasty taste in his mouth and the unsteadiness that came of sleeping at the wrong time.

Kamala and the M.O. were standing over the man. He hadn't been there when Krishnan fell asleep. He was wasted and ashen, the stare of the end in his eyes, convulsed again and again by fits of vomiting that seemed to tear open his insides. His mind must have turned the corner already, though his body fought on with a detached animal frustration, as if beyond the gray, angry leaving of life, there might exist an even deeper bitterness.

His wife crouched at the foot of the prostrate body watching it, the sweat-beaded skin, the mouth bared back, the moan first trembling then tearing out of the coma as he doubled up, retching and gasping painfully. It was written in her face also, but not as despair to which the numbness in her had not yet reached out, but only as the opening of a loneliness her life would walk through to its own ashen ending.

"You should have brought him earlier," the M.O. was telling her, shrugging his shoulders.

"I was afraid, Sahib," she explained, "of what might be said. I did not dare bring him while the others were coming."

"This is a hospital," the M.O. protested, angry with the woman. "It is a place of healing. Perhaps we could not have saved him, but if you had come earlier, we might have saved the others."

"It is God's will," she said a little distantly, her intonation sing-song, her eyes dark with a different preoccupation.

"We will do what we can," the M.O. assured her. "Remember that that is his will also."

Kamala helped her to her feet and she left, shuffling away, looking back over her shoulder as if she expected recognition to leap on her from the night and as if, when it came, there would be nothing for it to possess.

The man groaned, his body twisting, his legs lashing out, and Kamala shivered as she held his hand.

"Is there any hope for him?" Krishnan asked the M.O., swallowing uncomfortably, wishing he could say something a little less banal to the reality of the tense body and its struggle.

The M.O.'s face was serious, his voice emptied of its customary truculence. "He's sick enough to die like anyone else. The trouble is what he's sick with. It's cholera. It's all we need to tear this place wide open."

It was some seconds before any of them spoke. They realized that they should have expected it, that it was really only good fortune which had enabled Shantihpur to escape an epidemic, but the settlement had lived from ordeal to ordeal, each shutting out the imagining of the next.

The M.O. was the first to break the silence. "You can leave if you want to," he said to Krishnan and Kamala. "You've probably caught it already, but there's no need to stay here and die of it if you haven't. It'll be six days before the vaccine arrives."

"Nothing doing," said Krishnan. "The civil service is worse."

It was feeble, but enough to turn the trick. The M.O. smiled and patted Krishnan's shoulder. "It's my duty, but thanks for making it yours."

His manner became more businesslike. "Only the three of us

are to come near him. The water is boiled as a matter of routine but the routine is to be checked. Nothing uncooked is to be eaten by anyone. The excreta and the vomit must be burned. Everything that touches him and every utensil must be sterilized."

"But what about those outside?" asked Kamala urgently. "It's they who matter and about whom we should be thinking. He may not live but they can, if we warn them now, if we tell them what to do and how to fight."

"It may not be possible to warn them," said the M.O.

Krishnan saw the bewilderment in Kamala's face and hit out, the exasperation rising, spurred by resentment with that fatalism which he thought he recognized and was coming to hate.

"What the devil d'you mean we can't warn them? You and your lousy do-it-yourself pride. It's everyone's business. Stop carrying the Punjab on your shoulders. Go out there and tell them. Or if you can't, I'll be the town crier myself."

The M.O. looked at him as if he were not enjoying some grim joke. "Just think a little, puddlebrain," he said, "before mounting your centipede and going off to fight the dragon. She wasn't wearing a veil, of course, but that was because she was too afraid to wear it. The trouble isn't simply that he has cholera. The trouble is that he's a Moslem also."

He had timed the revelation well, and there was a smile almost of satisfaction on his face as he disclosed it. Even when the drama was that of his own defeat he couldn't resist exploiting the theatrical niceties.

They stood before him, his bewildered audience, nonplused, their determination stopped dead, trying to feel the edge of it with their minds. It was shocking to them, but not beyond expectation, as they began to realize. The Moslems were leaving but many still remained, and it could begin among them as well as anywhere else. It wasn't unexpected and it had the irony that was proper to disaster. Death was beyond distinction and would poison the living who were not.

It was time to resist, the strength of the facts proclaimed that, but who was the enemy to be? Was it the sick bodies in the constricted houses with the whimpering, fear-tainted voices beside them, or the fever in the mind flashing to violence, as the more ordinary everyday contagion was revealed?

Kamala was the first to break the silence with that decisive simplicity of hers that could have been obstinacy in anyone less convinced.

"It isn't different because they are Moslems," she said. "It just makes it more difficult to do what has to be done. They're sick, they're in danger, and our duty is to care for them. If they're afraid to come to us because they don't trust us, or because they can't risk being discovered, then it's our responsibility to go out and bring them in."

The M.O. looked at her, admiring but incredulous. "You may as well broadcast it," he objected. "They've only to see one stretcher coming out of there and they'll tear every Moslem in the town to pieces. It's all that's needed in order to spark the dynamite."

"She's right," declared Krishnan, coming in on Kamala's side. Loyalty restrained him from adding that what was right was probably not practical. His mind groped for the matter-of-fact, sensible justification. He laid it down like a defensive wall. "Cholera can't be concealed," he began to reason. "Sooner or later the whole town will find out. Once they do it'll be too late to help anyone. But maybe we can do something to stop it if we act now and act without hesitation."

"It's more than we can handle," the M.O. said. "There's trouble enough here without our looking for it. I've never asked patients whether they were Hindu or Moslem, and I've taken this man in, knowing clearly that it's dangerous. But if they need help they can make it their business to come here."

"But it's your business too," Krishnan protested. "This may be the beginning of an outbreak, and it's your responsibility to get it under control. It isn't for me to tell you how to do it, but you certainly can't curb an epidemic by sitting here twiddling your thumbs and inviting it to report to your front veranda."

"Show me a better way," the M.O. challenged him. "I'll listen to you with respect. You've been so brilliant in solving lesser problems."

Krishnan remained as unruffled as he could. "I know nothing of medical matters," he said soothingly. "But it's possible, isn't it, that the outbreak is still localized and that only a few people are infected? If we can bring them in, we might still be able to keep things under control. And even if we can't, we'd be helping people who'd otherwise be abandoned to die. It's half past twelve now, and I imagine that by eight in the morning everyone will know. It's a question of using those hours to the best advantage."

He became aware as he finished that the M.O. hadn't been listening to the argument. He was looking at them both intently but not with the manner of a man trying to stare them down. There was a faintly guilty cast to his expression, as if he were fighting something in himself.

"You're right," he said, uncomfortably and slowly. "They're going to find out, the mob will take it over. Only, if we're in it they'll destroy the hospital also."

So that was it, thought Krishnan. Even the M.O. was in love with something. Even he listened to a voice beyond pride. The words, sarcastic and eager to be rubbed in, rushed up in his mind, but, catching Kamala's look, he held them back.

"You're a doctor," she told the M.O., not rebuking him but rather as if she were pulling him back to a conviction and a law within himself. "Do as a doctor should. Whatever the consequences, do the right thing, do as your calling tells you."

"I'm a doctor," the M.O. agreed defensively. "That's why I can't decide. What good am I without my tools, my hospital?"

"Your task is to heal," she said quietly but with her typical, relentless, almost persecuting gentleness. "Whoever the sick are, whatever their religion. You've always been equal to your duty. It makes no difference if it's suddenly bigger."

She saw his expression wavering and pushed home her advantage. "You're a doctor and an Indian. You can build nothing if you don't begin with righteousness."

It seemed to convince the M.O. He spoke with something of his old belligerence, as if part of the burden had been taken off his mind.

"You're right," he agreed decisively. "I'll do it the way it ought to be done, without compromises, every inch to the end of it. I'm an Indian and I want to do it well. I want no white man *tut-tutting* in my ashes."

If Kamala was taken aback by the unexpected reasoning she didn't allow the chagrin to reach her face. Perhaps it was because she wanted overwhelmingly to have the right thing done. Or perhaps she believed that in the clarity of crisis the right deed would eventually pick out the right reasons. She looked at Krishnan and the M.O. with relief, as if a principle had been saved and not as if an argument had miscarried.

"It's night and a dark one," Krishnan reminded them. "Perhaps we can bring the sick in before day breaks."

"Good idea," agreed the M.O. "We'll bring them around the edge of the settlement and then in through the least congested part."

He saw Krishnan getting ready to leave and shook his head.

"Nothing doing, my dear fellow. It's work that needs two hands, and you're in no condition for it. I'll take one of the bearers; it's about time they did something besides smoking those filthy *bedees*. You'd better stay and look after Kamala. She's having a hard time and mustn't wear herself out."

He went out by the back door. It took only a few steps for the night to engulf him and the bearer completely. The darkness would help them, Krishnan realized with relief, and might even enable them to complete their work undetected. He began to feel almost a friendliness toward the night, to the velvety richness sequinned by faint stars, to the new moon stifled in the gray, billowing clouds. He had touched it often in his thoughts, melodramatically, as a cloak for treachery, or as a dissolution making more insistent the prowling, ambiguous incitements of the jungle. It had a different texture in his imagination now, with its concealments serving a better end than violence.

Kamala busied herself with the patients, with the man going down, inexorably, to a different darkness, the seed of the unknown relentlessly branching out, spreading through, strangling the defiant body. His struggling was still convulsive, but feebler. His agony seemed to come from a different world.

Kamala sat by him, her face pale with the tenseness. She could not help him, or slow the recession of his life, or hold back the blossoming of the tree's livid branches. She could not even reach him through the thickening numbness. Yet she seemed unconscious of her own futility, and Krishnan wondered whether she stayed by the clenched, prostrate figure to soothe away pain, or to bestow compassion, or because in the clarity of his struggle, she saw for herself some pitiless understanding. He went into the anteroom, and the Nataraja was there, the hurricane lamp that hung from the ceiling creaking and swaying so that the shadows behind the bronze image lunged and leaped with a demonic, concentrated energy. But the god itself was still, as if the quintessence of motion were repose, as if only the reflections moved and maimed, and as if, beyond them, shaping them, discarding them, one could reach the source of change and its serenity. The mind went over the exultant, lusting body and was tranquil, as if ambiguously blessed, as if no matter how deep the emptiness or obsessive the violence, the infinite arms reached out, the great foot trampled, the desperations came back to a meaning, which conferred truth because it was beyond desire. It was not the catharsis of art—there was no purgation, no refinement, no transmutation of the strength of darkness. It was as if one were raised into the mystery's center, into the transformation of the god's eye, as if the destruction shimmering on the leaping muscles, sucking down the thin wail of the dying man, was not a barbarism to be subdued, a violence to be disciplined, but a jubilation that absorbed the flesh, the rivers and the peaks of comprehension being but one hair of the unanswered stillness.

He always felt so toward the singing chain of destruction—the aging, the tarnishing gradually to green—and toward the enchanted circle which the branching arms broke open, so that the inner darkness joined the outer. Perhaps, like Kamala, he could watch the man go down and feel the seduction of a different whirlpool, the merciless, impartial vortex of the truth.

The cool air blew in and he shook the thoughts out. He must have been tired. Lack of sleep made one dizzy. The M.O. was back, wiping the sweat from his face.

"That's one more safe," he said matter-of-factly. If he had any feeling of relief or of achievement there was nothing in his manner to suggest it.

"Are there many more of them?" Krishnan asked.

The M.O. shrugged his shoulders. "I wouldn't know. I wasn't able to investigate."

It angered Krishnan, and the exasperation was evident in his voice. "Fine lot they are, I must say. We take the man in even though it's risking a riot. We stick our necks out going back for the rest. What are we supposed to do next, cut our throats in order to gain their confidence? Or haven't they even the sense to save themselves?"

The M.O. shook his head. "You've got it wrong, my dear fellow. It isn't them, it's the bearer. He's found out what the job meant and he isn't likely to go back for more. It was all I could do to get this one to the hospital."

Kamala had come in and heard his last remarks. "You shouted at him, didn't you?" she asked.

The M.O. looked uncomfortable. "I threatened to knock his teeth in, of course. I'd have done it too if he hadn't got down to his job."

"You've no right to behave as if you owned him," Kamala protested.

"I can imagine what's around the corner," scoffed the M.O. "Free India and the dignity of its people."

Kamala flushed slightly and her expression stiffened. "It isn't a question of whether we're free or not—"

"Don't mind him," cut in Krishnan. "He's carrying the white man's burden so he has to do it like a pukha sahib."

"It's easy enough to preach," retorted the M.O. "I have to get results. These people obey you only if you convince them there's something worse than obedience."

"You can't convince them with fear," Kamala said, in that characteristic way of hers, as if she had always lived with the big words and put the precision of her trust around them. "You can only convince them with the knowledge of rightness."

"Try it," suggested the M.O. skeptically, angrily. He shouted for the bearer, and the man came in, slouching, dragging his feet, shuffling them over each other, looking at the ground first, then mulishly at the three of them.

"The Memsahib wishes to speak to you," said the M.O. "She is under the delusion that you have better instincts."

"We know how you must feel," Kamala began. "We only want you to do what you know is right."

The bearer's eyes met hers in resentful deference. "I'm an honest man, Memsahib. I do whatever I'm paid for."

"This is something for which you can never be paid."

The bearer respected her, and Krishnan could sense the effort he made to reach up to her thoughts, before his mind, failing, slipped back into its familiar groove.

"I'm a poor man, Memsahib." The tune had begun to play, and he went on mechanically with its rhythm. "I'm a poor man I've children to protect."

"Then do what you're told to," exploded the M.O. "If you value your job. If you don't want your sisters and your daughters to curse you."

"You won't be dismissed," said Kamala reassuringly, soothing away the familiar fruitless threatening. "Not even if you can't bring yourself to help us."

"Memsahib," he said imploringly, "I'm a poor man and all my life I've walked in the footprints of my betters."

"No man deserves to do that," she replied. "It is for every man to make his own path."

He shrugged his shoulders and looked uncomfortable, dejected, as if he were twisting away from the responsibility. "I'm worth very little but at least I'm worth something alive. Dead, I'm not even worth the cost of throwing my ashes in the Jumna."

"You're a coward," the M.O. said contemptuously, as if he were kicking the word into the man's face.

The bearer bristled a little for the first time. "I do what I'm paid for. If they're as ill as that, they can take the risk of coming here. I'm not paid sixty rupees a month to stick my throat out over a Sikh's *kirpan*."

"Don't you understand?" urged Kamala. "Don't you understand that they're too afraid to come here?"

"They're Moslems," he snapped back, with a sudden revealing flare of anger. "If the hand is gangrenous we must cut off the hand."

"You couldn't cut off anything," sneered the M.O. "You're a coward pure and simple. Just plain blue funk behind the holy excuses."

"Take it easy," Krishnan intervened. "It's no use charging into the poor blighter like that. I wouldn't do it either for sixty rupees."

"Well, it was your precious idea," said the M.O. "Going out and bringing them in. If I'd had the sense of my instincts I'd have sat here and let them come to us."

"Don't crowd me," Krishnan warned him. "The great escapist always gets out of corners. It was my idea, just as you said, so I'll carry the other end of the stretcher myself."

"With one arm?" the M.O. asked incredulously. "Even the ox in the movie couldn't do that."

"I don't need to use either arm," explained Krishnan. "It can be slung from my shoulders with the webbing from one of the *charpoys*. I'd simply hold one end up and carry it back and forth. Of course, you'd have to arrange to get the patients on it."

The M.O. shook his head. "Your shoulder isn't in such good condition either. It couldn't take the strain. It would open the wound and slowly tear your arm out."

"I'll go then," said Kamala decisively.

Amazed but also reluctantly admiring, the M.O. stared at her.

"You're crazy," he said. "Stark crazy, like any saint. You're carrying conviction beyond the limits of reason."

"Please," appealed Krishnan. "You've done enough, Kamala, much more than enough. Leave it alone, for heaven's sake don't do it."

The M.O. turned to the bearer. "Take note," he thundered. "You unworthy son of an illegitimate father. You see now what your miserable obstinacy has accomplished. Be warned, you abominable concentration of cowardice. If anything happens to her, every God will curse you."

"Stop it!" protested Kamala. "He's not to be bludgeoned in that way."

She turned to the bearer, speaking to him simply but with her deepest gentleness, as if she were reaching out with her convictions, trying to make them part of him.

"Don't do it," she appealed, "only because you want to stop me from doing it."

Perhaps the film had always been over the man's eyes, the refusal to look at the sun, the veiling of a routine that, day after day, shut out the light and its cruelty. Perhaps, thought Krishnan, he wasn't really seeing anything more clearly. But at least there was something else in his expression, the proof that his apathy had been touched and not tormented, the thankfulness of an additional misting over.

"I'm a poor man, Memsahib," he began familiarly.

"We've heard that one before," the M.O. scoffed.

"I'm a poor man," the bearer repeated, suddenly putting dignity into the words. "My life is not worth the sandals of your own. I'm poor, Memsahib. In the eyes of better men I count for nothing, but my gratitude is richer than myself."

"Please," appealed Kamala. "Don't think of yourself in that way. Whatever you do, don't do it because of gratitude."

The man touched her feet with his hands, in the everyday gesture of obsequiousness, which his emotion managed to make gracious, a recognition of her instead of a humbling of himself.

"What other reason can there be, Memsahib? Day after day the years walk over a man, and then all of a sudden he stumbles into kindness. It is not in order to repay. How can a poor man give back only the seed of a little happiness? I do as I should, to do honor to you, to make that seed a garland."

"Let's go," the M.O. interjected loudly and uncomfortably. "It's getting late. We need every possible second to bring them in."

The bearer was ready to leave also. He had reached a little out of the shell of himself and now he could go back, and all his habits made him eager to return to the ways of obedience with a different feeling. Hastily they disappeared into the night and into the cloak of action.

"Do you really think it worked?" Krishnan asked Kamala.

"I don't honestly know," she answered. "I wish it hadn't happened that way. I'd rather, much rather, have done it all myself."

"I think you touched him," Krishnan said. "It doesn't matter how one comes to the change. I think there's a difference, that there's going to be a garland."

She looked at him, her eyes shining a little, and then the gravity came back to her face as she pushed away the feeling of achievement.

"I want no flowers," she said.

"You certainly deserve them."

"Not I," she protested with intensity. "Everyone but I. It's deserved by the thousands who've made a little grow from less. By the small dignities that have become ever so faintly larger."

"It's you who made them grow," he reminded her quietly, feeling a little of the pride himself.

She was in the doorway, on her way back to her patients, and then, unexpectedly, she held her arms out, letting the compliment float through her body. He forgot where he was and drew her to him. She was taut and smooth and reassuringly fragile, her pliancy pushed against the curve of his praise, her tranquillity sung to by moonlit water, like the restoring of a law within himself. Whenever he held her now, he had the feeling of a truth suddenly springing to life inside him, the repossession of an ancient remembrance.

"I don't know why," he was saying. "Of all places, this isn't the one for happiness."

"But it is, Krishnan dear," she answered, the promise looking up in that earnest oval face which emotion stripped only to a deeper serenity. "Because the edge of disaster must be hope. Because short of death there must always be a healing."

4

He must have fallen asleep while sitting down, trying to keep awake; his lolling head must have created the whirlpool. The stabs of light were the groans of the man dying. He had been sucked away, he and Kamala, away from the flotsam and jetsam, the fainting pretexts that a hand held on to. He was groping for something, treading not water but emptiness, trying to shudder himself away from the truth.

His eyes broke open, and he saw the M.O. back, looking happier, wiping his face with a towel.

"It's better than I expected," he said. "There are only four of them—two in the same house, the others across the street. I had the bearer nose around and make inquiries. Four in the morning isn't the best time, of course. But that's the picture as far as one can tell."

It was a limited optimism, but Krishnan found himself unable to share it. He still had the recollection of the vortex. He screwed his eyes up, looking at the M.O., trying to squeeze out the weariness, the haze of impending and accepted disaster.

"How much do you think we've really found out?" he asked. "It's difficult enough to know in ordinary circumstances, but now there's the other danger in addition, the danger of setting off a riot. It must make them twice as afraid of the facts."

"I suppose so," agreed the M.O., but the admission did not seem to discourage him. He had been recalled to his duty and convinced of his code, and the acceptance seemed both to have relaxed him and to have made him more confident.

"It's too much to expect the whole truth," he continued. "We just have to go on with what's been told us and hope that when the rest of it comes out, it won't be too late to do something useful about it."

"Maybe the woman told them," Krishnan conjectured. He was beginning to realize that he and Kamala might have pushed the M.O. into a fool's errand, the only result of which would be the endangering of the hospital.

"We're doing everything possible to reassure them," he went on, reasoning his way to the more hopeful outcome. "She must have realized that our only interest is to find out the size of this outbreak and get it under control for everybody's good. We're taking risks that we don't have to shoulder, and we wouldn't do that if we weren't eager to help them. But we need their co-operation. We can't succeed without it. Surely she made them understand that."

The M.O. shook his head. "Not if I'm any judge," he observed discouragingly. "She had her own private sorrows to worry about. It was hardly a time to think of public relations. Of course, I've tried to conduct my own propaganda campaign. I've told them I'm risking my skin to protect them and that as a doctor and a man of conscience I've got to stand outside this communal mess. They may have believed it, and we have to hope they did. But they're suspicious blighters, and fear has made them more so. They could have thought I was spying, looking for an excuse. They might have imagined that if they admitted anything I'd let it pass around and that would be reason enough for the rest to come in and tear the place wide open."

"I'm afraid that's the truth of it," Krishnan admitted dismally. "We've pushed you into something without thinking enough about it. We've been too concerned with the principles and not enough with the practical difficulties. We've probably done nothing except send you out on a limb."

The M.O. patted him reassuringly on the shoulder. "Success isn't everything, my dear fellow. With your superior education, you ought to know that. Besides, there's trouble enough for all of us to digest without our worrying about what we haven't been told. Let's just concentrate on our climbing the hill in front of us and not ask ourselves if there's a higher one behind it."

He stepped outside the entrance and called for the bearer.

Krishnan looked at the first streaks of dawn coming over the tent tops, fingering the darkness.

"Isn't it time to call it a day?" he suggested. "It's taking too much of a risk. There's light enough to see you, if you go back for the last one, and we aren't even sure that it's really the last."

The M.O. looked at him squarely but securely. He didn't have to protect the hospital any longer. The fears were out of him, a body in the room, a discarded justification, which he could heal dispassionately, like any other patient.

"This isn't much of a hospital," he said. "If it gets burned down maybe we'll have something better. I read an article once on the Coventry raid. It was supposed to be a quick way of slum clearance."

He looked at the place almost shamefacedly, as if it were a mongrel cur he ought not to have befriended.

"A sick man is a sick man," he concluded. "This is a place for the sick—the little there is for the little it may last. Kamala reminded me when I had forgotten. All I can do is live with it and defend it. If I didn't my backbone would never forgive me."

He went back with the stretcher, the wryness wrinkling the edges of his mouth, holding the picture of himself erect, the ironic redemption of a third-rate movie. It was all he had—the routine of duty, the escape of pride. Yet it gave him dignity and the beginnings of rightness.

Krishnan went in and found Kamala asleep, too tired even to stir when he caressed her. The first cholera victim was in a coma. He hadn't the courage to look at the man's last struggle. He drifted on to the veranda to stretch his limbs and rub away the weariness. The temperature had dropped farther, and the wind stirred briskly as he stood beside the doorway looking out, letting the dawn air rinse his perceptions clean.

The tents stretched away in the endless, recurring monotony of defeat. There were no hills, only the undulating sand dunes. There was nothing defiance could climb. But day would come soon, and the sun, avid and vigilant, would climb in the all-seeing, all-enclosing prison of the blue sky.

Inside, he put some food on the fire and slapped some of the boiled water on his face. He came out again and began to count the tents. They blurred, sliding over each other into the meaningless shape of the avalanche. The minutes ticked by—how many to the bomb burst, how many to the demon beneath the dancer's limbs?

Could it have happened otherwise? Could there be peace in the town named after peace? Could Kamala's love and the M.O.'s devotion to the image of duty reach into the desperation huddled beneath the white tops, soothing away resentment, curbing anger? Was it malignant fate, the arbitrary stamping of the god's foot, that opened the fissure, broke loose the avalanche? Or was the gathering weight condemned to havoc, so that the thunder of destruction had to come, the darkness ordained, devouring, ready to leap, on the wings of the butterfly, the fluttering voice of the sparrow. Perhaps no prudence could avoid disaster. Perhaps all that one could do was to salvage from the forbidding slopes a little more than the last wrecks of bitterness.

He must have reached some distance into depression with his thoughts because the M.O. was back, the last man safely in. He tried to feel the appropriate sense of relief, the satisfaction with a mission completed. Instead he had the feeling that the door was closed, that hostility surrounded them, that the rickety walls and leaky roof must be strengthened against the gathering, grinding siege of hate.

"Not bad," the M.O. was saying. "He hasn't had it for more than a few hours. This time we ought to be able to save him." He wiped his forehead with his sleeve and stepped into the back yard, where he lifted up the brass vessel with its dented rim and poured out the water for his face.

The scream of the first victim cut through the silence; the morning air shuddered with it, so that it trembled out to the far tents, shivering among the people flowing into the streets and the faces struck with horror in the hospital.

The name of Allah was clear on the last lips, a clarion call, a prayer like a curse, a dying man's desperate, beseeching supplication, hung in the tense air, Shantihpur's sentence of death.

5

The M.O. was the first to move, and he moved fast. He pushed the swing off the packing cases, the bottle of ink on top of it tipping over, spilling across the floor. The revolvers were there and he took the first of them out from the two cartons he had forbiddingly labeled "poison."

Kamala watched him, her eyes widening with dismay. She started toward him, her face going slowly paler, her hands held out, her voice imploringly tense, almost a stranger's voice to Krishnan, who had never known it to plead.

"No, no, please, no!" she cried. "Not that way. Don't do it, please. You have no right to do it. You can't stop anything. You'll only start more hate."

"Stay out of this," the M.O. told her warningly.

She reached awkwardly, vainly, for the weapon. The M.O. hit her on the cheek with the butt of it—not violently but hard enough to hurt her. She moved back, quietly erect, not even putting her hands to her face, her mouth trembling almost imperceptibly, and the tears stopped at the threshold of her eyes.

Krishnan plunged across the room, forgetting the sling on his left arm. He caught the M.O. square, and the man went down, sprawling on the floor, clutching the revolver, his trousers absorbing a generous quota of ink.

"You lousy sod," said Krishnan between his teeth. "Try it again and the first murder will be in here."

The M.O. grinned unexpectedly. His arm reached up, offering Krishnan the revolver.

"Go ahead," he mocked him. "If you're man enough to do it.

It's an improvement in you. You've come a long way from lavatory pacifism. Only, please shoot as if you believed in something."

Krishnan glowered and pushed the revolver back. "You know very well I can't kill anyone in cold blood."

"You can't kill," taunted the M.O., "no matter what the temperature. If a tiger walked into this office you'd reason with it until somebody else shot it or it died of old age."

Kamala made another bid for the revolver. It was even more awkward than the first one. The M.O. had no difficulty in eluding her. He rolled over the weapon so that she couldn't kick it away and then picked himself expertly off the floor.

"Your dainty wife isn't like you," he told Krishnan. There was a hint of admiration in his eyes and voice. "In her nonviolent way she's really quite a killer. She'd be a real Gorgon, she would, if she ever turned it on anyone but herself."

He backed into a corner and released the safety catch. "I'm in charge here," he said with firm finality. "The regulations say so. I run this place and I'm going to give the orders."

"Take it from him," Kamala pleaded. "He mustn't do anything with it. There's a different way. We've got to speak to their goodness."

"You can have your choice," the M.O. said to Krishnan. "You can sulk in the corner with Kamala if you want to and blow your nose in her pacifist handkerchief. Or you can come out and do a man's job in a man's way."

Krishnan looked at the torment in Kamala's face. He thought of the avalanche outside, the white tents waiting for the dancer's foot to stamp. The right action would be the one that worked, the one that stopped it. Was the proper course persuasion, the reasoned, dispassionate appeal to the mob's conscience, or the obstinacy of a different force, demanding its penalties, implacably raising the price of self-indulgence, staring down passion with the threat of the blue barrel?

"I'll take the other gun," he decided eventually.

He was still her husband and she a Brahmin wife, and the dis-

cipline went too deep for her to protest. Or perhaps, as always, she
was making him make his choice, even when the consequences
hurt her. She was looking at him, not saying anything, but this
time she couldn't keep the tears back. He could have hit her other
cheek with the gun butt and watched the blood flow and considered himself kinder.

"Now you're being sensible," he heard the M.O. reassuring him.
"Believe me, it's the only way to stop them."

Krishnan took the other revolver from its carton, weighed it
in his hand and snapped open the magazine. Deliberately he emptied it of its contents. With the M.O. watching him, too flabber-
gasted to react, he opened Kamala's hand and put the cartridges in
them.

"It's my life style," he explained. "I'm V. S. Krishnan, the uncom-
mitted philosopher. Nobody ever succeeded in making me choose."

"What the devil d'you suppose you're doing?" howled the M.O.
"You're crazy, stark crazy, to face a crowd with that."

"I'm scared," admitted Krishnan. "I'm scared stiff because I don't
know what I'm in for. But at least I'm scared only of the tiger, not
of myself."

6

It was nearly noon when the crowd came. The M.O. had shut
and bolted everything, put the *almirahs* up against the windows,
barricaded the back door with his desk. The servants were frightened and resentful. They did as they were told to out of habit and
because of the gun barrel slapping at the M.O.'s thigh. The feelings of the patients came together in subdued and hostile murmurs,
sick eyes watching the four sick men beyond them, with Kamala
between, making a screen of her gentleness. All the acid bottles
were out of reach. The scalpels had been locked up together with
the meat knife and the matches. He was as ready as he could be
for whatever he could think of, the stab in the back, the battering
ram of the mob on the front veranda.

When they had taken the precautions they went about each day's tasks as if nothing had happened, as if nothing ever could, as if the routine established the only reality, the restoration of the ailing bodies in the walled-in seclusion of the darkened room. But they counted the minutes, and as the minutes went by they didn't know whether to be relieved at their safe passing or tenser because they had come closer to it, because another and yet another heartbeat had cut down the suspenseful, desired space of waiting.

Perhaps they were glad when they heard the stamp of the crowd's feet and the throb of the other fever rising, approaching. The M.O. and Krishnan went out on the veranda. There were a hundred or so of them carrying a crowd's random armaments—staves, stones and pieces of timber made deadly with barbed wire. Not all of them had murder in their faces. Several had only bewilderment, others that fixed and faraway look, the atrophy of many and minor defeats, so that the expression was the same, the same transfixed, half-stupefied surrender, whether rebellion or submission raged beneath it. They came up slowly to the steps as if they were groping for, measuring, their strength, the hurried slogans flaunting, tentatively chanted—Justice for Shantihpur; They shall not destroy us; This is our town; We have a right to live here.

They stopped dead when they saw the revolvers leveled at them, Krishnan holding his and wondering if it held him, the surprising steadiness of the squat weapon going back to the body, firming his muscles, steadying his insides. He reminded himself that there was nothing inside the gun. It made no difference; the barrel didn't waver. Out of the corner of his eye he saw the M.O., the gun in his hand as if it were a whip, eyes snapped open, determination steely, staring the crowd down as if he had always owned it.

"What have you come to this hospital for?" he demanded.

His voice was steady, even steadier than the gun was. It had authority enough to keep the crowd back. Some of the raised weapons were put down. The angry turmoil of voices was less intense.

The ringleader stepped forward. He was a large man, his complexion pasty, built heavily enough to convey some impression of strength, though with more than a hint of flabbiness in his muscles and in the slow-footed way he handled himself. His shirt was torn, his face unshaven. He wore the marks of hooliganism with a self-conscious, unaccustomed pride, as if he were wearing new clothes at a wedding. He wouldn't have been threatening if he had not been a figurehead. But with the crowd's emotion gathering weight behind him, he could stand there, the sun at its zenith gleaming upon his knife blade, drawing in the substance of an angrier shadow, the concentration of a more potent authority.

His feet were planted apart, and as much as it could be, his body was poised and vigilant. His attitude was hectoring; but the bluster was pulled down into the postures of reason, the crowd's indulgence with its victims, perhaps, but perhaps also the opening of a misgiving, the first hint of uneasiness, as he watched the muzzle of the revolver trained upon him, the bullet ready to take off for his heart.

"We wish you no harm, Sahib," he began with reluctant, ostentatious courtesy. "May God protect your hospital and the lady who looks after us."

"You haven't come to pray for us," said the M.O. "But if you want to you are permitted to begin. Recite your *mantrams* and depart in peace. God will look after us when you leave us alone."

"We want no trouble, Sahib," the man repeated, fingering his knife. "We want only the four Moslems."

"There are no Moslems here," the M.O. said.

The man's face flushed and his eyes hardened. "You trifle with us, Sahib."

"This is a hospital," the M.O. explained calmly, looking at him but speaking to them all. "Whoever comes in leaves his religion outside. There are no Hindus or Moslems here. There are only sick bodies waiting to be healed."

The ringleader's voice dropped another two notches in deference. He was the crowd's nominee, so he would first be the spokesman for its patience, its readiness to explore all honorable alternatives. A mob was more deadly when it felt it had justice on its side.

"Huzoor Sahib, we are peaceable men, we wish to kill nobody. We have suffered at their hands, each of us, Sikh and Hindu, we have lost our property, seen our wives and sons die. We have never taken vengeance, Huzoor Sahib. But in our own country, in this home we have built with the little we took away, is it right, Sahib, that the poison of them should kill us?"

Brandishing knives and staves, the crowd growled its assent. Krishnan tensed instinctively, forgetting the emptiness his hand held. The M.O. continued with patient severity, as if disciplining some recalcitrant child.

"This is a hospital," he repeated. "Within these walls the purpose is to save life. It will not be otherwise. I will permit no murder."

"We do not want to murder them, Sahib," the man protested. "We wish only to send them away. This place is all we have, Sahib. We were driven here, we have taken refuge with you. They burned down our old homes. Must they destroy us in our new homes also?"

"You came here," agreed the M.O., "and you have a right to live here. They were born among us and they too have the same right."

"It is enough, Sahib," the man replied, impatience beginning to bristle in his voice. "We wish them no harm but we will not be slaughtered by them."

The crowd closed ranks and slowly began to edge forward. The M.O. held his ground.

"You want to be safe," he warned them, playing his last card. "Touch them and you're certain to be poisoned. If the cholera spreads I've nothing with which to help you—no vaccine, no medicines, no facilities. Touch them and Shantihpur will die. Leave them alone and maybe I can stop it from spreading."

They fell back a little, the piled-up anger subsiding, knots of discussion forming among the voices.

"Leave them alone," one of them suggested. "The doctor knows what he's doing."

"It isn't as contagious as he says. It's safer to put them where they cannot harm us."

"Some of us must be immune."

"There are Moslems in the town. They can carry them out and get out of Shantihpur also. It's their poison so let them die of it."

"We can burn down the hospital."

"That would be killing our own."

"We can cut their throats and burn them in the back yard."

"But we promised the doctor."

"We've a right to protect ourselves. Besides, I never made a promise."

"Nor I."

"Nor I."

"It's the same thing as murder."

"Murder, he says. What d'you suppose they did to us?"

"My wife."

"My only son."

"I couldn't even recognize my daughter. There's a limit to tolerance; they're not fit to be vermin."

"We raised no hand against them and they killed us."

"Kill them."

"It's only four. It's not even retribution."

"Kill them."

"We wouldn't do it if it weren't to protect ourselves."

"Kill them."

They began to move forward once more, weapons raised, watching the man with the revolver watching them. They had a different look now, pulled together by a common abandonment, the vacant white of the glassy eyeballs showing, the grin over the suddenly wolfish teeth snapped back in animal, standardized elation. The flash of hysteria glittered its way among them, more deadly than the gleam of the avid knives.

The M.O. looked back at them, his gaze narrowed, focused, pinpointing the core of their recalcitrance. His eyes neither flickered nor relaxed their vigilant composure. It was as if he were reminding the tiger of its tameness, after the memory of the jungle had slunk in. He stiffened his body, and the whip seemed to be lifted, flowing out of his determination, uncoiling in his voice.

"Another inch," he said to them distinctly. "Another inch, and I'm going to open fire. We've got you people covered from every window. We've sent for the Rampur police. Try anything and the law will finish it."

"We demand entry, Sahib," the ringleader shouted.

"Then go on demanding till you're blue in the face."

The man leaped forward, his eyes blazing. His knife ripped upward in a scythelike movement, a haymaking operation that only assaulted the air. The M.O. had stepped back, his revolver barking at the same time. There was a half-throttled, attenuated scream, partly anguish, predominantly terror. The knife clattered to the ground. The man kicked it away himself with a reflex of repulsion, as if it had slashed at him and might do so again. His eyes were focused unbelievingly on the darkening stain of blood as he watched it flow with horrified fascination.

"It's only in your arm," the M.O. told him. "You don't have to howl as if you were trying to get into heaven. You can come inside and be my latest patient. Or you can stay outside and argue and be carrion."

The man glowered angrily at him. For a moment he held his ground shamefacedly, as if he were waiting for the crowd's momentum behind him to carry him over his own humiliation. Then, as nothing happened, he came reluctantly forward, nursing the injured arm, sullenly, eyes downcast, his face crimsoning with the implicit disgrace. The crowd stood still, uncertain, passion hushed, irresolutely fingering its weapons.

The M.O. stepped forward, raising his left hand. His finger eased off the trigger. Deliberately he let the revolver muzzle drift down until it was pointing harmlessly at the ground.

"Go home, my friends," he said. "This town is Shantihpur. Not peace alone but peace with wisdom also. Go home and let the law preserve you."

"The Doctor Sahib is right."

"We meant no harm, Huzoor."

"If we're protected from it we have no cause to quarrel."

They lost their cohesion, broke into groups, and drifted back to their everyday pursuits. Soon the space before the veranda was empty of everything but the memory and the blood stain, solitary and warning on the gravel.

"It's over," said the M.O. "For the time being, that is."

He shepherded in the latest of his patients. The man seated himself on the edge of the bench. He was suspicious, dejectedly defiant, still clinging to the tatters of bravado, apprehension flickering in his face as he watched the M.O. sterilize his instruments.

"It is not serious, is it, Huzoor?" he asked. "No more than the removal of a bullet."

The sweat had formed in anticipation on his face, dribbling away his pretense at indifference.

"It will hurt as it should," the M.O. said discouragingly.

"I can stand it," the man assured them, "as long as I know what I'm in for."

He wanted to force the confidence into his voice but he couldn't succeed in getting it out of his throat.

"You'll have to," warned the M.O. "We've no anesthetics. Nothing, not even cocaine. And as for brandy, there are nobler causes."

It was not the truth by any means. There was some cocaine and a small supply of morphia. It was on the tip of Krishnan's tongue to point that out. He hated inflicting unnecessary pain and he couldn't have accepted the M.O.'s probable argument that it was the only way to teach the swine a lesson. But he restrained himself, being aware also of the advantages of a united front.

The man's hands twisted as they laid him on the table. He wailed and writhed as the bullet was extracted, so that Krishnan had difficulty keeping him rammed down. The tears came out, diluting the perspiration. He sat up, choking the sobs back angrily, humiliated by his own behavior, looking down almost with hostility at the body that had unexpectedly betrayed him.

"Water," he pleaded. "A little water, Sahib."

The M.O. threw a tumblerful into his face. The man flinched away from the insult, then sat more erect, wiping his face slowly with the sleeve of the other arm. His eyes, which had been downcast, were beginning to smolder.

"Don't make too much of it," the M.O. told him sternly. "It's only a flesh wound. You can thank your lucky stars I'm such a good shot."

"You don't have to be ashamed of it," said Krishnan, his better nature reasserting itself. "It's bound to hurt, hurt terribly. There's no reason to behave as if it didn't."

"Rubbish," the M.O. declared contemptuously. "I've done far worse to people who never batted an eyelid. It's cowardice, that's all. Deflate a bully and you have a funk. If he had even a teaspoonful of courage he wouldn't be whining the way he is."

The man waited a little before he answered, trying to get himself outside his feelings, letting the pain and the disgust subside. When he spoke he had recovered some of his self-assurance. His voice was even, but his face was grim.

"This isn't going to be the end of it, Huzoor Sahib."

"Of course not," agreed the M.O., unperturbed. "It isn't the end; you'll have to come back for more treatment. Now go home and see me at ten tomorrow."

The man went out of the front and down the road. He kicked the gravel as he slouched away and looked back threateningly, as if to say that he would not return alone.

"Nice customer," commented the M.O. "I was certainly lucky to manage to hit his arm. If I'd killed him by accident we'd have really upset the apple cart."

"But surely that's what you wanted," said Krishnan, surprised. "You intended to wing him, didn't you? So that they'd be shocked into their senses, but not shocked further—shocked into revenge?"

The M.O. patted him jauntily on the shoulder. "You mustn't believe everything I tell my admiring public. I'm a terrible shot, really. All I can do is hope for the best and aim for the middle of the beer barrel."

Krishnan looked at him bewildered. Everything in the M.O.'s bearing had suggested the expert shot, the practiced riot-queller. It was difficult to believe that it had all been a pretense. Nevertheless, what took him aback was not simply that he had been taken in but the knowledge of how differently he might have behaved if he himself had not fallen victim to the deception.

"You're joking," he objected. "That wasn't the way it looked to me at all."

The M.O. was obviously pleased by the consternation he had produced. "Acting is easy enough," he said. "It's what every man does when he wants to seem something better."

Krishnan smiled wryly, trying to hide his feelings. He put the best face on it by pretending to mop his brow. "At least," he told the M.O., "you were never really alone. Standing resolutely beside you was an even flimsier fib."

"A crowd is like an animal," the M.O. concluded more seriously. "Quite often what subdues it isn't really strength. It's the way you are able to look into its eyes. You've got to keep calm if you want to be able to tame it."

"I hope so," said Krishnan. "For all our sakes I hope so. Because they're going to come back. I could see it in the man's face. And then you'll need all your talents as a hypnotist."

"You've hurt it," Kamala declared, breaking emphatically into the conversation. "You've hurt its body and you've hurt its pride, and there's nothing more dangerous than a wounded tiger. They're human beings. Don't you understand? They're frustrated, they're frightened and they need to be helped. You can't treat them as if they were circus performers."

There was a hardness, not far from bitterness, which Krishnan had never known in her voice. It took him aback but seemed only to entertain the M.O. He sat down almost exuberantly on the bench, laying the revolver aside to massage his forearm.

"You're jealous, plain jealous," he taunted Kamala, grinning. "Because I did what your pacifism couldn't do. There's no point in listening to a frustrated woman. I'll ask your husband, the ethical Houdini."

"You did a slick job," Krishnan conceded. "It took all the nerve there is. And all the time you knew what you were doing."

The M.O. grimaced in pseudo-disappointment.

"Heavens!" he said. "What a tight-rope artist you are. You're like a Nataraja that never puts its foot down. Slick job, you say. Can't you even admit it was a good one?"

"I'll do the embroidery when they don't come back."

"It isn't in my contract," said the M.O. "My job is only to keep them out of the hospital. Reforming them is the business of saints and philosophers."

It was more than Krishnan could let him get away with. "You've got a nerve, haven't you," he expostulated. "Telling me that I'm a tight-rope artist. And all you do is duck out from every problem. It doesn't exist if it isn't in the hospital."

"Easy," the M.O. said. "I'm not assuming that they won't return. We've done the obvious thing, in the circumstances, by asking Rampur to send us reinforcements. So it doesn't depend on me now. It depends on whether Kamala really convinced the bearer."

He looked at her, challenging her with the responsibility, waiting for her to protest that it wasn't fair to expect her to work miracles.

"If I'd really convinced him," she retorted unexpectedly, "he wouldn't have gone at all. A gun is a gun. It doesn't matter if you use it or the police do. It's using it that's wrong. The law can't be bludgeoned into people. It isn't real if it doesn't come out of their hearts."

"Out of their hearts," the M.O. repeated, angry and incredulous. "The only thing that's in their hearts is murder. And it's real enough too, heaven knows. Why don't you go and lecture them for a change? Tell them they only have to be forgiving and that God and the Government will look after everything else. I'd like to see it work. I'd be happy to take personal charge of their weapons. But until I've seen miracles, I'll pray for the police."

"We'll need to pray," said Krishnan, the thought striking him suddenly as he looked at his watch. "It isn't more than fifteen miles to Rampur. Two hours at the most on a bicycle. And it's at least six hours since the bearer left. If he ever got there something should have come back."

There was a moment's silence, and then the M.O. nodded his head in agreement. "You're right," he said depressingly. "My mathematical friend is infernally right. He'll never get there; he's probably sold the bicycle. For a potful of toddy if Kamala didn't convince him. And for a copy of the *Gita* if she did."

"What are we supposed to do now?" Krishnan asked. It was an aimless question, expecting any answer, any routine that would impose a direction on the uncertain breathing space they had won.

"Whatever is practical," the M.O. concluded, going back almost with relief to the solidity of his profession and its limited, normal defeats. "This is a hospital; we'd better get back to our patients. We'll bury the dead and put salt into the living."

Kamala had done what she could with the patients during the barricading and the brief hostilities, plying them repeatedly with the saline solution, doing the pathetically little that she could to keep the shrunken, waxen bodies warm. But it was too much for her: the waste of the disease relentlessly flowing, the last spasms of vitality drained away, the prostration on this side, the clammy terror on that. It was a losing battle, a delaying action fought without a purpose. They could save one perhaps if they concentrated their efforts, if they stood by him, watching him, pumping in the fluid, before the terrifying convulsive cramps reached up into the transfixed sunken face, petrifying the blue skin and the dried-out body. They could save one if they abandoned the others, but justice demanded that they dissipate their efforts, surrendering all to a democracy of despair. They did what they could, mechanically, mute, without a question. They were the servants of a law even if it seemed to condemn them. The minutes slipped threateningly over the prostrate silences, and outside the four walls as well as in they felt the shadow of the dancer leap, the resignation to a deeper rule of violence.

The dead man had to be disposed of, and the only servant that was left refused to help. The other had made his exit when the crowd came. Even the scavenger wouldn't touch the remains. Krishnan and the M.O. managed to get the cot out, and they dug a grave for him hastily, untidily, looking over their shoulders at the living. It was right not to complete it, to leave the earth heaped high and finality unsettled. It was right to be provisional since there would be other deaths.

The night dropped, clamping down over the horizon's ring of suspense, jagged with the tent tops and the blistered houses. The stars shone, extravagantly clean, as if bedecked, a light of foreseeing that would remain when those who fought for lesser loves had perished. The air was cool, a velvet, palpable blackness, a body that seemed to flower and reach up, giving a singing and a soothing to thought. There was a beauty, a tension, in the darkness so much one's own that one could almost finger it. It could be the glimmer of truth, the deepest beckoning. Or it could be the taunting of a different enticement, the silhouette of anger walking into the mind, welcoming, inviting, the obsession growing with the challenging nearness, till every alternative was blotted out and all that remained was the organized provocation of the violent body and its call to revenge.

They took their turns with the ambiguous night, one resting at a time in a four-hour flirtation with the ghosts of sleep, while the others went on with the remedies, endless quantities of salt fluid pumped in, the clammy flesh disgorging itself of nothing, while the buckets of waste, as pallid as rice water, were unceasingly removed, and the sunkenness in the faces caved in, shriveling closer to the livid tree that branched from the grim core. They were not succeeding, but the treatment continued because there was comfort in the motions, the prescriptions applied for extraordinary deaths.

Kamala was the first to sleep, and the four hours went by without event. It was too easy to be true; there wasn't even a stone thrown, a windowpane broken, abuse or a challenge flung out of the darkness, a flag run up, the outpost of a warning. It was too solid to be reassuring. There was an erosion of confidence in the thick, insinuating silence, the contrivance of an unnatural anger so deep that even the jackals on the outskirts did not scream, and the night seemed a party to the sickness it enveloped.

Krishnan's turn came next. It was easier than he had thought to pull his mind away from the possible shapes of disaster. He had reason to be tired, and the pain was thickening, spreading from his arm, sinking him into a dizzy, unanchored drowsiness. The smoke filled his dreams no more thickly than it should have, considering what was burning. He was being shaken, being angrily reassorted, and the meaning would come when he was disorganized enough.

He swallowed his way out of the suffocation, his eyes winced open, and the acridity was real. The hand on his shoulder was the M.O.'s and behind the smoke he could see the *almirah* burning. It was the rosewood one with the splintered back. They had pushed it against the window as part of the barricading. But in their haste they had forgotten to take the clothes out, and somebody, hoping for that, had thrown in the match.

He flung himself into extinguishing the threat, and it needed all three of them as well as the lone servant. The flames had spread to a corner of the matting, and they had to remove the rest of it. Then the water ran out, and more minutes were lost while they dredged some from the well. They beat it, sloshed it, choked it into harmlessness. It was the present danger and they thought of nothing else.

It must have absorbed them as it was designed to, because none of them remembered what they all must have heard—the thick, terrified gasp of recognition and the unavailing, doomed, diminishing struggle. When they went back to the patients, the trickle of blood had already reached the doorway. The two cholera victims lay with the knives in their hearts, the sunken eyes identical in fear and in death, looking up to the same hole in the roof.

For a while they couldn't react to it. They were looking for the one twist in the evidence that would make it clear that it was all a dream and indeed there was something unreal in the symmetry, the rigid bodies with the accurate knives, arranged fastidiously in a tableau of frozen violence. It must have been over before the victims even saw it. There could never have been any question of recognition, of turning away from the thrust, or of taking its deadliness in the arm or the shoulder. The steel had flashed down as the understanding leaped up. Perhaps their minds had already dimmed into its shadow, and the transfixed terror was also an acceptance. Perhaps the surrender had already overwhelmed them and only the guise of the claim was unexpected, so that the call came rightly, the familiar stranger, the bright end tapering in the fanatic starlight.

The M.O.'s face showed his dejection, his hands trembled a little, and if his voice didn't, it was because his anger with himself had stiffened it.

"We should have known," he said. "Anybody could have seen it was a ruse. We should have had sense enough to think about what they were planning."

"We couldn't help it," Kamala consoled him. "All of us were needed to put out the fire."

"She's right," Krishnan chimed in, trying to reassure himself too in the process. "The whole place could have burned down. We've done the best we could; we've kept as much as possible alive. Now we've got to concentrate on the one that's left."

"Hear! Hear!" the M.O. chorused grimly. For the first time there was a touch of desperation in his manner. "The moment has come for action. Bang the big drum and let the trumpets call out. Three corpses and a fourth man that we can't save."

His voice broke down into rebellious helplessness. "What reason, I ask you, what reason is there in all this? For all that we're doing we deserve to have some of the luck. Somebody up there has a nasty sense of humor. If they had to take two they could have left me the last one I brought in, the one with whom I might have had a chance."

It was a mood that Krishnan could not but share, and he had to force his own exhaustion out of it and compel himself to be deliberately cruel.

"It's your job," he told him as harshly as he could. "You're supposed to be able to face it. And as for worrying about justice in Heaven, you'd be better off looking for your celebrated backbone. Climb back into your hospital suit and go on with your duty. The show isn't over till the characters are dead."

He had been more vehement than he had intended, and he realized that he was slapping at his own weakness. But he could see the scorn reaching the M.O., working its way where the consolations hadn't.

"So you think I'm a quitter," the doctor said, glaring.

Krishnan continued with the contemptuous barrage. "You're beginning to ask *why.* Your untortured mind will never stand the strain of it. You'd better go back to what your fingers can do. There isn't much of you, so you can make it stand up."

The M.O. got together the ghost of a gleam in his eye. He wasn't unaware of Krishnan's motives but, like every man clutching the slipping sense of purpose, he had to advance to the pretenses that would save him.

"I don't know why I listen to you," he protested. "If I've any pride it ought to have taken a holiday. But you're perfectly right: I mustn't look for the answers. I was brought up an urchin, with my shirt tails hanging out. I don't need to be propped up like your English heroes. I can do without the cummerbund of a philosophy."

His fingers and mind went back awkwardly to their obligations. It was a mechanical duty at first, an effort of will rather than of conviction, but they pushed on with the attempt even though they could not push it forward. They realized that the impossible task had to continue, not simply for the sake of the victims but, more fundamentally, for their own protection.

They bent their energies on the man remaining. It simplified the problem. It meant that one of them could keep continual watch, circling outside, peering into the light's clearing, for the danger that would never come now that it had done the damage. It meant that the other two were completely free to apply themselves single-mindedly to a single hopelessness, pumping in while the body dredged itself out, injecting hope into the hollowed eyes, a purposeless, self-canceling operation that for a short while showed the net gain of life. They could feel the slippage as they worked against it. They had never had a chance. It was the enemy's turn and it had always been his. The delays and the small gains were contrived only to magnify the denouement. There was a purpose in it, not for those who were overwhelmed by the action but for whatever force of perversion held the cards and looked down ironically in the clarifying starlight. It was necessary to go on, to complete it. The macabre logic required to be played out. The courage and perseverance had to be totally futile.

At two in the morning the last man died, and they could look with lucidity at uncompromised defeat.

"We did our best, we couldn't do more," said Kamala and, even in her, the tiredness was showing, not simply in the voice but in the spirit.

"We might as well pat our own backs," the M.O. agreed despondently. "Nobody else is going to do it for us. There's no one around with the old school spirit to tell us that losing doesn't matter and that the game was played in the right spirit of sportsmanship."

Krishnan tried to strike a more cheerful note. "You kept trying," he told the M.O. "After all, that's what counts. If you were seven feet high you couldn't have done any better."

He was aware as he spoke that he was being driven into a kind of childishness. It was the consequence of the long chain of defeats. If one were to resist their gathering weight at all, one could only do so with the easier pretenses, the smart remark, the jaunty simplification. There was no other way not to be cowed by the facts.

His effort was ineffective, as he feared it would be.

"That isn't the point," the M.O. said dejectedly. "It's no consolation that others could not have done better. The point is that no one could have done worse."

Krishnan tried again. It was surprising how easily the clever words came in that unexpected belligerence of the spirit which was less a will than a stubbornness of existence, a carrying on until life yielded a reason. "In a democracy any man is as lousy as the next."

He was more successful this time. Perhaps they appreciated his persistence more than the justice of what he said. At any rate, the remark brought a smile, and the smile the beginnings of a revival of confidence.

"Krishnan's right," said Kamala. "Not to have tried is the only real failure."

It was said a little patly, a bolt on the lid below which the emptiness still smoldered, but it was enough for the time being, for the tribulation, enough for hope to wind around, strengthen against.

"You can take it easier now," the M.O. said. "You can rest if you want to. It's the reward of failure."

The child was asleep, yet, as they turned to it, its presence wakened them out of a routine that had been almost sleepwalking, the actions impersonal, mesmerized by crises. The itch and the pull of littleness came back. Krishnan could watch the boy cupping his face in his hands, then look across the truculent tadpole shape at Kamala's eyes and the serene surrounding of her fondness, which unhappiness could not harden or dejection melt away. In the center of the storm the child lay naked, its ambiguous pose ready to kick and to welcome. Krishnan thought of Lord Krishna, the infant doomed to death by the tyrant king, carried into the safety of a different storm, into the welcoming of a different torrent. Perhaps this foundling had a destiny also. One day, perhaps, it would grow up into justice, into the playing of mischievous music to milkmaids, one day into the captivating of the truth.

She was too tired to smile, to edge herself toward him, but her arm reached out in the surety of sleep, and against the blue and green striping of the mattress, his hand held hers, enclosing a beginning.

He awoke early next morning because of habit, the unvarying mental alarm clock, not because his body would not have slept, not because tomorrow was any degree more dangerous. He went out to watch the sun rising. The hospital was set on high ground, and from the veranda one could see the orange light spread and persuade oneself that it was the growth of a difference.

The air was crisp, bringing a premonition of winter, tasting of blue water and the memory of mountains. He let it brush over him and tangle his hair. A mongrel dog wandered across his vision, and in a reflex action he threw a stone at it. When it yelped he felt charitable and gave it a rotten banana.

He had gone halfway down the square to make his apology, and it was only when he came back that he saw the bicycle propped against the veranda railing. The grips on the handlebars had been pulled off. The spokes in the front wheel were bent and the mudguard dented.

On the Brooks saddle with the leather torn away, the note had been pinned. He opened it and read the forbidding, childish handwriting:

THE PEOPLE ARE THE LAW, NOT THE POLICE

He had heard the echoes of the words before, gallant echoes in the struggle against foreign occupation, standing for bravery and the humblest rights. It was the same force still, the same compulsive gathering of littlenesses, he told himself, casting his mind back to the deep springs of obstinate hope and minimal dignity from which the torrent, whatever its nature, had to flow. What was it that made the flood good or evil—its origins, its purpose or the particular obstacle that it seethed around? And were the police the answer to the people, any more than when they stood in the despised past, the mechanical bludgeons of an alien interest, and equally now the guardians of an emptiness, the law's prohibitions applied because they were legal. They were against vengeance but they were not above it. They were the dam the water would flow over, not the counterforce that would drive back the torrent, and the scrawled, melodramatic, red-ink defiance was right, the people were the law, this was their anger, and the answer, not the reaction, had to come out of the same desperation and no degree less passionate.

He took the message back into the scarred house with him, dragging it reluctantly into that different meaning which the obstacle of their convictions had helped to create. He added the new loss to the sequence of deaths. But he could see from Kamala's face that this was not an addition only, a further weight in the tilting balance of defeat. This man had not been struck down by lightning, by any conspiracy or malignancy of accidents which could be pointed to under the impartial stars and damned as fate or instinctively resisted. This man had been sent out into the storm deliberately and if he lay now under some far-off culvert, blood soaked, the rotting leaves upon his body, the dignity she had given to him led him there, and she was too thin-skinned, too logical, to forget that.

"He should never have gone," she said, her expression rigid. "It was an impossible errand. He'd never have done it if I'd left him alone."

The M.O. awkwardly attempted to console her. "We don't have to jump to conclusions; he's probably safe. He may simply have given up when he found he couldn't get through. And even if he resisted, it doesn't follow that they saw fit to kill him."

He had left out the other possibility, the cynical possibility that the bearer had joined the other side, with which he had earlier taunted Kamala. It could not be totally ruled out; but leaving it in would have been only a theoretical concession, and Kamala could not have been persuaded by any hope not offered in terms of the bearer's loyalty.

So he had put the hope down in front of them, unconvinced himself, for the little it was worth, and none of them could look at it and believe it to be real. The bicycle bore all the marks of a struggle. The message was meant to threaten, to exult; there was aggression even in the flourishes of the scrawling. The death followed in a sequence, in a progression of failure. It was as it should be in the unraveling of defeat.

The M.O. saw that the flimsy hopes were dissolving, that they had no choice left except to live with the worst. He tried, with forced confidence, to establish a different approach.

"It wasn't really anything you said," he told Kamala. "You're fooling yourself if you think you're that important. It was his sense of duty, really; the poor blighters don't know how to live outside it. Rebellion to them is like straining against a spring. When they're tired enough the spring pulls them back to what they've always been doing."

"He was forgetting all that," she insisted miserably, too honest, too sensitive, to accept the consolation. "It was I who pushed him back. He was grateful for something and he wanted to help. He'd be alive now if it hadn't been for me."

"Nobody made him go," Krishnan assured her gently. "It was his choice. It wasn't gratitude. He was just doing with a different dignity what he always did. He was a *chaprassi;* his business was running errands. It's the same pattern day after day, only this time the pattern ended in death."

"I didn't have to end it," she said. "I should have left him alone. I got you into this position, didn't I, and no one but myself ought to have taken the risk. When a life is so poor one has even less right to ask for anything from it."

"It wasn't for you," Krishnan repeated stubbornly. "Remember what you said yesterday: that he wouldn't have gone if you'd really convinced him. He did it because *he* thought it was the right thing. In the end a man listens only to himself."

He couldn't persuade her, even with her own words, though she was grateful for the effort, and he was glad when the child cried and she could give it her sweetness and watch it respond with its pure pleasure, uncorrupted by defeat experienced or even seen as a cloud in the mind's foregathering. It had no memory, no chain of the past to bind it. It would grow and become, and the time of its failure was far off, a pinpoint in the fuzzy fascination, and perhaps when the failure was touched it would shrivel away like the sensitive plant in the back yard, like the floodwater under Lord Krishna's feet, under the pedicure of the armed and magic innocence.

There was a knock at the door, and Krishnan opened it. It was yesterday's hero, with the smile creamed in, the satisfaction bulging in his face.

"You're three hours too soon," the M.O. pointed out curtly. "We aren't open for your kind of business."

The man held up his uninjured hand in a gesture of mock appeasement. He looked around, pretending to be unaware of the havoc.

"Huzoor Sahib, I'm a working man. I have to earn my living. I know that the great are always indulgent. I've taken advantage of your generosity and come early."

He rolled his eyes slightly, as if he were following the impact of his humor. The M.O. stared back at him, detestation in his look, but with the frustrated intensity of one who had no alternative but to heal the thing he detested.

"I don't have to treat you," he protested. "I'm not your judge but

I don't have to be your doctor. If I had any conscience I would let you rot."

The man grinned amiably, completely in control of the situation.

"I'm a changed man, Huzoor Sahib. I have confidence in your wisdom and your promises. He who comes in leaves his religion outside."

He spread himself on the bench, admiring the scenery. He offered his injured arm with an almost jaunty confidence, sure of the outcome now that he had quoted the text. He was so pleased with himself that he did not even complain when the M.O. stripped off the bandage more roughly than he needed to. His eye fell on the charred *almirah,* which he had been ogling for the past five minutes.

"What *can* have happened, Huzoor Sahib?" he exclaimed, his jaw dropping in simulated concern.

"Somebody wasn't able to find an ashtray."

"It is terrible, Sahib," the man commiserated. "I myself do not smoke. I hope that this calamity will teach others not to do so."

His eyes shifted expectantly to the curtain screening off the sickroom. "But all will be well, will it not, Huzoor Sahib, as long as the ailing recover?"

"They won't be sick any longer," the M.O. said.

The man knew which side of the ambiguity was real, and the satisfaction catwalked in his face. "It is good, very good, Huzoor Sahib. No sickness, no infection. It is a good day for a humble patriot."

He watched, beaming, as the M.O. reluctantly bandaged his arm. "What will you do with it?" the doctor asked him.

"I'm a poor man, Huzoor Sahib," the man replied, assiduously rubbing in the humility. "What can a poor man do but earn his living? And acquire security, if the gods permit that?"

He looked around, serenading the room with his satisfaction, putting the word *security* unmistakably into its context.

"It's healing," the M.O. said, pretending to be unaware of the innuendo. "It's coming together much better than I had expected. In another week you ought to be well again."

The man shook his head vigorously, discouragingly. "Oh, no,

Huzoor Sahib. It ached and bled all morning. It made me think, Huzoor. I couldn't stop thinking. I'm a sick man, much sicker than I thought. It is doubtful, Sahib, that even your skill can save me."

He was overcome eventually by his own wit, and he picked himself up, his plump sides shaking with the silent laughter, as the three of them watched him in anger and disgust. He had sobered up by the time he had got to the door, but then he looked at his arm and at the ruined room. The resemblance, or the lack of it, tickled his fancy, and this time he couldn't resist being explicit.

"It is more serious for you, is it not, Huzoor Sahib? For my modest injuries I have an excellent doctor. But, alas, alas, who will look after your pain? Who will sit down and cure the doctor himself?"

CHAPTER EIGHT

The Dark Dancer

WHO COULD TELL precisely how it all began? The observer could point to a moment of time, the edge of a knife, a watershed leading to another country where the rivers flowed differently and the faces were altered. It might be possible to say these were the links, these were the events and processes of destruction. Even after the wind whispered over the footprints and the sand erased them, one could filch back the story. It was possible to examine the scars, sift the conflicting evidence, research could always reconstruct the illness and prescribe the remedies that were never administered. It was always possible, since wisdom always looked back, to show that there had been an implicit coherence of error. Wars were not started by apples or misfits alone, but by the complications contriving in the context, which the diagnosis could isolate so that they were never repeated. If the impartial report were ever written— the report for which the Commissioner didn't have the time or those concerned in reading it the interest—it would be said that much could be said on all sides and that the burden of responsibility was anonymous, with everyone standing in the common guilt.

Undoubtedly at eleven-ten on that October morning the incident did take place, the match was applied to the tinder. But it was only the kind of quarrel that always took place, day after day in the huddled and blustering shops, and which on any other day would not

259

have done more than give vitality to the bargaining process. And even if the *ghee* didn't actually have maggots in it, it was probably not in the best condition anyway, and there was undoubtedly some basis for the complaint, which had been made several times earlier to the same merchant. The invective may have been more than ordinarily colorful, but even among the purchasers of *ghee,* some had to be gifted with a special eloquence and others with the tongues of vigorous wives. There was certainly no need to come to blows, but on any other day the fact that the quarrel went this far would have been merely unusual, and any residue of ill feeling that it left would have been rubbed out by the next but one transaction. Unquestionably, it was a precipitate act (a word the D.C. favored in his noting) for the shopkeeper to hurl a vessel at the complainant, for, as the unwritten report would no doubt have said, in times of great tension it was all the more imperative that the maximum extent of moderation should be exercised. But in avoiding the missile, it was hardly necessary for the customer to tip over the oil lamp. Even then, the stall would not have burned down if it had not been jerry-built, as was indeed the condition of any shanty in Shantihpur, or if the shopkeeper had put out the fire instead of pursuing the culprit, or if the crowd had done something practical instead of debating the pros and cons of the case.

However, while the mishap was regrettable or unfortunate (the particular nuance remaining to be decided), it should not normally have led to anything worse, since all in Shantihpur had lost their belongings, and that in truth was the reason they had come there. Situations which seemed superficially more dangerous had, in other circumstances, been successfully handled by the prudence and resolution of the forces of law and order. There would have been no consequences if the man had not been Moslem.

But that he was Moslem was an incontrovertible fact, at least to the extent that no one who might have known better denied it. In addition, the shopkeeper said so and he ought to have known what he was talking about, having sold *ghee* to every person in Shantihpur. Moreover, the crowd bore out the shopkeeper completely. Finally, the man ran away, which he would not have done if he had nothing to conceal, particularly when some of the spectators (most of the women, in fact) had tended to be on his side during the course of the argument. It was, moreover, not simply the shopkeeper's testimony but the view of all those who had rushed out on to the street to ascertain the cause of the disturbance that the man, when he eluded his pursuers, did so by disappearing into the Moslem quarter.

It might have been argued that he was really chased there. But, whatever his reason for going in, he was never seen to come out, and when the crowd demanded him he was not handed back, which would have been common prudence at the least and could have led to no harm had the man been Hindu. Even so, it was certainly excessive to start throwing in incendiaries; yet if the culprit could not be produced, the least that could be done was to undertake restitution. The effort to retaliate was ill timed, to put it at its mildest, which was probably the right way to phrase it, with the customary politeness of post-mortems. As for the employment of the two rifles, that, if not deplorable, was foolish in the extreme, since even if no one was killed the suspicion could only be that more arms were hidden, and this led, naturally enough, to rumors of a fifth column, a sinister and unnecessary substance.

Nevertheless, the interim conclusions might have stated, the misfortunes closing in might have been avoided had the surrounding tensions been less explosive. And in the creation of these circumstances some responsibility had to be attributed to a certain medical officer, who, in the application of his principles, displayed blind loyalty at the expense of judgment. From this it was not to be inferred that any surrender of principles was recommended, since that would be contrary to the nature of a society both logical and hierarchic, and which, moreover, since the days of Manu, had called only for minor modifications. But the business of all medical officers was to heal illness, not to seek it out. Civil servants, by their nature, sought nothing, not even greatness. Since, moreover, the jurisdiction of the M.O. (which was only his nominal, not his substantive, rank) ended ten feet outside the front veranda of his hospital and could not have been extended without specific orders from Rampur, he had in fact exceeded his competence, in an immoderation of zeal which was palpably unjustified. Had he not chosen to reveal the problem, it might either have dissolved itself in due course or, alternatively, have grown to the point where it required the intervention of a higher authority. The essence of responsibility was, surely, to understand when it ought not to be ex- exercised.

Thus it could be proposed, for insertion in the tentative record, that the tactics employed were lacking in flexibility, which indeed could be held true of all tactics that ended in defeat. In order to know himself, an officer had to know his limitations, which meant, eventually, that he should know the rules. This certainly was a challenging requirement, yet it should not be forgotten that the very fact of existence was a challenge. It was true that, due to a bottleneck in production, some rules were unfortunately out of print and others had not been applied for so long that they could not be remembered. Yet the truth was that no rule, by its nature, could ever be out of date, and if certain of them had been forgotten, so to speak, that could only be because they had been inwardly absorbed. While it was to be hoped that printing facilities would improve, it should also be clearly and intensely understood that publication was not the same thing as knowledge, and that the aim of every civil servant should be to reach that state of administrative bliss and identification where he experienced himself and the rules also as one. This indeed was the point of those fundamental service rules known popularly as the *Gita,* and the fact that their application at Kurukshetra led to havoc greater than any inflicted at Shantihpur could not reasonably be held as an objection against them. The point was not to avoid disaster, a hope ridiculous in the age of Kali, but to confront it with dignity and in the appropriate degree.

Plainly, it seemed not improper to conclude, there had been a sequence of accidents, malignant, as might be presumed from the stars, to which had to be added a failure of understanding that exacerbated an already inflammable situation, to quote the Commissioner's longest words and therefore his strongest, which the clerk seeking promotion would expectantly insert. But would the house have burned down if it had been fireproof? This was perhaps not a legitimate question, since not to be fireproof was the condition of *Kaliyuga*. Yet, since the purpose of historical inquiry was to ascertain what conditions might have led to a different outcome, it would be misleading to pretend that such incidents could be avoided in the future by the recruitment of better medical officers, or by an overwhelming ordinance requiring *ghee* hereafter to be uncontaminated. Thus it was evident that the civil service was not to blame, being but one strand in a web of failure, so that the roots of disaster reached deeper in and further out than the superficial, in a sense arbitrary, findings of overzealousness and economic avarice. In the end all men were involved in the death of each other, the report should insist, pointing the forefinger firmly, so that each could look inward and revise his understandings, in the sudden luminosity of a collective death.

It is possible to go back, to remember, to review, to disinter the chain, remodel the footprints. Yet there is a distance where impartiality stops and one is aware of the shadow, of the dancer's leap clanging in every disaster, of the thrust of the *gopuram,* however blunted, frustrated, upheld unyieldingly, from the obstinate earth. Intelligence can seize and contrive the facts enough for today's explanation and for tomorrow's prudence. But the meaning was different for those whom it overwhelmed. If there is a consolation that the darkness can live with, justice demands that it be like the body ambiguous, that it inherit something of the dancer's effortless grace, that the truth it contains should have been washed through by terror. Each has a beginning that is not public history, the pros and cons affirmed, the balance struck, the mind moving through, adjudicating, sifting only that which it can measure and unravel. Each has his beginning, his condition of darkness, from which the road runs out, the purpose branches, as each man grows separate and singular in his loneliness, to a different discovery and a different death.

So it was for Krishnan also, and for him the beginning was not the quarrel in the shops, which neither he nor anyone with him had witnessed, and which he was told of only long after in the stirring of the ashes, in the contrivance of an explanation. It was not even the immediate web of antecedents, the fear of the epidemic, the refusal to hand over the patients, the problem which their principles had created, and which had been dissolved by death and murder, leaving only the passions it had helped to solidify and had brought to the inflaming edge of violence. It was not the pulsating pressure of desolation which came down, endlessly denuded, from the north, it was not the mechanics of anger and reprisal, locked as they seemed to be in their endless cycle, piston and cylinder in the movement of hate. The beginning was not the tree trunk in the cutting, or the other face he had abandoned to go onward, and which now appeared only in the softening of a recollected distance, the haze of an idyl that once held his contentment. It had begun that noonday when he came home, up the four steps between the pitted pillars, and opened the door into an alien emptiness. It had begun when he looked into Kamala's eyes, suddenly sensed her power of acceptance, and knew, with that flash of recognition which is not love but an angrier necessity, that she had the strength to give that emptiness meaning. It was at the wedding feast, amid the bangles and tinsel, the mendicant dreams and the brocaded gossip, when the voice of the singer glissaded, the dancer leaped, and he felt the lurch, the nausea almost, of an absolute loneliness and the abrupt recovery, the sensation of a seed planted, without his knowing what germ it contained, or what demand its darkness would grow into. It had begun then, and this had to be the end of it. There had to be a point of no escape. The flirtations were over, the family gods had been appeased and overturned, he had lived in the garden and had chosen unhappiness, and now the circle had drawn tight and it had come to pass as he had once reflected: there was a precipice where both of them would stand and the night would close on them, hunting them into a meaning.

And what was the beginning for her? She had always been true to her nature, consistent even in crisis, her road was straight and clear, a striking forward, not an exploration or a discarding of uncertainties, but gently, peremptorily, an assertion of herself. She had let him go with an almost passionate reticence, never qualifying by any appeal his freedom to choose, or even by the shadow of any reproach. She had received him back with the happiness that was due to her, but not with bells ringing, not with apparent elation or even satisfaction at a commitment rewarded. Was it because she knew of the greater test? Was the first vindication only gone through in order to strengthen her for the next ordeal? Looking at her serenity, one could admire its quality, come to cherish it, and yet realize that it contained something that attracted unhappiness. She was uncompromising, a creature of the storm. She was the erect tree which demanded the lightning, and so for her also the beginning stretched back into the roots of her life, and the angry faces outside were her failure.

He watched her as she went about her duties, and her face was not so much set as settled. There was a poise in her expression which he found vaguely disturbing. It was less a physical change than an inner one, a kind of unsparing watchfulness of conviction.

He tried to draw it out of her. If she could be persuaded to talk about it, it could be made harmless, he told himself, and then he wondered why he had presumed it to be harmful. He told her that failure was not the same thing as error. One could be right and yet could be defeated, and often failure was the eddy on the surface, with a different tide of reality beneath it. He was angry with himself after he had said that, because he might have put the thought of failure into her head, but she talked about it reasonably, levelly, as if she were outside the fact, too much outside it to be entirely reassuring. He began to be more specific, arguing that it was everyone's idea to bring in the cholera victims and that if the crowd was goaded, it was because of himself and the M.O. fooling around with revolvers. He didn't explain what would have happened without the show of force, and, to his relief, she didn't ask him. She was considerate to everything that he said, and he thought he was making progress until he noticed that she was considerate in the same way to all the hospital cases. But there was no hopelessness on which he could put his finger. She kept telling him that he was right and she never said it as if she didn't believe it, yet all the time he had the feeling that there was another part of her, away from the whole conversation, involved in a struggle to which she would not admit him. He had an inkling of it when he started to mention the bearer, and she told him unexpectedly and with a startling vigor that she agreed with everything pinned on the Brooks saddle: the people *were* the law, not the police.

"But it isn't so now," he protested, taken aback. "It belongs to a different political order. When the forces of law were alien and unpopular."

"All force," she said, "is alien and unpopular."

It was the sort of generalization that always made him angry, and he was going to give it some of the treatment it deserved, when he realized that she was saying it to herself and not to him. Even so, it left him feeling puzzled. What could it possibly mean to *anyone,* he asked himself, with the flames outside and the tumult in the streets? Wasn't the mob the embodiment of popular emotion?

She must have seen the bewilderment on his face because she started to explain. "I mean it's alien to one's real nature. To everyone's nature, if they go down deep enough. You shouldn't be surprised. It's what I have always felt, and I said it only the other day, remember. The law can't be bludgeoned into people. If I honestly believed that, I'd have to agree with what was stuck on to the saddle."

It was an unnatural consistency, and he wrinkled his brows at it, trying not too successfully to make it clear to himself. His efforts amused her, or perhaps she made them do so, because she smiled at him and put her arm around him, with a demonstrativeness so unusual for her that he had to brush the questions out of his mind and accept the reassurance she offered.

"Krishnan, dear," she said to him, pointing at the child. "You mustn't worry. Let's worry about him instead. Poor boy, he doesn't understand. He's being denied the pleasures of confusion."

She took the infant up, put her hand behind its uncertain head and rocked herself with it into a kind of happiness. All her old tenderness was there in her behavior. But there was something else

—a hint of avidity, almost. The look on her face was too tense, too dedicated, to convince him—as it was designed to—that all was well.

2

Looking back at the shadows of failure and error, measuring the anticipation against the actual shock of it, Krishnan realized that it was not quite what they had expected it to be. There were reasons for the small margin of deliverance if one was prepared to stare at the facts long enough. Firstly, the violence was diffused, with the hospital no longer the mob's object. The writing had been on the wall for a long time, and those who could do so had already left; the assault, when it came, struck a shell that was almost empty. Those who remained did so because they had too much to abandon or because they were too old, or too desperate, or too rooted in remembrance to think of an escape. When the alternatives were forced on them, when they were compelled to choose, they chose emptiness rather than death, as nearly everyone did in that stubbornness of life which is poverty's condition. Many of them were allowed to make the choice. The roads had not been systematically blocked, and the victims had not been driven back to the carnage, as had been the virulent, vindictive pattern of other sackings on both sides of the border. Yet the savagery was there, the terror flowed in the streets, the flames leaped up, crackling against the evening sky, and an almost Olympian sense of detachment was needed to say that, in truth, the anger was unorganized. It was not much more cruel than elimination had to be. But the end was elimination—nothing less—and that was cruelty enough—infinite cruelty almost—to those whose positions made them pay the price or who watched from the white hospital the death of an ideal.

In the hospital itself there were respites, available breathing spaces, which seemed unnatural, a deception almost, after the tensions of the earlier nights. For that too there was a plausible reason. The principal casualties were among those being driven out. The way of escape did not run past the hospital, and desperate choices permitted no detours. It was a question of an arm or a life. As for the majority, casualties among them were not beyond the hospital's resources, since the attackers were overwhelming in numbers and since it was recognized that too determined a resistance would only make destruction more complete. It was better to leave something other than the ashes. There was always the hope that the flight would not be forever, that the anger would pass, that the future would offer a way back, that what was abandoned could be flimsily restored.

But if there were respites, it meant there was time to think, to be aware of the meaning or its mocking absence, and each time they had to ask the questions of themselves, as the casualties came in, and left, perhaps to do it all over again but certainly not to repent because they were wounded. It was all the more difficult to appeal to them, since all had been victims of the same ordeal and since perhaps there was no one in Shantihpur who had not suffered as much as he inflicted. It was unreal to argue that vengeance must have an ending, and if one did so, it was angrily pointed out that a hospital had its proper position in violence, law was a matter for the absent police, and the law of the furies for the people themselves.

Krishnan tried to steer Kamala's thoughts away from it, from the hurt minds that trickled in and out, each one an installment in the desolating knowledge that a more primitive logic was now dominant. It could have been so much worse, he told her, and surely all that she had done must have been responsible for at least a little of the difference. It could have happened much earlier—in fact, as she knew, it had happened in other places, and violence postponed was always violence diminished. If the cholera hadn't broken out, or if it had broken out anywhere else in Shantihpur, the other outbreak might never have taken place. In times of great tension the margins of tolerance were always stretched thin, and on other occasions they had been overwhelmed by far less. Something must have been accomplished, there must have been a gain in self-restraint, because when the barriers broke down, they yielded only after a long siege and under extraordinary pressures.

She listened to it all and even allowed it to soften her expression, so that he might have thought he was making progress if he hadn't watched her hands or been aware of the slightly unnatural erectness of her body. She tidied the room because she felt it ought to look more cheerful. She played with the child more than she usually did, piling bangles upon its wrists and legs and expressing concern because its toenails hadn't been manicured. Unexpectedly, she did her hair. He had become so used to the neglected tiredness of it that he found himself almost startled at seeing it in a condition approaching its vernal, velvety glossiness.

She was probably trying to reassure herself, he realized, but if the will hadn't been there she wouldn't have made the effort, and it might be, he told himself, that he had helped to strengthen it. He was glad when she opened her suitcase and took out the most ornate sari she possessed. It was orange, with a border of gold and peacock blue and the figure of the Nataraja worked artfully into the recurring motif. Her face lighted up when he asked her if she had designed it. She was fond of these extravagances, she said, she indulged in them periodically, and then she was horrified by their cost and for weeks afterward would live on rice alone.

She put on the sari, and there was no question that it suited her. The fabric was pliant enough to go with her petiteness, and the restrained pattern, dignified but not heavy, seemed to give her an extra inch of height. He told her she was beautiful and that there was a mirror other than his eyes to prove it, but she said she was happy with the compliment and wouldn't want the truth to tarnish it.

Five minutes later, though, she was making chagrined faces at her reflection, and he was so pleased at this minor accession of vanity that he took special pains to appear to be otherwise occupied. She was putting *mye* into her eyes to make them more lustrous. When she had finished she came to him for his approval, but he pretended not to see her and to look everywhere else.

He took her out on the veranda, arranging their exit carefully, so that, looking at him, she was looking away from the flames. Then he became aware of the change in her face and told her that the moonlight had fallen into her eyes. Gallantry was not something he had practiced, but he found himself complimenting her with no sense of affectation, and she was so unspoiled that she made every triteness not only true but totally original, as if the words had never before been spoken and as if the praise in them had been given nowhere else.

Unexpectedly, she wanted to take a walk. It was such a beautiful night, she said. Its freshness gave her a feeling of tranquillity, and she wanted the stars to bless her with the knowledge that there was something beyond the hospital walls, beyond Shantihpur itself, which would remain to forgive them after it all had ended. He said, a trifle curtly, that there was nothing to forgive when people had done their best. Perhaps she was thinking of those who had started the violence. Probably that was what she meant, she answered, though no one could be entirely free from blame, but all she wanted now was to be at peace and not to argue about meanings on a veranda.

He told her that leaving the hospital was dangerous, and it was her turn to reprove him. She knew that he had said it because he was thinking of her, and she was grateful and a little proud because of that. But she could never be happy hiding behind four walls. She had the feeling of being imprisoned, she added, putting into the word a quiet but unmistakable vehemence. She turned around to face the flames, and he had to let her do it even though he moved in front of her mechanically, still trying to be the screen. There was really no alternative. She had always been possessed by that stubborn clarity, and there was only one direction in which she had ever wanted to look.

"Please, Krishnan," she appealed, her voice caressing, as it seldom was. "It's only because I'm tired of being cooped up. It's just a mood, really, but you know how tyrannical a woman's moods can become. Won't you indulge me just this one time, Krishnan? I promise to obey you ever afterward."

She pouted a little as she spoke, so that his refusal, had he insisted on it, would have been reduced to the level of petulant boorishness.

"Very well," he agreed, uncomfortably and gruffly. "I'll do as you wish, but don't say I didn't warn you."

"Oh, Krishnan," she said, teasing him. "You must at least smile when you're trying to be nice to me. And you're so much less handsome when you want to look severe. It's only an impulse, honestly, Krishnan, like suddenly pining for a brocaded bag or like an expectant mother wanting an orange. I've been under a strain, and you have to forgive me a little."

She put her hand in his and led him out, swinging his hand with an animation that might have seemed almost childlike if her constant seriousness had not qualified it. But this time her seriousness was different. Her face was not pulled together by the concerns and questions which her reaching out to others must have collected or even by the will to overwhelm despondency. It had relaxed into a serenity, friendly and yet aloof, as if something within her had been settled but as if, also, the happiness that the settlement had brought her had already been given to something else. Her lips, finely chiseled, always fastidious, now seemed almost sculptural in their chastity. Her eyes remained lustrous, but under the softness he was aware of a brilliance which was not just the reflection of the starry, enveloping night. She walked with her diminutive shoulders squared a little, as if a strength in her had been touched into life, the circlet of white flowers floating in her hair's blackness, she walked with a blossoming, a queenliness almost of dignity, and there was no question that she was now at peace.

They were about a quarter of a mile down the street when it happened. It was still some distance from the area of hostilities. The girl must have run a long way, which was what her two pursuers wanted her to do. They were loping behind her, not exerting themselves to cut down the intervening space, waiting for her to collapse, exhausted, to the ground.

Kamala's eyes flashed, her grip on Krishnan's hand tightened, and before he fully realized what was happening, they were between the two pursuers and their quarry. The street was narrow and there was a bullock cart left at the right side, constricting it further. There was no way through unless the two of them were prepared to give way.

Krishnan wanted sickeningly to give way. It blazed into his mind that this was what Kamala had come out for, this was the rendezvous to which she had led him with that erect, queer, now frightening determination. With his arm strapped, he couldn't even protect her. He tried to pull her to one side against the cart, but she fought him off with a startling accession of strength and stood squarely across the path, unflinching, not with the defensive force of resolution but with an eagerness bordering upon happiness, as if the seed of recognition in her, the leaping echo of the dancer's foot, had confronted at last the meaning for which it was born.

Even then it could have ended quietly if the girl had simply kept on running. They would have been cursed for getting in the way but they could have apologized and also blamed the owner of the bullock cart. She needed ten seconds to be lost around the corner, and whatever the motives for which the time was bought, they could have told the two men it was either confusion or clumsiness.

But she didn't keep running. She stopped, turned around, and looked at the scene with a fascinated, suicidal curiosity. It was incitement enough for the two men. They tried to brush past Kamala, but she barred their path decisively, and Krishnan, trapped at her side, wanting to protect her, didn't know whether it was they or she whom he should watch.

"Get out of the way, *Bebeji,*" the larger man said thickly. "Her people burned my house down. My mother and father were killed. My sister was taken away. If she's alive now she's somebody's chattel. Get out of the way. It's time for them to pay now. It isn't half of what they've taken from us."

It was the usual justification, and Krishnan was about to respond in the usual way, making his appeal to the men's better instincts. It would have no effect, he realized, but it might gain them a few more moments, and meanwhile the girl might come to her senses and run. It struck him overwhelmingly that he had to make her run. Her staying there was an incitement, not just to the two men but, more dangerously, to Kamala also.

"Run, you poor fool!" he shouted out suddenly, agonized. "For God's sake, run before it is too late."

The shorter man lashed at his face with the iron-tipped stave he was carrying. Krishnan took the blow on his uninjured arm. The pain dazed him, but he bored in desperately, trying to get between the two men and Kamala. The other man kicked at him and, as he twisted aside, hit him square and viciously in the strapped arm.

Krishnan had to back off, and Kamala stepped in, her eyes blazing, but less with a sense of pity for his predicament than with the force of the determination driving her. She did not reason with the men, or appeal to them, or use any of the compelling resources of her gentleness, with which she had so often brought back others to their dignity. She seemed oblivious to everything but the starkest alternative. Her bearing was passionate as he had never known it, passionate as if all compromise had ended.

"You're not going to touch her," she declared, and even her voice was brilliant and ringing. "If you do so, you'll have to kill me first."

He knew what was coming now and he tried vainly to prevent it, plunging in once more, oblivious of the pain. The bigger man brought his foot up, smashing it into his injured arm. Krishnan kept going, trying to reach up, twist away the knife. The other man hit him savagely with his *lathi,* and he went down clutching vainly, the pain seeming to sweep the two men away, impossible inches beyond his fainting fingers. He rolled over, desperately stretching out to Kamala, her sari aflame in the suddenly crimsoning distance. He couldn't touch her, couldn't even cry out to her, he could no longer join his nightmare to her fate. The haze flooded in, with the man's body big as all darkness, crushing the pouring edge of it, and through the haze he saw Kamala not simply standing fast but thrusting erectly, passionately, forward, seeming almost to float against the knife. He was shocked

274 The Dark Dancer

by her beauty, her inwardness suddenly stripped bare, the un-wavering and almost eerie arrogance, as if for the first time she was meeting her true lover. Then the crimson stain welled over her rigid breasts and the serenity came back, a luster to her loveliness, as she drifted down, the taper of her scream faintly clutching at the edge of his senses, down endlessly, a leaf, a reality falling, her hair cascading into a deeper blackness, till the darkness reached out where her eyes could see him no longer, and the nightmares joined at last to overwhelm him.

CHAPTER NINE

Son of Kunti

THE FOG drew back, focused and separated. It became the four walls and then the tomb of an emptiness. The singing was a sound and not a weight. He watched the room forming, becoming a thing apart, no longer an extension of his own pain. He could hear the fan clattering, arguing with the air, and see the precise shape of the window bars, where the sun riveted them upon the calendar.

It was yesterday still upon the fingermarked sheet, and yesterday was a time beneath the lotus, under the erect poise of Lakshmi's blessing, standing forever in that woundless fragility. Goddess-upholding, the flower must always float; there would always be the fragrance of its serenity, no matter how dark the raging of the waters, how deep into disaster the remembrance.

So it had to be and had to be without her, even though wherever, however, he looked, the colors reminded him of what she wore, the whiteness pulled back the flowers from the red torrent, even though the sun, whatever lengthening of reminiscence it fingered, fingered only the last luster of her hair. There would not, could not, be a world beyond her, a wall, a grave where she had never existed. There was no new life that could wipe the remembrance clean, no entrance she had not already passed through. However distant, different, the horizon, it would possess a meaning because she had lived in it.

But he had to look forward also to an emptiness. The body was

gone, the quiet, still grace had slipped into the silence, the gentleness would be a reminder, not a presence. He had to look forward
to a world without a reason, or nourish her reason—reason or
sacrifice—whatever dust of a purpose he could sift and bring back
together in the huddling of the embers.

In the end there might be no purpose at all, nothing that could
be written or imagined, on the brass urn that would hold the handful of her ashes and give back her littleness to the ocean's peace.
There were people who died for slogans and for causes, to alter
in some way the movement of the earth. The words would stand
green and challenging above them, and as long as the grass grew
and the flowers flourished, it was needless to ask if the words
contained the truth. She had not died thus in a marching and
singing of meanings, or proud upon the pyre, killed by her people,
but unavenged, futilely on a back street, a shrinking stain on the
conscience of two drunkards that would be licked over, dissolved
by the next violence. Her death held no reason, only a pitiless logic,
the lonely assertion of an unrecognized dignity. Her death was no
more than herself—the pure light of her uncompromising nature,
the meaning no further than her eyes could look, and since she
had fallen thus, committed to no cause, pledged to no strengthen-
ing and exterior loyalty, what else but grief could grow on her
death's borders?

He tried to call back the truth as she would have had him hold
her, forgiving and yet proud, compliant and yet aloof, the bride
of an arranged marriage, daughter of duty, not by love given but
by her fate bestowed. He had had to abandon her in order to
understand her. The pull was so deep that he was unaware of
its strength. He had come back not to the conventional intensities
but to a quiet and deceptive happiness that, since it made no claims,
had come to be taken for granted, so that it was only when the
light went out that one suddenly recognized there could be no
other shining.

On the white wall, the blankness, he felt he could sense the
softening of her presence, and he had the conviction that he would
find a shape in which he could remember her belonging.

With the emptiness ebbing, the pain became more concrete, taking on the contours of his body. It throbbed and tore at him continuously, thrusting in wherever the dullness moved back. His head pounded threateningly in a room of its own. He felt dizzy and sickened as he tried to fight the haze off, to isolate the slings and bandages that encased him. The window swam up to him, and with a final effort he pushed the confusion through it, stuffing it all into the enormous back yard. He saw the other patients pulling themselves together out of the miasma, looking at him unsympathetically and with bewilderment, unaware of the efforts he was making on their behalf. The roof withdrew, the walls moved reluctantly back, and he could judge more clearly where he began and ended. He was aware now of his limitations.

One day, he thought to himself wryly, he would come out of the *nth* coma, the great transfixions that interlaced his life, and would look up at the wall and see the trophies, the great bull's horns, the Himalayan rhododendron and his own head grinning among the *kirpans* and *lathis*. He would eye it then with the appropriate detachment, knowing that a wiser head was on his shoulders.

He watched the door open and saw the M.O. drift in. The doctor eyed him with the ultimate bedside manner, implying that it was the supreme height of good fortune to be alive and also to be in bed.

"They really gave it to you this time," he commented. "You're a genius, that's what you are. If there's a blow around, you'll get your thick head under it. You've got more stitches than my fingers can count, you look like roast beef that's been taken through a mangle, and you've seen more stars than the Astronomer Royal. Anyone reading your record would think that being beaten up gives you a secret happiness."

"It's the last time," Krishnan assured him. "If I live through this I promise that I'll never again leave my Secretariat desk."

"You'll live," the M.O. said. "What else can you do but live? Nobody ever knocked out a punching bag. All they can do is pound it into a different shape. And then it goes back into the same shape anyway."

"It isn't necessary, you know," said Krishnan. He had sensed that the diversion was the M.O.'s way of saying that he didn't know how and didn't want to begin it. "It isn't necessary, because I saw her die. I was conscious long enough. I couldn't do anything but watch her to the end of it, and I know there's no room for even the thread of a hope. All I want is to see her for a little, to be alone with her body for a few moments."

He saw the uncertain look on the M.O.'s face.

"You *were* able to find the body, weren't you?"

"Of course, of course," the M.O. assured him hastily. "There was no attempt to conceal it. The Moslem girl ran all the way here and told us, and we were there ten minutes after it had happened. Her blood was still warm. We waited as long as we could, hoping we could bring you back to consciousness. But in the end we had no choice but to cremate her."

"But it's twelve hours," Krishnan protested, levering himself up angrily on his elbows. "The limit for cremation is twelve hours. I'm her husband and it was my right. It was the last thing I could ever have done for Kamala. However weak I was, don't you understand, it was my business, as long as my fingers were able to light a match. Now you've taken away even that little tribute."

"You've been hurt badly," the M.O. said soothingly, trying to ease him back on the bed with his manner. "You've been unconscious a long time."

"It's morning," retorted Krishnan, his voice trembling. "The sun's coming through the window, isn't it? Any fool can see it's seven o'clock in the morning. It isn't more than eight hours since she died."

"You're right about the sun," the M.O. agreed. "But you haven't noticed the calendar. It's seven o'clock, yes, but the day is Wednesday." He waited for the implications to soak in and for the bewilderment to form on Krishnan's face. "You see," he added gently, "you *have* been unconscious a long time."

The tension slumped, and Krishnan was able to lie back. "I'm sorry," he said wearily. "But I'm glad it was you who did it. You knew her, and I think you respected her. If the feeling was there the rites don't really matter."

"We performed all the rites," the M.O. assured him. "Nothing was left out. Everything was done scrupulously, according to the book."

He saw the question come into Krishnan's eyes.

"My dear man," he said, "people have died in Shantihpur before now. And this was no ordinary person; this was Kamala. If I didn't detest being sentimental, I'd say that a little of many people died with her."

He had made the last remark straightforwardly, out of his respect for Kamala, not intending it to carry the weight of a large meaning. Watching Krishnan's almost eager response, he began hastily to whittle it away.

"Don't think her death changed anything in Shantihpur. She was good to a lot of people and they liked her. In a purely personal way they wanted to help. But don't try to convert that into some kind of symbol."

"I don't want to fool myself," Krishnan answered, his eyes blurring as he called the memory back. "She was little and lonely and walked into her death. She wasn't efficient, as holy people ought to be, dying professionally under some sleek, fat moral, arranged to give everyone the proper sense of guilt. Her death was simply being true to herself. It wasn't meant to change the ways of others."

"It didn't change them," the M.O. assured him cruelly.

"Hers wasn't more than a little light," said Krishnan. "One day it was trampled to nothing. You were right to remind me. I've no business to single out myself. Murder is something that keeps on happening in Shantihpur. But it's still murder, and I'm demanding justice."

He sat up bolt upright, his eyes blazing, completely oblivious of the stab of pain in his back. "I know the swine," he said. "I saw their faces and I won't forget them. If the law doesn't kill them I swear by Shiva *I* will. I'm a vegetarian, pacifist, South Indian Brahmin, who's been sat on by everyone else's *Karma*. I get beaten up at political demonstrations and I sit around, frustrated, in lavatories, not having the guts to kill those who would kill me. But I can fight too when what I love is murdered."

"Lie down," the M.O. told him. "Maybe I was fond of Kamala myself. Or perhaps I can't stand having my subordinates bumped off. Anyway, when the girl came screaming up here, I went out with a gun looking for trouble. The two boozers, as it turned out, had completely forgotten the girl. They'd stripped Kamala of her diamond earrings and were messing around her body, fumbling idiotically with the clasp of her necklace. Why they didn't simply break open the fastening beats me. Anyway, when they saw I meant business, they did what the brave men of Shantihpur always do and headed hastily for the nearest exit. The crowd was coming in at the other end of the street, and of course that meant that if I missed either of them I was going to plug some innocent bystander.

"They made their escape, didn't they?" asked Krishnan, drawing the conclusion that the facts seemed to dictate. He was tired by the persistent sense of failure, recurrent, invariable, like a malignant heartbeat, almost too tired to want to hear the rest.

He realized that he ought to thank the M.O. "You didn't have to make it your business," he said. "So I'm grateful, really grateful, that you did. In the end their getting away won't make any difference. I'll see to it personally that the scores are settled."

"It didn't happen the way you think," said the M.O. "It was the oddest thing, really. The crowd didn't open up and close over them as I had expected. They just stood there, refusing to give way, as if there was something they had to understand and as if even before they understood it they realized that a time had come for judgment. One of them recognized Kamala and whispered her name. There was a sigh at first, as if they couldn't grasp it, and then the anger came bristling among them as in an animal whose young ones have been killed. The two men ran right up to them waving their arms and screaming to be let through, and beat at the people, trying to force their way in. When they saw the look on the faces they started to beg. They were spun around and flung flat on their faces. I could almost hear the thing behind them snarling. They got back onto their knees whining and wailing and coming toward me because they feared me less. I let them have it; it was what I had come out for. But it wasn't I who killed them. It was the knives in their backs. Then the whole terrible juggernaut went over them. They weren't just trampled. They were absorbed. It was as if the entire force of that awful engine were wiping them and their sin out of existence."

His hand passed instinctively over his face as he spoke. "You've had your justice," he ended. "I only hope it helps you to sleep better. Some nights I'll wake up scared remembering it."

"They got what they deserved," Krishnan retorted. He tried to say it solidly and with finality, as if the execution made no difference to the judgment. But he was aware of the uneasiness telling him that it did.

"There's another side to it," he added, unwilling to face the violence, attempting to see a different meaning in it. "They wouldn't have done it if they hadn't been stirred by her death. Perhaps it shows that we've been too pessimistic and perhaps now that the first rush of their anger is over, the shock of how she died may make a difference."

The M.O. shook his head. "She'd have been horrified at it," he pointed out. "She'd have died all over again to stop it from happening. Is that what you call making a difference, making the crowd a more bloodthirsty animal? I was there, I *had* to look right into them, and if anything happened to them I ought to have known it. I never saw anything but fury in their faces."

"The riots are ending, though, aren't they?" asked Krishnan. "I don't seem to hear the shouting any longer. I look out of the window, and the street is as it used to be, with the people walking, not running, and with nothing in their hands. Perhaps I talk this way because I've only just awakened. But couldn't it be the beginning of a difference?"

"It doesn't mean what you think," the M.O. protested. "It's only because every fever must come to an end. The patient dies or he gets back to normal. You think they've stopped because they've looked at themselves, because they've suddenly seen the face of conscience. It's a handsome feeling, and you want Kamala framed in it. Only, it doesn't happen to fit the facts. They've stopped because they've done what they wanted to, satisfied their appetite. They've given up because there's nothing left to burn down."

He was unaware of the expression on his face as he spoke, and Krishnan found himself reassured by the man's intensity.

"It must have affected you a little," he suggested to the M.O. "You wouldn't be denying it in that way if you weren't a little afraid of being convinced."

"Rubbish," the M.O. exploded. "I'm just telling you what's good for you, that's all. You've got your life in front of you once you've come to your senses. There's no point in spending it among a lot of cobwebs."

"I'm sorry," said Krishnan. "It's a weakness of mine to want to look for meanings. Particularly after I've been hit on the head. But you're a practical person and you can find better things to do than to bother yourself about the stars I shouldn't see. The cholera, for instance. That's much more important than my hallucinations."

"The cholera's over now," the M.O. said. "The Moslems we took in have been buried. And the centers of infection were burned down in the riots. The contagion never spread to the rest of us. They cauterized the wound before it could."

His eyes lighted up as the force of the argument seized him. "What stopped it?" he asked Krishnan triumphantly. "It wasn't Kamala's principles. It was the crowd's violence, the thing she had fought against and which she died uselessly trying to prevent. She never taught them anything. All she succeeded in doing was to die. You want me to believe that death achieves something? What sense can that possibly make to me? All my life my business has been to fight death, to postpone it, to confine it, to take away a little from its claim. Her death wasn't different from any other, except that, being avoidable, it was even more futile and senseless. Put it among your cobwebs and set fire to it. Kamala never did anything but die. It's all that can be done by any death."

His face was flushed and his voice crackling with the excitement

of his conclusions. He looked at Krishnan pityingly for the first
time, and with relief, as if he were no longer dangerous. He strode
out almost jubilantly into the solid world of cleaner realities and
unthinking patients.

If there had been a door he would undoubtedly have banged it.

2

Kamala's father arrived on the following day. He had come as
early as he could, after the M.O.'s letter had reached him, but the
space on the air line had been completely taken, obliging him to
fly by a longer route. Remembering Krishnan's experience, he had
borrowed a car from a friend in Delhi. It had arrived safely, with
only the hubcaps stolen.

He was too late for the cremation, of course, and too late even
for the ceremony that followed, in which the water and milk had
been scattered over the pyre, the bones collected from each part of
the frail body and the ashes arranged as her body's silhouette, as
the last earthly reminder of her shape. There was nothing left now
but the small urn that enclosed the dust of the past, all that remained of the pride of obedience, the sculptured sense of duty,
the gentleness that floated through the littleness, all that he had
given seventeen months before in marriage under the *pandhal,*
letting her light pass out of his emptying life.

He was told of the meticulously performed ceremonies, of the
many who passed gravely by the bier, hands folded, as if the ob-
lations fell upon them also, so that in the small town which had
known many dyings there was a stillness of meditation gathered
around the frail flesh. There had been few formal repentances,
little of breast-beating, and of the conventional griefs that said
farewell. Even in leaving she had bestowed a deeper peace.

If he was impressed by the account, which had been dressed
up a little for a father's benefit, he allowed no appreciation to form
upon his face. He was tight-lipped and frozen-willed, yet it was
evident that he wore his manners as a protection, that he resorted

to the mask of dispassionate dignity only to keep his thoughts from the withering emptiness. Sometimes he fumbled for a word, but more often than not the sentences came as they should, polished, precise, deliberately balanced, reminding himself and Krishnan of a symmetry in all minds which it was proper to keep above personal grief.

He said he regretted that the marriage had failed. It was a remark so far below the level of the event, so incidental a reaction to her spent life, that Krishnan found himself impelled to protest. It was all his fault, he said and was going to add, but suddenly found it pointless, that in reality there had not been a failure. How could her father care about the lamps she had lighted in Krishnan's mind or want to count them against the darkness of her death? He told him that Kamala was a wonderful person, that she was more, much more, than he could claim to deserve. He had meant it sincerely, and in different circumstances he could have made the words live, but they sounded false now, a cinematic superlative, reminding them garishly of an inappropriate plot. It was remarkable how her father's tone, the solidity of his attitudes, dictated the quality of their exchanges, so that without his realizing it, everything fell within the polished periods.

She was a Hindu wife, her father said. Krishnan would have thought the ideal tyrannical once, a condemnation to a life of drudgery, toiling consumptively in the smoke-filled kitchen, waiting upon the men, eating apart, walking behind them in appropriate deference, bearing their children and accepting their sins. Now, under the severity of the judgment, he recognized a nobility, not one that he would want to inflict upon others, but which he could understand as a principle and pride in Kamala's life. She was a Hindu wife, he echoed, and watching her father's eyes glow, he knew that in his strict world of dignity and duty it was not possible to pay a higher compliment.

He added impulsively that he could never forget her. It was too personal a phrase, he realized later, being reminded by the other man's look that praise being treacherous had to be rendered objectively and that a wife was not simply all she had meant to her

husband. They inhabited a code, husband and wife, in which
happiness was only a by-product, not always born in the exchanges
of duty. Her father did not, however, reject the tribute. He inclined his head slightly toward the well-meant words as if he could
take them as meaning part of the truth. There was, he implied, a
space for personal grief. But the world would forget Kamala, and
it was not wrong that it should. And a man belonging in the
world had also to share in that forgetting. Six months from now,
he said, Krishnan would be looked on as an eligible widower and
he, Sankaran, as a man without a daughter. God had not been as
cruel as he might have been. His son remained, earnest, intense,
bred to the family tradition, admitted to a university at sixteen
and already receiving unprecedented distinctions. The line would
continue and would not degenerate. It was all that a father had
any right to ask.

He continued thus, impassive and unyielding, and little by little,
as the formulas of responsibility were repeated, the sense of blind-
ness was taken out of the tragedy and he could look at it, live in
its aftermath, with due emotion but without hysteria. Krishnan
let him come to his reconciliation in his own way. He himself felt
differently about the meaning of Kamala's death, but the other
man would not have accepted his answers and probably, in his
eyes, even to talk of a meaning was a mistake. One died as one
should. Nonattachment, Kruger would have called it. To perform
the action because of its own rightness, irrespective of what the
action accomplished, so that one's purity stood above it, even above
the ultimate action of death. But was it philosophy or only a ferocious etiquette? Was it only a question of dying in the right dress?

He asked himself the questions as the day passed, and Sankaran
went in and out of the hospital, performing the minor rituals that
remained. In the evening he was regaled by his parents' arrival.
They had waited for space on the direct route, since detours
through Bombay were too expensive for his father's taste, notwithstanding his mother's protestations that her only son, if not at
death's brink, was in dire danger. She had reached her destination
bedraggled but determined, ready for the ordeal of Shantihpur as

if it were the siege of the Red Fort. A formidable array of utensils
had been imported since Krishnan obviously needed South Indian
cooking and since no cooking could be authentically South Indian
if it was done in North Indian pans and pots. Also in the cargo,
paradoxically, were some soggy English cereals and several tins
of stale biscuits, but these, it was explained, were to remind him
of the happier moments of his British heritage. There was then
unpacked an enormous contraption for filtering water, of the
kind found only in superior hospitals and railway station restau-
rants. Then came the toiletries: oil of exceptional quality extracted
from hand-picked coconuts, *neem*-flavored toothpaste made to a
special formula, which could cure anything from warts to low intelligence, and sandalwood soap with that rare and special fragrance that was achieved only in the mills of Mysore.

It must have required most of a plane to carry it, so his father's
decision not to detour through Bombay was evidently no more
than a token resistance. The inhabitants of Shantihpur had at
first looked askance at the invasion; but being largely unem-
ployed, several of them perceived in it a golden opportunity for
economic progress. The result was a rash of applications to serve
the noble cause of V. S. Krishnan's recovery, principally from mendicants and vagrants who claimed great devotion to the memory
of Kamala. As night fell, Mother was immersed in a multitude
of *chits,* almost all of them from men of great eminence in Lahore
and Delhi. Some indeed were in the name of the Prime Minister,
and while this made it obvious that a process of fabrication was at
work, judging the extent of it reduced Mother to confusion.

At this point Father stepped in brusquely and informed the local
citizenry that they could best demonstrate their undoubted devotion to Kamala by consenting to work for half the usual wages.
This immediately thinned the ranks of the applicants, reducing
them to a meager twenty-seven who were either telling the truth
or were more than normally hungry. From them, five were selected who seemed the least likely to complain of overwork or to
collapse from unaccustomed labor.

The retinue was now complete except that there was no place

to deploy them. Recognition of this fact, which her earlier recruiting enthusiasms had obscured, reduced Mother to her deepest dejection. She had not expected to be confined to transactions in tents. She had been told that Shantihpur was a place of violence and that her only son lay beleaguered in it, but, like Tippoo Sultan, whom he excelled in virtue, he deserved at least to be beleaguered in a palace. Her campaign of relief, which was now approaching military dimensions, was based on the premise of adequate housing. On any lesser assumption the panoply of her logistics would collapse.

All would have been lost if the *ghee* merchant who had started the Shantihpur riots had not, after Kamala's death, been subject nightly to Kali's visitations. On three successive nights the grisly image of the goddess had appeared to him clothed in what was undeniably pig's fat and his own blood. The merchant could have taken the obvious course and blamed the quality of his own *ghee* for the nightmares; but professional stubbornness obliged him to conclude that Kamala was the goddess Parvati incarnate and that since he was at least indirectly responsible for her death, her minions would pursue him to the ends of the earth. His fears were brought to a climax when, rising from his bed on the third day, he discovered a cobra coiled expectantly under it. With a shout of dismay, and making use of an unsuspected ability for tap dancing, he extricated himself from this unnatural jeopardy without injuring either himself or the snake. Fleeing to his shop, he enjoined his trembling assistant to feed the reptile with buttermilk and honey so that in due course the evil demon in it might come to prefer these delicacies to his blood.

After the day's *ghee* had been sold, he arrived at the hospital quivering and panic-stricken, ready in principle to retreat to the Himalayas but doubtful that from so remote an altitude he could successfully direct his commercial ventures. The M.O. listened gravely to his story and then advised him that the only possible course was to surrender his house to Kamala's relatives. If a sacrifice on this scale were made to Kali's wrath it might not be necessary to flee to the mountains. The merchant would probably be doing sufficient penance if he took up his abode in Shantihpur's worst tent.

The man listened, reflected, and after some hesitation accepted the proposal, though it was difficult to say whether the tears in his eyes were of gratitude or chagrin. He added, by way of additional propitiation, that free *ghee* would be provided for all of Kamala's relatives. Then, recollecting that Krishnan had a tendency to keep on living no matter how often he was hit on the head, he hastily limited this concession to the time it would take to dispel the evil spirits.

Thus, at ten o'clock on a moonlight night Krishnan was removed to what his father-in-law euphoniously described as more commodious quarters. He was tired and would have preferred to spend the rest of the night sleeping, comparatively undisturbed, where he was; but his mother was emphatic that he had already spent too long in that ghoulish place of staring refugees and burned *almirahs*, where hidden death stalked among the rickety tiles. So the bed on which he lay was duly raised on four uneven pairs of scraggy shoulders and carried down the street with the frantic motion of an ailing tramp steamer in a China Seas typhoon.

It was somewhat over a mile to the *ghee* merchant's residence, which the cobra was now reported to have left, proving to everyone's satisfaction that it had arrived there at Kamala's behest. A large number of Shantihpur's citizens joined the procession, several because they had nothing better to do, and others because they had convinced themselves that by taking part in it nothing but time could be lost, while on the other hand much merit might conceivably be gained. Drums were beaten and torches set alight. There was piping of flutes and dancing around the figure propped up like an effigy in the perilously swaying bed. Krishnan's mother, happily aware that her son had achieved a recognition not normally given to minor civil servants, enhanced the occasion by distributing sweets.

It was a quarter to eleven when Krishnan, exhausted and disgusted, was set down in his new home by his weary retinue. He pretended to be fast asleep. This saved him from the nightly glass of Horlicks which his mother was otherwise determined to dispense.

"Never mind," he heard her saying, undaunted. "When he wakes up in the morning we'll give him a steaming tureen of Bovril. Of course, it's beef broth and he's a vegetarian. But he's our only son also, and we've got to make him well."

He knew what to expect, at any rate, and he awoke with the sun, on the principle that it was best to complete the ordeal early and have the whole day ahead of him to mend his tattered condition. She had not exaggerated when she had said "tureen." She watched him solicitously as he gulped down the body-building fluid, searching his complexion for the beefy glow of health. Illness, she informed him, should be assaulted from every direction. He would have Wincarnis at lunch and Sanatogen at teatime. She would make him better than new, she said implacably. No stone would be left unturned or avenue unexplored.

She looked at the room with its vivid bowl of flowers, zinnias, acacia and sprays of queen of the night, at the ominous tins of potent restoratives and at the sun gleaming in on the pornographic pictures which the *ghee* merchant had forgotten to remove in his flight.

"It's so much nicer than the hospital," she said. "We really owe it to Kamala. Her passing away was a terrible thing, to be sure, but it's fortunate, isn't it, that it had such a happy effect."

Krishnan's irritation reached the simmering point. "I'd rather she were alive," he retorted shortly.

"Of course, of course," his mother blandly agreed. "The poor girl ought never to have died. But when you do die it's always so reassuring to know that your death is accomplishing something useful. How happy she must be, sitting up in Heaven, to know that she's helping her beloved husband to get well."

"She was a Hindu wife," Krishnan protested indignantly. "She never compromised with what was right. Her death was noble, inspiring in itself, one learns from it, without its accomplishing anything. She did her duty, and that's its own reward."

His mother looked at him, her face shining with admiration.

"You love her still," she proclaimed ecstatically. "Such touching and tender devotion! It's just what I expected from my only son and it's going to make you so much more eligible. But you must look forward, dear. Your whole life is before you. You'll never get well by moping. You simply can't live entirely in the past."

He felt helpless before her fond irrelevancies. He could never change his image in her eyes. He reasoned with himself that the best course was not to argue but to endeavor to create a diversion.

"Please," he suggested despairingly. "That *dacoit* in the kitchen who calls himself a cook. Can you be sure he's really making *iddalis?*"

With relief, he saw the consternation on her face.

"Oh, Krishnan," she wailed, dejectedly wringing her hands. "All the Wincarnis has been left in the storeroom. Supposing he drinks it up thinking that it's port. Then you won't be able to get well for weeks."

She shuffled off, leaving him mercifully to his thoughts. He was startled to realize that it was almost twenty-four hours since he had had the privilege of being left to himself.

All of a sudden he remembered the child. He blamed himself angrily for not having made inquiries. The commotion of the past day, the grinding pain, from time to time searingly localized, which seemed to be all that existed of his body, were not, he told himself, reasons enough to forget.

When his mother came back he went on strike and refused to touch the Wincarnis or smell the *sambhar* until the infant's fate was ascertained.

It was an hour before the M.O. could be reached. His mother stood piteously, while Krishnan glared and glowered, watching her only son slowly starving to death. When the messenger returned it was with the perplexing news that the child had been given to a gracious, generous and completely penniless lady, who had a husband afflicted by dengue, a daughter in an advanced stage of expectancy, and a deep desire to serve the memory of Kamala, even if only by bringing up her adopted offspring. Within forty-eight hours of the infant's arrival, the husband had miraculously been cured and the daughter safely delivered of a son. To the mother's disinterested affection for the orphan there was thus added the hope of heavenly good fortune and of rising in life to a modest and sober prosperity. Was it not cruel to expect her to relinquish the gift which Providence had so unexpectedly bestowed?

It was superstitious rubbish, Krishnan snorted—dengue hardly ever lasted for more than a fortnight, and the man was already in his twelfth day. As for the daughter, she was just as likely to give birth to a son as not. There was nothing miraculous about the infant; it was a typical, normal, ordinary, two-legged brat and if it were not returned immediately to its foster father the holy memory of Kamala would be much agitated. These facts were conveyed to the recalcitrant woman, who replied that Krishnan, as the husband of a wife of celestial goodness, deserved to have his opinions treated with vast respect. However, the truth was that the goddess Parvati had appeared to her in a dream the previous night and had enjoined her strictly not to give up the child. Parvati, needless to say, had the face of Kamala. Thus the woman was now inexorably tied to the infant by a combination of holy love and terror. Whither it went she was determined to go.

It was plain as a pikestaff now, Krishnan's father said. All the wretched woman wanted was a job, and blowed he was if he was going to let her have it. Expenses in this lunatic operation kept on rising, his limited finances were dangerously strained, and merely to get the bilge and biscuits to Shantihpur, one third of the coconuts on the plantation had been mortgaged. Why was it necessary to add to the family circle a brat of unknown and probably obnoxious origins and a cadaverous ayah of unlimited appetites?

Father was right as always, Mother said. The child was almost certainly not a Brahmin, and if Krishnan carted it along wherever he went, how could he ever expect to get remarried? He was better off without it. If it brought the woman good fortune she would sing Krishnan's praises forever; and if it didn't she could only blame her own stupidity.

Knowing the probable outcome, he didn't argue about it. He

merely said that until the child was produced, no food whatsoever
would be permitted to pass his lips, and that included Wincarnis,
Sanatogen and Bovril. Then he lay back, feeling considerably better. The hunger strike was a potent political weapon, and besides,
he had already had far too much to eat. He was prepared to die if
need be, he added horrifyingly, and that was all that was needed
to make his mother dissolve. Having done that, she liquidated his
father's resistance also.

The child arrived, and its compulsory guardian with it. The
woman was wizened, with the impassive face and parchment skin
of those who were born from the earth and sealed in its wisdom.
At least that was his initial, romantic impression. When he studied
her more closely he found that she was covetous, superstitious and
a chronic liar. Sandwiched between these two images was a feeling
for the child and, through it, for Kamala, in which affection and
reverence were inextricably mingled with avarice. He began to tell
himself that it could not be otherwise. He himself was aware of a
purity in Kamala's death, the flight of an arrow, the fall of a leaf,
the exact, relentless movement of a beginning to the terrifying end
which its nature ordained. And yet had the end come to her? Or
had she sought it, thrust herself upon it? Had she done the action
solely because it was right or because it was also the means of her
deliverance? Was not the lovely and unnatural arrogance, the erect
exultation with which she went to her death, the confession of the
small seed of her failing?

He was glad that he could see the flaw now and hold it in his
thoughts without its opening his mind to its fissures. Her act was
brave and gallant. It haunted him, not because it was totally pure
and perfect, the nonattached act all philosophers contemplated,
but because it was her act and hers alone, true completely to her
pride and loneliness, and because even in its imperfections it ex-
pressed her. It would glow in his mind only because she did, because he had known her body, shared her quiet happiness, and
followed her to that angry uncompromising climax from which
she had not wavered, but had entered proudly, with the strength
of a lover's consistency. And for the outer world it would be what

each man wished—courageous, foolhardy, an idealistic death, a willful suicide, the occasion for a fat man's fear, an old woman's superstition, a crowd's pulverizing, orgiastic vengeance.

The act was not totally pure, and even if it had been so, the response, being human, had to be corrupt. She would go, diminishing, down the river of death, borne away by quacks and charlatans and astrologers. They were part of the living stream, the inevitable degradation. They were in the procession which carried every idea.

3

The timetable of ritual was specific and detailed, as precise as any conventional timetable. It called for Kamala's ashes to be cast on the waters immediately after the pyre had been extinguished, on the second day following her death. Because of her father's impending arrival the ceremony was postponed and, at Krishnan's insistence, postponed further, until he himself was well enough to perform it. It was not a situation that the family relished. Sankaran, they said, could have done it quietly, consigning the ashes to the Jumna, which was sufficiently sacred and not too far away. If matters were delayed they usually became more complex. Once Krishnan had recovered enough to perform the ceremony, the financial as well as the moral responsibility was his (a point which his father duly emphasized), and since Krishnan would have nothing less than Benares, there was, in addition to the considerable expense, the logistical problems of moving the whole caravansary to that distant city, foundling and ayah inexorably included. Krishnan's thoughts of Benares made evident his devotion, from which his future wife would undoubtedly benefit, and indeed, said Mother, pursing her lips, the ambiguous nature of Kamala's death might make Benares desirable as an atonement. But her father, who must have been aware of the circumstances and perhaps of other failings that their brief knowledge of Kamala had not counted, had not even mentioned Benares, and why should they, who had only taken her, give what those who had borne her did not even expect? It was not right to dwell too much with the dead; one was expected to return to normal on the thirteenth day, and Krishnan should moderate an attachment that was in truth beginning to be morbid. Life was real, life was earnest, she declared intimidatingly, and the poet, with his usual penetration, had added that the grave was not its goal.

Unless he resorted to hunger strikes, Krishnan realized, he was unlikely to get the better of the argument and he could see his father chafing in the corner, grimly counting the coconuts in bondage. The situation was not improved by the ayah, who was the family's sole means of communication with Parvati and who had been told directly by the goddess herself that anything less than Benares would be fatal. Was there no bottom to avarice, Father exploded. Not content with obtaining a free job, the cadaverous crone was cadging a free pilgrimage. Krishnan, weighing the mounting odds against him, told himself that someday he would go to Benares on Kamala's behalf and that it was the fact and spirit, not the timing, that mattered. That was the evening before Kruger's letter arrived; it was a barbed and blistering exercise in scholarship. North Indian priests, snorted Kruger, apart from their vulgar habit of swallowing their last syllables, were given to dangerous abridgements of ritual, being victims of the two-anna-an-hour mentality. Had they, for instance, he queried thunderously, properly lined the palms of the corpse with silver. (They had not, and Father, in retaliation, lined their palms with only half the silver they expected.) Since they had not, Kruger proclaimed, devastatingly confident of the answer, it was to be presumed that these semiliterate priests had also neglected other vital elements, such as giving a milch cow to a Yama-fearing Brahmin. After such gross and cardinal omissions it was hardly to be expected that Kamala's soul could be given safe passage, and Krishnan, as the person technically responsible, would pay fully for the negligence of the priests. According to certain authoritative texts, it seemed likely that he would be rendered impotent or, like certain eminent poets, made partially blind in one eye. At any rate, he would certainly never remarry. There was only one course of action, Kruger concluded, and he wished to emphasize that he was promising nothing, only prescribing an obvious antidote. A proper redemption must be made at Benares and he himself would be on hand to see that scholarship was not defaced and that ancient wisdom was not further dishonored.

Only one conclusion was possible after Kruger's letter, and that entailed propelling Father, despite his mechanical protests, even more deeply into the moneylender's embrace. He did indeed remark sourly that it was better to pawn the biscuits than the plantation; but Mother, who was becoming tired of the pretense, reminded him crushingly of the size of his bank account and, with tears streaming, told him that she would rather be impecunious than live to see her only offspring impotent.

Though Krishnan's recovery was speedier than the M.O. had expected, it was ten days before the expedition could depart. The atmosphere was sultry, and Sankaran, aware of what was charging it, offered tentatively to take care of a portion of the expenses. But Father replied curtly that his family was quite capable of looking after itself and had often mended the deficiencies of others. It was certainly nobody's fault, Mother added with sweet impersonality, if as a result of someone else's rashness her only son was beaten half to death, and if he should now turn out to be sterile and one quarter blind, because of omissions made when he was unconscious, which other people did not find it their business to remedy. Not that she was complaining, she insisted. If it was fate one had to bear it with fortitude, and of course the whole principle of justice was to do it without expecting it of others.

The journey was consumed in veiled allusions, and Sankaran, who was no novice at the art, pointed out that justice was traditionally blind, which was no doubt the reason some people were unseeing. Far be it from him to complain either, he retorted. It was obviously no one's fault if a loyal and guileless wife found herself suddenly abandoned, and it would be churlish not to recognize that a foreign education enlarged a man's horizon so that country chattels might not be to his taste. Although he was careful not to look at Krishnan as he said it, the line of fire was distinct enough, and Krishnan, by no means anxious to have his past actions made into a verbal battlefield, was more than relieved when the threatening journey ended.

Kruger met them at the station and lifted the hostilities to the higher plane of scholarship, where all were able to unite more or less happily in a common anger against uneducated priests. He led them to the *chatram,* the rest house, which he had chosen personally after rigorous investigation. It was not the best among them—in fact, there was no furniture whatever, the taps did not work, the roof was leaky and the place smelled of urine—but it had been built by a moneylender who had never charged more than 20 per cent interest and who was therefore not undeserving of the great merit that would be bestowed upon him when a Brahmin such as Kruger made use of his facilities.

Next morning they were at the brink of the teeming river early enough to catch the burnish of the sun upon the waters, as it fingered the long, irregular, downward-sloping steps, worn with the weight of untold pilgrimages and even now bearing the milling onrush of hastes and hesitations, as the thousands came once more to the edge of holiness. By rail and by river and by airplane, or marching along the scorching, pitiless roads, stumbling, starving, dragging their blistered feet, they all came, rich and poor alike, in the plain clothes of mourning and repentance, the differences stripped away, merged and reborn in the torrent of a common identity. The narrow streets which opened on to the *ghats* were filled with the incense of the temple's shadow. The shuttered spaces had the scent of infinity. Everywhere, hemmed in by the hustling crowds, jostled by a will that seemed to be beyond one, one felt nevertheless a sense of liberation, not of being alone but rather of being unhindered, of a common strength born into a personal blessing.

Along the river's length the bodies burned, the cry of the lost rose and fell in wailing, chanting abandon, the breasts were torn, the black hair rent, partly in grief and partly in the solace of the ceremony that subdued the sorrow. Over the charred pyres, the sickening odor of the consumed flesh drifted. In the turmoil, the holy men sat and stood transfixed, as if the screaming were a distant numbness and only the bright light in the mind existed, spreading and devouring the world's false flame. And the less holy, those of a lower discipline, who had quelled the body but had not as yet abandoned it, and at their fringes the salesmen of holiness— flagellants, agony-swallowers, the star performers of a spiritual carnival—displayed their mutilated selves to the world's judgment, the scantily filled begging howls thirsting for the charity which flowed out of the smoke pall, under troubled minds, and around the bodies of the newly dead.

At the river's edge the sacrificial fire was lighted, the flame that had burned in their two hearts since their wedding flaring now in the last rites of death. The water was cupped in the stiff, dried blades of sword grass and sprinkled, exiling evil once more to the earth's four corners. Drifting into the half-familiar ceremonies, which in their unison joined marriage and death, absorbed in a purpose with no precise beginning, Krishnan found himself say- ing the soothing words, making them form in his own voice, not simply repeating but possessing what the priest chanted, with the reassuring, slowly solidifying feeling of more than Kamala's loss being washed away. The details of the scene in front of him seemed to recede, as a different reality moved into its foreground and he was aware only dimly of the participants in the ceremony, of Kruger criticizing the priest's pronunciation, stopping him once because of a textual inaccuracy and on another occasion because he was not facing due south, as was required under the funeral rites. He saw Mother indistinctly, her face dimmed for the first time with the tears she had never before given to Kamala's mem- ory, and, vaguely also, Sankaran's drawn, malaria-drained features, gradually frozen into a strength of stone, from which the pain remorselessly ebbed, leaving only a frightening Buddha-like benev- olence. Then even the people seemed to dissolve in Krishnan's eyes. The chanting and the tumult softened to silence, and all that was left was himself and the endless river, the small brass vessel that now held Kamala's ashes and the words of supplication that would send her to her destiny.

Agni, do not afflict her, consume her not, entirely.
Scatter not her skin and body to the emptiness
Let her be born first in your fire of wisdom
Schooled in God's truth, give her to her ancestors.

Out of the ashes, he knew, would come more than the ashes, and watching the sacred water lap the steps, throwing up the scum line of its debris, he could imagine himself being brushed for a brief moment by the sensation of a different life evolving.

Ripe in the truth, yield her to her ancestors.
Into the world of spirits let her float
Subject to no will but to law everlasting.

It was time now for the last rite of dissolution.

Let the eye repair to the sun, the breath to the wind.
As her virtues befit her, let her body be given
To the ocean, the air, and the greenness of the earth
The growing life of the plants, the mingling waters.

The urn was emptied, the ashes cast out upon the gentle current and the world focused again, the sorrow and the elation, all those whom desire had jostled down the steps, to be healed, to be blessed, to wash away the dead, the weight of error, gathered together in superstition and fear, in charlatanry and the throngs of the truth, in the temple's silence and the clanging of carnivals, the deep sincerity mingling with the gaudiness, so that each was the condition in which the other found itself. He saw the ashes fan out, crumple, melt away from the reaching hands, the singing rising and falling, and watched the devout, who had come from distant places, plunge ravenously into the cleansing stream, oblivious of the cattle and the corpses, the refuse, the leaves and flowers swirling, the flotsam and jetsam and the hubbub of life.

4

When they had trudged back to the rest house, Mother was ready to sigh with relief and Father to count what remained of his blessings and to make inquiries about the earliest train home. Kruger, however, reminded them sternly that under the ceremonial rites, donations had to be given to not less than thirty-two Brahmins. Father must have been more tired than anyone thought since he raised no objection beyond suggesting mildly that this might be a good time to dispose of the surplus biscuits. Mother, who had not been entirely carried away by her visit to Benares, asked with unconscious cynicism where thirty-two deserving Brahmins were to be found. This gave Kruger his opportunity to agree that moral standards were undoubtedly relative. However, there were many, he said, even in his own limited circle of acquaintances, for whom a little help would go a long way. There were men of more than ordinary piety who, because their children or wives were ill, could not undertake essential pilgrimages. There were scholars of almost desperate diligence whose minds would not function because their bodies were nearing collapse. Finally there were holy men who had truly mastered the flesh and who could sit on nails or stand for two years on one leg, with the correct air of absent-mindedness. He had a list, he said, producing the much erased piece of paper which he must have begun to prepare several days earlier, and of course any list that Kruger compiled would be judicious, thorough and unswervingly logical, given its assumptions. One could quarrel with the assumptions, certainly, but Benares was hardly the place to begin. There was, in fact, no real room for argument. Father asked resignedly what the total damage was and, when he had paid the final costs of death, weakly wished Krishnan a long and prosperous life. Kruger dispensed the largesse; it was technically Krishnan's responsibility, but he was far from well, and the ceremonies at the *ghat* had demanded more from him than he had realized.

Mother could not yet breathe her sigh of relief. There was still

the ceremony of the thirteenth day, which Kruger insisted on performing, and a further round of gifts to worthy Brahmins. Then
the house was blessed, life formally came back to normal, and
Father began to consult the railway timetable. Mother opened the
newspaper and read aloud two offers of second-hand bicycles as if
they were earth-shaking political events; at this point her eye was
able to pass felicitously to her real concern, which was the marriage
advertisements.

"Isn't this interesting?" she announced. "A Vadama girl has no
objection to a widower. She's a Bachelor of Arts, in public finance
and European history. But she sings well and plays the *veena* also."

"Krishnan can do better," his father said. "He's a Government
servant on the way up. He shouldn't settle for less than a Joint
Secretary's daughter."

"A Joint Secretary with a house," responded Mother, her face
shining with expectancy. "Krishnan isn't an ordinary match. He
isn't like those young men of twenty with poverty-stricken parents,
whom the bride's father has to educate in England."

"Fine kind of education," Father snorted. "Half of them can't
pass their examinations and they sit around taking the Bar, or so
they call it, though it's really monkeying with the landlady's daughter. A girl's father can put down twenty thousand good rupees
and what's he got but a Socialist in the front room?"

"Come, come," protested Krishnan. "I've known Conservatives
who sleep with the gardener's daughter."

His wit was lost on his dedicated audience.

"I wasn't trying to define a political type," Father pointed out,
ostentatiously pained by his son's irrelevance. "Perhaps I can put
the point to your limited understanding more adequately in financial terms. Instead of a potential waste you're an expanding asset.
It isn't such a common thing in India, and if people want it they
must pay the going price." He realized that he was unconsciously
rubbing his hands. He sat back, embarrassed, trying not to look
like a stockbroker.

"Father's always so right," said Mother enthusiastically. "Besides, you're not just a Government servant but a kind of romantic

hero. Just look at all that you've suffered for Kamala's sake. Any girl who marries you can be sure that you'll defy death in order to protect her from evil."

"He's a true Brahmin also," Kruger added. "He's the only one among you who sincerely desired to come to Benares. He came out of a sense of piety and duty and not, like you, because he feared the wrath of the gods. He performed the rites well, even though his body tormented him."

"Brahmin, hero and Government Servant also!" Mother exclaimed, clapping her hands, her expression starry-eyed. "What greater paragon can a fond father-in-law request?"

"This particular paragon," Krishnan said brusquely, "is going to make up its own mind. I'll marry whom I wish and when I please. And when I do so I'm going to marry the girl. Just her, you understand. Not the Akbar Road house, the Frigidaire or the Buick."

"Just listen to him," Mother commented, entranced. "Any normal father-in-law would give him two Buicks for saying that. You're quite right, Krishnan dear. Your business is just to look masterfully into the girl's eyes and leave us to negotiate the details of the dowry."

"By all means negotiate," said Krishnan. "A dowry can't be paid without the groom. As the potential groom, I'm sorry to inform you that the odds are heavily against my marrying again."

Mother didn't seem to be at all perturbed. "My dear boy," she said, trying to soothe him. "It's the natural way to feel. After all, it's less than four weeks since Kamala passed away. But in a few months you'll begin to realize that every man needs a mate and that it isn't good for one to be alone. When you feel that way we'll have all the candidates ready."

"I'll stay single," Krishnan repeated, making the discouragement stronger. "God knows I've made enough mistakes."

"That's just it, dear," said Mother. "You've made so many, you can't make any more. It's written in your horoscope. If you mount the pedestal of an appropriate marriage there's no telling how far you can climb the ladder of success."

She was swept away by the heady mixture of metaphors and began enthusiastically to count her prospects.

"Menaka's gone," she said, "but there are others just as good. There's Lakshmi. Her father owns a quarter of a cotton mill, but business is getting quite respectable these days, and it's nice to be always sure of having saris. Then there's Radha, who went to Shantiniketan and personally knew Tagore. I don't know, though, exactly what *her* father owns. Everyone says that Urmila's quite brilliant, and when one is an aspiring civil servant, it's good to have a dancer in the family. And then there's Meenakshi, and Sarada and Rekha and that Congressman's daughter who played Damayanti so well, though personally, I must say, I've never trusted actresses, and Sambasivan's eldest—I nearly forgot her—particularly if he's made Commissioner next month."

She went on, increasingly oblivious of her surroundings, and Krishnan let her talk, knowing that nothing he could say would ever convince her that time had passed, that a world of experience had gone by and that the force of events had altered forever the image which she held unchanging in her fondness, with the names of the eligibles, the would-be wives and courtiers, joining hands in an admiring circle around it.

5

They went home, and he had to go on. His mother wanted to be with him in Delhi, to set up a household and minister to his needs, but the funeral was over and the wounds were healing. The thirteenth day, according to the texts, was the day of return to the normal life, the desk at one end, the rickety bed at the other and the car commuting between the mind and the body.

The regular motion of the train becalmed him and he sat back, adjusting various tensions, watching the clear sky float uniformly past and the earth green with the relief from heat and the approaching coolness of winter. He got himself out and went to the place called home, the night end of the shuttle where his suitcases lived. He put everything into its place, including his own mind. He walked in the groove and it no longer felt like a trap.

He'd told Cynthia he wanted to say good-by and he drove up to the farewell. She was a little slimmer, so it seemed, and dressed with a quiet elegance. He was aware of the carefully chosen details but realized that she no longer dressed that way for him. He looked at her, and all he did was see her. If his eyes closed she would be there no longer.

"Krish," she said gently, "I can't tell you how sorry I am."

She kept the distance even in her voice. She too was aware of the small space between them which neither of them would ever again invade.

"We were happy together," he said to her very simply.

The words didn't sound inadequate. They covered all of the truth, and for the first time he was able to speak to her directly, without having to devise a brightness over which both of them could parry and thrust.

"I know," she responded. "I know you found something, Krish. That's why I'm so sorry that you had to lose it."

"I haven't lost anything," he answered, and saying it with conviction but without vehemence, saying it like that to the other side of his life, he knew that he was finding himself and not simply leaning on the strength of Kamala's love.

Some of her impatience with the symbols edged back. "She *is* dead, isn't she? When you love someone deeply and the person dies, don't tell me you haven't suffered a loss."

"Her ashes are gone," he answered reassuringly. "They're forty-six miles below Benares by now."

"You mean her memory is going to live with you always?"

"Not her memory," he corrected her, "but the difference she's made within me."

She looked at him levelly, trying to make him fidget. But he wasn't going to retreat from the words. They were what he intended to say. It was good to walk up to the simple, steadfast truths and not have to maneuver a cleverness from them.

"You're different, Krish," she concluded.

"I'm just myself," he said.

She smiled a little, but to herself, not at him, and watching her face soften, he felt it was safe to say it.

"You're looking lovely, Cynthia."

"Thank you," she said, and her satisfaction was simple, not the brittle thing it had been in the past, the recognition, however deftly smoothed over, of an advantage gained, an opportunity opened. "Thanks, Krish. It's good to hear you say that. And I'm glad that her death did something. That so many have stopped and are thinking. That her people, those among whom she worked, are going to live in a world that's a little farther from the edge and the trigger."

This was the big temptation, and he could hear the voice in him inciting him to agree, erect the memorial, raise the flag above her, let the achievement grow green from her death. Then he thought of Kamala's loyal littleness, and her quiet pride of duty, and it was enough. With a sudden happiness he knew it was enough; there was nothing else, no meaning required to make the truth.

"It isn't a question of what her death did," he said. "It's done other things also. It's made a crowd savage, an old woman superstitious. Maybe it did stop the riots. I think so myself. But if it didn't, then it still doesn't make a difference. She was true to herself and that is all that matters. It's a question of what she was, not what she did."

Cynthia furrowed her brows and then good-humoredly gave up. "I can't understand, Krish," she said. "I don't even know that there's any point in trying. People act in order to accomplish something. You can't give more to action than your life, so you've got to give it for the largest possible purpose. If her death didn't achieve the ends she wanted, that's failure, and failure *can* be heroic and noble. But if there isn't even a question of what she died for, if there isn't a purpose to measure it against, what else can it be but mean and futile and horrid?"

"It's how I feel," he said with quiet finality. "Even if I can't be understood. Maybe I loved her and her death was her too."

She reflected a little more about it. "I suppose I'll understand in the end," she said. "I'm not so terribly unlike her, you know. I don't like compromises either."

"Don't I know," he said, teasing her. "I still remember the night you threw me out."

She protested a little, but amiably, at his saying that. "All I was doing was trying to cut my losses."

"It was good of you," he assured her. He was glad to see her eyes light up and to know she was grateful for his gratitude. "It was gallant and good and it put me on the right road. But be sensible, Cynthia. Don't be a perfectionist. Go home and settle for ninety-eight per cent."

"Yes, Krish," she murmured. "You know I always obey you."

"You're a wonderful girl, Cynthia."

"Don't let it bother you."

"It doesn't any more," he said.

It didn't, and he kissed her on the cheek and went out, down the corridor, into the disciplined emptiness, out of the dream and back into the groove.

6

There was one more call, and he made it immediately afterward. The white house had been repainted and the garden was tidy and bright. It was recovering fast from the annual illness of summer.

Vijayaraghavan was there, slumped in the easy chair, as if forgetting were a kind of duty. He was bonier, more angular, the fire in his eyes a little further burned out. He looked at Krishnan as if he had seen everything through his spectacles.

"You've killed her, haven't you?" he accused him abruptly.

"I got half killed trying to stop her from dying."

"You've killed her," he insisted. "Why did she go to Shantihpur? Because you walked off with that English baggage. She could have led a decent, ordinary life, growing dahlias in front of the house and rearing children and waiting for you to bumble back from the office. It was you who pushed her to the end of the road. So don't tell me that she died a heroine's death."

"She died as she had always lived," said Krishnan. "Yes, I know it's a hollow thing to say. It isn't even big enough to contain the emptiness. But there was more than happiness in living with her. There was a sense of order also. It hasn't gone entirely with the ashes."

"There's nothing left," said Vijayaraghavan quietly. "Neither her body nor her gentleness. There aren't even children to inherit her eyes. You can always trust a fool to kill completely."

"There's something that won't die," Krishnan persisted.

"She's dead, curse you," the other man flared back. "She's dead, and spare me your blundering holiness. I can't touch her with my fingers or my mind, and so she's dead. I want her living and not your morbid memories."

He sat up angrily, the sense of loss so massive in his slight body that he could no longer remain in his chosen pose, the urbanity of drawing-room contempt. Krishnan could sense him groping for the images of scorn, as if to build them into a shape around him.

"I think I understand," Krishnan said gently. "It must feel worse if you have loved but never known her."

Vijayaraghavan eased back in the chair a little. "Continue," he said. "Tell me what her death did. I suppose you'll say she stopped the Shantihpur riots. It would be a fine-sounding equation if I could make it mean sense to me. But I'd rather have her than all the people she saved."

"It isn't an equation," Krishnan began.

"I suppose her death made some kind of a difference to you."

"In a way, yes," Krishnan conceded, bracing himself for the answer.

Vijayaraghavan struck back much as Krishnan had expected he would. "Damn you, you pompous, preaching fool. She didn't die for your higher education."

"She didn't die for anything," Krishnan said.

"Not even to save a Moslem prostitute?"

"Not even for that," Krishnan maintained, surprised by his own firmness. "Not to protect her but to do what was right."

"You've learned your lesson," Vijayaraghavan admitted. "I've read the *Gita* too. Only, when I look at her death the *Gita* no longer makes sense."

He got up and opened the door for Krishnan. "Go home," he suggested. "Wrap yourself in red tape and the sacred books. It isn't my business to make you less of an Indian."

Krishnan went away but he didn't go directly home, whichever end of the shuttle home might be. He drove to the bank of the Jumna and watched the wide blue waters flowing serenely now in the waning sunlight, as if fear had never grown on their red banks. Hundreds of miles away, their holiness would join that of the Ganges, and both would flow into the ocean and the ashes of infinite memories.

The curve of the horizon and the sweeping, stretching spaces reminded him of Kamala's littleness and her death, yet, measuring it against the neutral emptiness, he felt himself neither helpless nor alone.

It was right that they should not understand her leaving— neither the M.O. nor Cynthia nor even Vijayaraghavan, with his tight-lipped protections stripped down to their grief. The world absorbed her absence in its own way, a crowd's way, the way of a frightened merchant, Mother bride-bent and Father calculating, and in Benares the way of the rapturous pilgrim to whom the body passed in a blaze of blessing. His understanding was his own, it grew out of his own life, and if by chance others had come to share it, it might have meant only that he depended on them once more.

He belonged to himself now, not to the family, or the code of conduct, or the rebellion against them, or the subtler persuasions of the mind and the heart. He didn't have to stand on a philosophy, be rooted in a scene. If there was a house around him, then the house would be his. He wouldn't have to come up the steps, between the pock-marked pillars, putting his shoulder against the hesitant door, fumbling for memories that made him remember the difference.

At last the hunger was no longer in him. There wasn't the ache to be part of something larger, or the other pining for the island's relief. He could look at the sky and the river and the emptiness without wanting to paint them with significance. It was as the Sikh had said: he wasn't owned by the remembrance, or by the future, or by longing or hope. He knew it was so because she had died the last death, making it true even without a result.

He thought of Lord Krishna's words to Arjuna in the chariot, not as a strange meaning, a light in a desolate sky, but as a condition to which his life could work, even through the repetitions and frustrations.

> *He who seeks freedom*
> *Thrusts fear aside,*
> *Thrusts aside anger*
> *And puts off desire:*
> *Truly that man*
> *Is made free forever.*
> *When thus he knows me*
> *The end, the author*
> *Of every offering*
> *And all austerity,*
> *Lord of the worlds*
> *And the friend of all men*
> *O son of Kunti*
> *Shall he not enter*
> *The peace of my presence?*

He looked at the sun going down, crimsoning the river. In a few minutes the orange light would fade and the velvety oblivion flow in over the emptiness. The shadows were stretching, reaching out toward him. There was nothing behind him, and ahead of him only himself.

He walked back slowly to the strength of his beginning.

About the Author

BALACHANDRA RAJAN *was born in Toungoo, Burma, in 1920. He was educated at Presidency College, Madras, and at Trinity College, Cambridge, England. In 1946 he received his Ph.D. from Cambridge University and went on there to lecture in Modern Poetry. In 1948 Dr. Rajan joined the Indian Foreign Service and after a period of duty at Delhi was assigned to New York, where for several years he was Advisor to the Permanent Mission of India to the United Nations. At present he is in Vienna as the Resident Representative of India to the International Atomic Energy Agency.*

Dr. Rajan was the founder and editor of Focus, *a series of books of contemporary criticism and writing. He has contributed poetry and criticism to many American and English periodicals, and he published, in 1947, a scholarly work on* Paradise Lost. The Dark Dancer *is his first novel.*

DUE

MAY 24 72

PRINTED IN U.S.A.